# MANCHESTER

Manchester University Press

# MANCHESTER

## Something rich and strange

### Edited by Paul Dobraszczyk
### and Sarah Butler

Manchester University Press

Copyright © Manchester University Press 2020

While copyright in the volume as a whole is vested in Manchester University Press, copyright in individual chapters belongs to their respective authors, and no chapter may be reproduced wholly or in part without the express permission in writing of both author and publisher.

Published by Manchester University Press
Oxford Road, Manchester M13 9PL
www.manchesteruniversitypress.co.uk

British Library Cataloguing-in-Publication Data
A catalogue record for this book is available from the British Library

ISBN 978 1 5261 4414 0 paperback

First published 2020

The publisher has no responsibility for the persistence or accuracy of URLs for any external or third-party internet websites referred to in this book, and does not guarantee that any content on such websites is, or will remain, accurate or appropriate.

Typeset by Servis Filmsetting Ltd, Stockport, Cheshire
Printed and bound by TJ Books Ltd, Padstow

For Isla (P.D.)

For Anne and Dave (S.B.)

# Contents

Introduction – Manchester: seeing like a city … 1

**Atmospheres** … 25
Spirit – Morag Rose … 28
Feel – Sean R. Mills … 32
Corridor – Sarah Butler … 36
Chimney – Jonathan Silver … 39
Night – Nick Dunn … 43
Moors – Cassie Britland … 47

**Monuments** … 52
Statue – Natalie Bradbury … 55
Museum – Jonathan Silver … 59
Shopping centre – Martin Dodge … 65
Stained glass – Clare Hartwell … 70
Sculpture – Natalie Bradbury … 76

**Movement** … 81
Exchange – Steve Hanson … 84
Stone – Tim Edensor … 87
Ring road – Nick Dunn … 92
Loop – Natalie Bradbury … 96

# Introduction
# Manchester: seeing like a city

### Sarah Butler and Paul Dobraszczyk

It is your foot placed on the cold concrete ground,
But how many others have begun that pattern?
There must be a beginning to our past.
But how far back do you have to go to find the first single
 memory?
You can visualise the fraction of bare lane before your eyes,
who knows what happened here a million years before,
But then a single building of a life is there.
This is the start of a first memory of our city a million
years ago.
But now as the city grows stronger there are more memories built,
thousands merging as one.
Our city is beginning.
But then the city that is in front of you now, overflown with its
 very own history.
If it wasn't for our city's first thought then where would we be
 now?
That building would still be bare and empty.
Look at the new city, the world is a fascinating place.
It is time to make memories of your own.

Over Time City (Anon)

Manchester is a city that inspires fierce loyalty. Some identify themselves with the city's industrial past – Manchester's century-long reign as the world centre of cotton production; some with its more recent rich cultural history (the music and nightlife of the Madchester period). Others' loyalty centres on the city's enduring sporting prowess, the ever-changing fortunes of the Reds and Blues. And all who choose to call this city home find themselves becoming attached to its people, its buildings, even its characteristic grey skies and wet cobbles. Whenever we return to Manchester, we feel that sense of homecoming, a flood of memories that are wedded to the fabric of the city itself – in the words of Elbow's 2005 song 'Station Approach': 'coming home I feel like I designed these buildings I walk by'.

Yet, for many, there's a sense that something has irrevocably changed. In this new century, the urban core of Greater Manchester has been in the throes of its most significant transformation since the Second World War. With purportedly more cranes in 2019 than any other city in Western Europe gracing the skyline of the city centre and the inner edges of Salford, dozens of high-rise apartment buildings and offices are being constructed at a frenetic pace: the culmination of over thirty years of private-sector-led urban regeneration.[1] There are many, of course, who see the city-centre transformation as demonstrating that Manchester is the epicentre of the 'Northern Powerhouse', finally sloughing off its post-industrial malaise and accompanying reputation for social deprivation. But many others are deeply concerned that the very soul of Manchester is being ripped out of the city and that its long-standing structural and social problems – first observed in the early nineteenth century – are being simply airbrushed out of the picture.

As damningly reported in 2018, not a single one of these thousands of new living spaces are classed as affordable.[2] They are also largely financed by profit-hungry global investors who have little interest in their effect on the city, let alone local communities. And, as these luxury towers rise, so the homeless population in

1 (Opposite) The Owen Street towers under construction in 2019 with the Beetham Tower behind

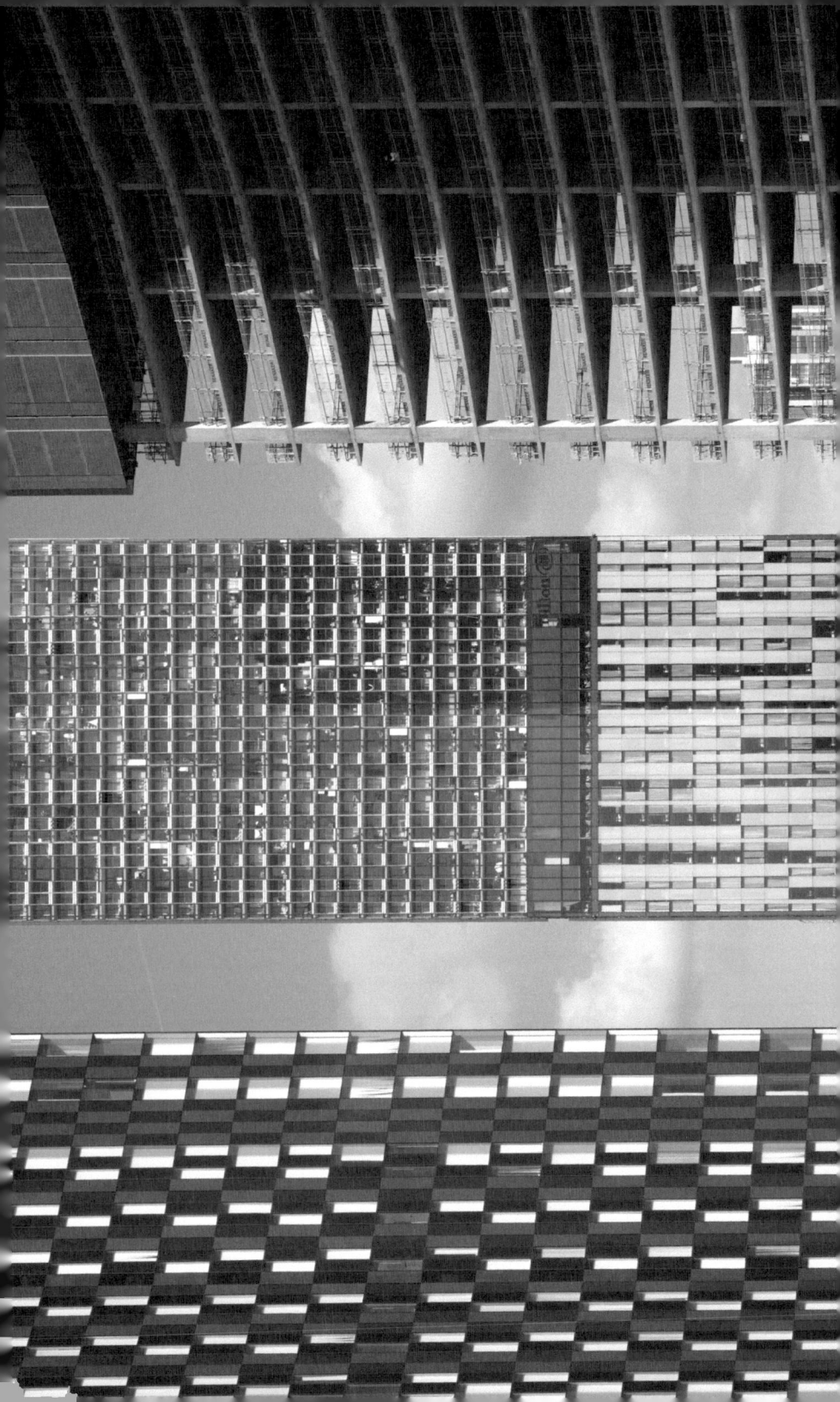

## Introduction

their shadows seems to grow even larger. Just a few miles from this hub of transformation, in both the city of Manchester and the wider metropolitan region, is an urban environment that is changing only very slowly, if at all: a place that has been systematically deprived of the kind of investment currently being funnelled into the urban core. There's nothing comforting here about the old adage coined by Sir Robert Peel: 'What Manchester thinks today, the world does tomorrow.' It's abundantly clear to anyone who chooses to notice that the growth first, welfare second policy that's now been in place for over thirty years has not led to the riches in the centre trickling down to the deprived suburbs.

From these places just outside the core, the rising towers feel like a gigantic gesture of contempt directed at the rest of the city, mocking the very idea of Greater Manchester itself, despite the growing rhetoric of regionalism – Devo Manc – that has characterised the area's governance since 2011.[3] What if all those new towers are actually a rejection of the ways in which the majority of its residents actually live? What if all that is happening is the building of a small fortress of wealth in Manchester's core that systematically shuts out the rest of the city? It is as if a new city is being created in the heart of the old one, the two diametrically opposed – a startling reminder that perhaps nothing has really changed since the Victorian period.

With rhetoric dominating both sides of this argument, few stop to reflect on what actually constitutes Manchester as a city. Is it defined by its formal administrative boundaries – that is, as just one part of a wider urban conglomeration, comprised of the city of Salford and nine other metropolitan boroughs? Or is Manchester really the whole urban region itself – that is, the Greater Manchester created in 1974, the boundaries of which still constitute a metropolitan county today? This is a deeply contested issue, both officially and in the popular imagination. Some hold

**2** (Opposite) Homeless encampment on Deansgate in 2016

## Introduction

fast to the idea that Greater Manchester is an aberration from older county boundaries: the Friends of Real Lancashire and the Saddleworth White Rose Society are extreme examples of this. Others understand that one's place-identity is always relative, depending on your audience. Thus, even someone living on the edges of Greater Manchester will likely say they're from Manchester, or the Manchester region, to a stranger to the area, while they might maintain a more specific local identity to those closer to home. And many living in Manchester's satellite towns, particularly the young, prefer to be identified with the metropolitan centre rather than its periphery, which is often regarded as impoverished and parochial in comparison. Clearly, whenever we talk of a city, we are using a fluid term, subject to change depending on who we're talking to and how we perceive the wider region.

### Greater Manchester: an urban region

The reason for thinking of Manchester as an urban region rather than an individual city is clear. From the early nineteenth century onwards, Manchester grew from a medium-sized town to one of the largest cities in the world, becoming the centre of an extensive geographic region overwhelmingly defined by one industry: the spinning and weaving of cotton. As the cotton industry grew, the city became the hub of a vast network of production that took in hundreds of surrounding towns and villages, each of which sent its goods to the urban centre for marketing and export. The same might be said of many cities in the industrial North – Leeds and Sheffield, for example – but, as pioneering urban thinker Patrick Geddes argued in 1915, Manchester's urban region was much more well-defined than any other, linked as it was by the dominance of one industry alone.[4]

**3** (Opposite) Derelict mills in Ancoats

## Manchester: Something rich and strange

Even as the cotton industry went into catastrophic decline after the Second World War, the region around Manchester remained unified by all of the factors that the process of urbanisation – and the gradual agglomeration of once geographically distinct towns – brought into being. These include a well-established infrastructural network, both above and below ground, that connects all parts of the urban region (and far beyond it as well), as well as an increasing recognition of the need for a wider form of government, first made concrete with the 1974 creation of Greater Manchester and attempted again, more recently, with the partial devolution of power from Westminster to the provinces, with the formation of the Greater Manchester Combined Authority in 2011. Thinking and governing an urban region is of course immensely complicated, and getting Greater Manchester's ten local authorities to work together more equitably has been problematic; clearly, the concentration of wealth in the urban core demonstrates that it is Manchester's authority which still dominates over the others.

Most people who live in the city, if asked, would be able to come up with a definition, however vague or generalised, of what constitutes the 'essence' of Manchester. Many existing books about the city – at least those that are sold in its bookshops, museums and cultural venues – tend to hone in on certain aspects of the city that are seen to exemplify its spirit. Music and football dominate, no doubt for good reason, but so does a form of nostalgia that fixates on comparing the present-day city with that of the past. While these books provide useful and interesting information about the history of the city, they tend to perpetuate a superficial way of seeing it – a fixation on what makes Manchester 'great', whether that greatness is supposed to exist now or at some point in the past, more often than not, the early twentieth century (when Manchester was still one of the world's largest and most important cities). Usually cast as a form of civic pride, this way of seeing the city is problematic because it prevents richer understandings

## Introduction

from emerging – it exerts a kind of stranglehold over alternative approaches, particularly ones that seek to reveal less comforting stories about Manchester and its past. We need reflections on history that speak more directly to the present moment – connections that challenge the pervasive idea of Manchester as a city in perpetual revolution, where the past is either quickly erased or frozen in time as heritage.

But it is perhaps no wonder that current books tend to focus on a limited range of topics or gravitate towards the city centre, for industrial Manchester was founded on what Friedrich Engels called the 'hypocritical plan': an unplanned but nevertheless conscious segregation of rich and poor, the exploiters and the exploited. In the early 1840s, Engels described the ways in which the city's street network kept the poor hidden from the rich so that they didn't need to be made aware of the terrible conditions in which they lived, lest they felt guilty.[5] And, of course, we see the same thing happening today around the edges of the city centre, where rich and poor are again being rigidly segregated. It is as if the current Labour-controlled city council has learnt nothing from past failures – or maybe it's just too overwhelming for them to think about how to radically change a city founded on inequality. However this is precisely what is needed if the city is to truly 'regenerate' into a progressive urban region: a radical reshaping that faces the more negative aspects of Manchester and transforms its long-standing – even foundational – social divisions. A place to start – and where this book begins and ends – is to simply see the city for what it really is, and not flinch from what we encounter.

We invite you to see Manchester more in the whole, encompassing places far away from and often in stark contrast to the glittering shopping districts and towering luxury apartments at its centre. This counters the general tendency in British politics to isolate and exclude – one that has been played out dramatically on a national scale in the Brexit debacle, but also at the local scale with the rapid development of many urban cores into citadels of

## Introduction

wealth. Thinking of conurbations in the round inevitably draws us away from narrow parochialism and the interests of one particular group. This approach need not run roughshod over local differences or seek to centralise power; rather it can maintain the local and the global together in creative tension – a tension that, after all, is always there in our everyday lives as urban citizens. Yet, the fact that only one in five Mancunians took part in the election of the region's mayor in 2017 suggests that such thinking is not prevalent right now. The legitimacy of any municipal government that claims to represent the whole region rests squarely on a dramatic improvement in electoral turnout.

What is required is a collective effort to renew the imagination of the city from below, a city that both anchors a secure sense of local identity but which also pulls us into a greater whole. This may seem like a rather tenuous way of generating a new politics of the city, but there is no doubt that this is where such a politics must begin – in the minds of the many rather than the powerful few. Seeing the city as a whole is a political act: how we feel about where we live is not merely a subjective impression; it is absolutely vital to how we engage with our environment. A mode of feeling is political because it has the capacity to change ideas, out of which come all of our actions. Getting beyond the local is about acknowledging that, in reality, everything always overflows and is wrapped in something else – everything is connected, even if we're not aware of it. These connections are like the invisible cities described by Italo Calvino in his influential 1972 book of that name, adapted into a stage production for the Manchester International Festival of July 2019.[6] In Calvino's estimation, it is just as much the hidden things that make cities what they are as the things we can see: the remnants of all its past stories contained in the built environment 'like the lines of a hand, written in the corners of the streets, the gratings of the window, the bannisters of the steps … every

**4** (Opposite) View towards central Manchester from Winter Hill, Horwich

segment marked in turn with scratches, indentations, scrolls'.[7] Finding those hidden connections – reaching out to touch the lives of others, past and present – is vital because of the ways in which the city is currently being polarised in its redevelopment.

Calvino invites us to think more imaginatively about cities and how their extraordinary diversity can be known more fully. Take, for example, the famous rain that all of us who live in Greater Manchester experience, and which often forms the topic of everyday conversation. When we talk about how urban regions are linked up we usually use infrastructure as the main focal point, either transport (trams, trains, buses) or utilities like water, sewage, gas, telecommunications and electricity. But although absolutely vital for the successful functioning of a city region – the ongoing disaster that is Northern Rail being a negative case in point – infrastructure is often rather dry and somewhat abstract in its appeal to our imaginations. In contrast, thinking about Manchester's famous rain humanises the idea of the city region. It allows for a much more direct perception of the city as a whole – a way of rediscovering the places we so often take for granted. By reclaiming our right to shape the city, we – each and every person in the city – can resist the current waves of development that are seeing the core of Manchester being turned into a fortress for the few. How that resistance is shaped into something coherent and powerful is beyond the remit of this book. But to begin with we need to think as big as we can, to try and connect ourselves with what is beyond us and embrace and work with whatever we see. Fundamentally, it's about finding wonder again in the places we think we know, and realising that it is us, Mancunians in all our glorious and troubling diversity, that hold the city together and have the capacity to make its future.

# Introduction

## Rain

One of us still vividly recalls the five consecutive days in November 2011 when it rained continuously in Manchester. Still a relative newcomer to the city, it was a rude induction to Manchester's reputation as the rainiest of English cities (it is, in fact, only the fifth wettest in the country). In dismal late-autumn light, those five unrelentingly wet days seemed locked in a strange time zone – the experience of the city was one of forced enclosure punctuated by dashes between buildings or steamed-up buses, umbrella always at hand. Outside, the rain marked the city's brick and concrete buildings with ribbons of water. Pools gathered in every available hollow, and little streams dribbled incessantly from lintels and eaves. For that seemingly interminable period, it was as if the solid architecture of the city had been blurred into the smudges of paint seen in the paintings of Adolphe Valette, teacher of L. S. Lowry – the city liquified into atmosphere; water everywhere.

As literary historian Lynne Pearce has observed, Manchester's rain looms large in nearly all fictional representations of the city, a way of framing it as a place of bleak monotony – a city with intractable problems.[8] Unsurprisingly, rain features strongly in much of the crime fiction centred on the city. In Karline's Smith's *Moss Side Massive* (1998), a novel which reflects on Moss Side's reputation as a centre of gang violence in the 1990s, the young 'Rasta' Zukie is depressed by the drizzle as he cycles close to a 'dreary grey block of council flats … awaiting demolition. Row upon row, block upon block of solid, grimy pigeon-shit concrete.'[9] Here, rain is a metaphor for failure – a reminder that Manchester seems condemned to keep repeating mistakes made in the past, unable to escape the depressing connotations of its predominantly grey skies. And, in *Moss Side Massive*, this is a failure by the city towards its black citizens – a municipal authority that, from the 1960s to the 1990s, repeatedly used demolition as a way of dispersing concentrations of ethnic minorities.[10]

## Introduction

Lemn Sissay's poem 'Moods of Rain' (1988) uses water to frame the poet's experience of being a black man on the streets of Manchester in the 1970s and 1980s – a time when racist abuse was encountered everywhere.

> I'm giving up dodging glassy-eyed puddles,
> My feet like the kitchen cloth,
> Face screwed up, no time for scruples.
> Head down, walk straight and cough,
> And silver speckled my licks are crowned.
> Melting black faces drip and shine,
> No smile by an unsatisfied frown,
> Same goes, I think, for mine.

When that discrimination became less blatant, rain came to mean something altogether more positive for Sissay. His 2008 poem 'Rain' was painted onto a wall above a takeaway on the Oxford Road near the University of Manchester. In order to make sense of the poem, one has to read it downwards, as if following the drops of rain themselves, assembling the fragmented words one by one. The 'triumphant' rain in this poem is equated with hope – the 'Man/cunian way' of the last line referring both to the motorway that bisects the city just north of the university and also the indomitable spirit of Mancunians themselves. Here, rain offers a shared experience of the city that strengthens the cohesiveness of its communities.

Mancunians may moan about the city's rain but, for many, it does indeed provide a means of connection with others, if only in shared conversations about the weather. Rain represents homecoming – a sense of belonging to the city. In Jeff Noon's futuristic cyberpunk reimagining of Manchester, *Vurt* (1993), rain provides an anchor point in a city where dreams have blurred into reality by means of powerful drugs ingested through different-coloured feathers. The novel's central protagonist Scribble remembers his

5 (Opposite) Rain-soaked windscreen in Levenshulme

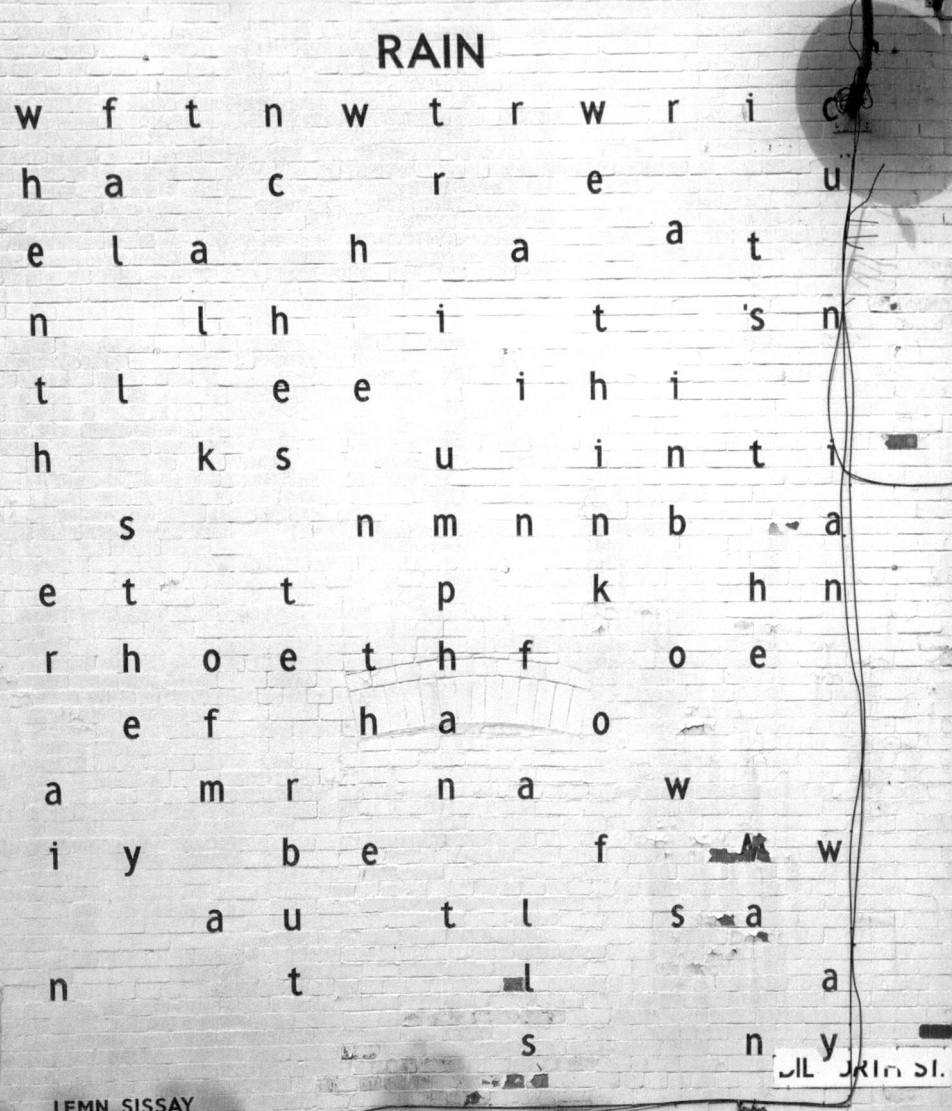

**6** Lemn Sissay's poem 'Rain' painted onto a building on Dilworth Street

youth through the rain: 'All I know is that looking back I swear I can feel it falling on me, on my skin. That rain means everything to me, all of the past, all that has been lost.'[11] The sheer physical reality of rain – the way it makes you feel its presence so strongly – is like a call to be truly present in a world which the virtual

## Introduction

threatens all the time to pull us away from: 'The raindrops on my face play a sweet refrain', in the words of The Beautiful South. For the Pakistan-born poet Basir Kazmi, the shared experience of rain allows newcomers to identify with the city:

> So that others may take pleasure in your talk, Basir
> Don't talk of your tears, talk rather about the rain.

That Manchester is indelibly thought of as a rainy city, despite the facts indicating otherwise, speaks more perhaps of its *lack* of cohesive identity – after all, Manchester has always been a city of immigrants longing to feel at home. In Mike Leigh's film *Naked* (1993), two young Mancunians living in London recite a traditional ballad where the imagery of rain encompasses precisely this kind of longing:

> Take me back to Manchester when it's raining
> I want to wash my feet in Albert Square
> I'm all agog for a good thick fog
> I don't like the sun I like it raining cats and dogs
> I want to smell the odours of the Irwell
> I want to feel the soot get in me hair
> Oh I don't want to roam I want to get back home
> To rainy Manchester

Mike Leigh knew the song from his own youth – he sang it with his friends in Habonim – the international socialist Jewish youth movement he joined as a schoolboy in Broughton, Salford.[12] Once again then, the imagery of rain draws us out into a rich tapestry of feelings and memories. Unlike most symbols of belonging – flags, coats of arms, monarchy or national anthems – rain doesn't allow any one social group to claim it as their own. That is why it is such a powerful way of conceiving the city as a whole – rain falls on the just and unjust, rich and poor, black and white, religious or heathen. It's a rich metaphor of unity that always reaches beyond any meaning that we assign to it.

## Manchester: Something rich and strange

### Many Manchesters

This word 'rain' introduces the central idea of this book, namely of the city as much more than the sum of any of its parts, an interconnected web of physical things both human and non-human that always invites us to enlarge our imagination. It should also be obvious by now that this book will not make any clear distinction between the city as a physical entity – its building and infrastructures – and the city as it exists in the minds of its citizens. Cities are a meld of matter and mind, and writing about cities often reflects this. But, unlike London, which has a very distinct and wide-ranging body of fiction *about* the city, Manchester does not, despite its reputation as a creative hothouse in the 1980s and 1990s and notwithstanding the vital role played by key literary texts in the city's history, from *Mary Barton* (1848) to *Vurt* (1994). Corinne Fowler has argued that the Londoncentric UK publishing industry has always favoured the capital as both a subject for books, and also because so many writers choose to live there.[13] In one sense, this reflects the difference in scale of London in relation to provincial cities; yet it also shows a lack of imaginative engagement over the years with secondary urban regions, particularly formerly world-leading industrial cities like Manchester that have declined in global importance since the Second World War. This book doesn't seek to reclaim or reassert Manchester as a 'world' city; rather, it acknowledges the fact that Manchester is still a global city, but one now shaped by global forces rather than the other way around.[14]

   The desire to see further, to open up new possibilities of perceiving Manchester, and discover countless 'cities' within the city, runs through the heart of this book. It's no exaggeration to say that current books on Manchester are let down by a lack of such diversity, whether through a disproportionate focus on certain subjects, such as football and music, or a lack of representation of areas outside the city centre. The diversity of Greater Manchester's

# Introduction

geographies often escapes mainstream notice – most guidebooks to the city focus only on the city centre, and when journalists write about the Manchester beyond the core, there's often an astonishing ignorance about those places. Even with the recent move of media production companies to the city region – the BBC being the most high profile – Manchester is often used in film and television programmes either in a generic way, signalling industrial decay, criminality or anonymous suburbia, or, more astonishingly, as a stand-in for London. Witness the late-Victorian John Rylands Library in the city centre posing as the British Museum Library in the BBC film *The Limehouse Golem* (2016), the gloomy Gothic interior of the Rylands preferred over the classical rotunda of the British Museum to signify Victorian squalor in London.

This inaccurate use of an historical site in Manchester points to the need to reinvigorate a much more engaged imagination of the city that can nourish an inclusive politics and urban life. In this book, twenty-five different writers provide their own individual takes on some of the pieces that form the vast jigsaw puzzle that is Manchester, from the centre to the periphery and beyond. We invite you to find your own way through this assemblage; it's a book that can be read both from cover to cover and also by dipping in and out, thereby discovering your own connections over time. The images – mostly photographs – are equally important. As those who market Manchester to investors know all too well, images of the city are a powerful means of attraction – they act as memorable lures in a highly competitive market of cities jostling for funds. But they can also work to instal a renewed sense of wonder at what is already there, or to lure us into more difficult terrain, whether places or pasts. They also remind us of the fragility of the things we so often take for granted: some photographs show buildings that have already been demolished. They also work to condense the texts into memorable visual pictures – some of which you might recognise at once, others inviting you to dig a little deeper.

## Manchester: Something rich and strange

Each chapter takes a single word as a starting point, and these sixty words are grouped into eleven sections: themes around which we, as editors, have curated this richly diverse material. The book begins with *Atmospheres*: the look and feel of the city that can't be reduced to the soundbites so beloved of Manchester's image-makers. *Monuments* takes us to the more tangible things that sum up the city: its statues, museums, shops and public art. *Movement* focuses on processes: how motion defines the city, from its transportation networks to the movement of materials and money within and beyond the city. What sustains all of this, of course, is *Work*; the brutal toil of the cotton industry that made Manchester such an important urban centre in the nineteenth century may have gone, but its remains are still everywhere to be seen. Developing this further, *Relics* asks what these remains signify and how we can think through what might be important to preserve for future posterity.

The next three sections – *Underworlds*, *Dregs* and *Secrets* – explore the enduring image of Manchester as a city with problems – or a problem city. Our writers interrogate the darker aspects of the city, from its literal subterranean spaces to the toxic residues of industry. Others write about the violence bubbling under the surface of the city, reminding us of the need to face up to Manchester's very real social issues and acknowledge their long histories. Yet other chapters in these three sections suggest that facing uncomfortable truths can also be liberating, because doing so roots us in the reality of the city rather than in superficial images of it. This encountering of the 'reality' of Manchester also extends to the non-human – the *Nature* explored in the next section. As is typical of most post-industrial cities, Manchester's nature is an often scruffy mixture of brownfield and greenfield sites that are usually ignored or feared, considered as places without value, or full of danger. This kind of nature is often the result of ruination: part of the city's endless cycles of death and rebirth brought to light in the section on *Destruction*. Death in the city can come

## Introduction

without warning – from the Peterloo massacre in 1819 to the 2017 Manchester Arena attack. Other times, it creeps slowly into the crevices of the city's buildings, spaces and social life. But despite all this – the problems and the pain – Manchester remains *Home*. The book ends with a sense of what home might mean to the city's vulnerable population – those without a permanent roof over their heads or those who are at risk of persecution. Even if most of us will never know the reality of having one's home taken away, we are all living in a city that is constantly under threat of ceasing to become our home, the built fabric that roots us always at risk from city-makers whose values lie elsewhere. As this introduction has argued, it's not something that we should ever take for granted.

Indeed, it is critical that we, as citizens, claim our right to the city. This doesn't necessarily mean that we all need to become directly involved in the governance of the city, or in building it (though some of us might), but rather that we don't separate the question of what kind of city we want from broader everyday concerns. In asking for a more inclusive city, we also ask what kind of people we want to be; what sort of social relationships we are seeking; and what values we want to hold.[15] Asking these questions from the bottom up will inevitably produce a multitude of different and often contradictory answers; but herein lies the great promise of cities – that this rich diversity of desires can be celebrated and brought together to create places that work for everyone, and not just the powerful and wealthy few. And, as this book shows, words are just as important as actions in this regard. With all the money and other resources currently being funnelled into the urban core of Manchester, there is an unprecedented opportunity to use this surplus for the greater public good. But this requires a new vision of the city as something much more complex, diverse, disturbing and contradictory than is currently being put forward by those who should, and probably do, know better. Reading this book, you will hopefully sense something of that alternative Manchester – the everyday city brimful of imaginative possibilities. We invite you

## Manchester: Something rich and strange

to take these and expand them further – we need yet more words and stories, an ever-expanding cornucopia of language – in order to germinate something more hopeful, humane, equal and *real* out of an uncaring and violently delusive global capitalist system that wants to remake the city in its own narrow and destructive image.

## Notes

1. In many ways, the policies being pursued today bear no significant departure from those documented in Jamie Peck and Kevin Ward's book *City of Revolution: Restructuring Manchester*, published in 2002 by Manchester University Press, and covering the years immediately after the IRA bomb in 1996.
2. See Jonathan Silver, *Cities are recognising the dangers of speculation and big capital: What will Manchester's politicians do next?*, Greater Manchester Housing Action website, 10 July 2018, available at www.gmhousingaction.com/cities-are-recognising-the-dangers-of-speculation-and-big-capital-what-will-manchesters-politicians-do-next/?fbclid=IwAR3o9zGrDHSvGV9IcZbc39oY2fHo1X4F4mHGQF2hBCL_vug2Qpwxn6-V5L8 (accessed 17 June 2020).
3. On the recent processes of devolution, see www.greatermanchester-ca.gov.uk/who-we-are/devolution/.
4. Patrick Geddes, *Cities in Evolution* (London: Williams, 1915), pp. 31–2.
5. Friedrich Engels, *The Condition of the Working-Class in England in 1844*; trans. Florence Kelley (London, 1891), pp. 57–8.
6. On the stage production, see https://mif.co.uk/previous-festivals/mif19/invisible-cities/.
7. Italo Calvino, *Invisible Cities* (London: Vintage, 1998; first published 1972), p. 9.
8. Lynne Pearce, 'Manchester: the postcolonial city', in Lynne Pearce, Corinne Fowler and Robert Crawshaw, eds, *Postcolonial Manchester: Diaspora Space and the Devolution of Literary Culture* (Manchester: Manchester University Press, 2013), pp. 55–60.
9. Karline Smith, *Moss Side Massive* (London: The X Press, 1998), p. 18.
10. See Laurence Brown and Niall Cunningham, 'The inner geographies of a migrant gateway: mapping the built environment and the dynamics of Caribbean mobility in Manchester, 1951–2011', *Social Science History* 40:1 (2016), p. 106.
11. Jeff Noon, *Vurt* (London: Ringpull, 1993), pp. 18–19.
12. According to Leigh, a retired schoolmaster from Prestwich claimed to have written the song for a school review at Stand Grammar in 1950.

## Introduction

13 Corinne Fowler, 'Publishing Manchester's black and Asian writers', in Pearce, Fowler and Crawshaw, *Postcolonial Manchester*, pp. 79–81.
14 See Peter Dicken, 'Global Manchester: from globaliser to globalised', in Peck and Ward, *City of Revolution*, pp. 18–33.
15 See David Harvey, *Rebel Cities: From the Right to the City to the Urban Revolution* (London: Verso, 2013), p. 4.

# Atmospheres

The river pours on its thick muddy current through the streets of the city … The blue heavens above are hidden from us by the thick black smoke of the huge factory chimneys which weave a close impenetrable veil of brown fog between the city and the sky. For half a century these bridges [over Manchester's rivers] have not basked in the warm glory of sunshine; only the cold faces of the moon and stars are permitted to look upon them, for at night the factories rest, and the clouds disperse.

German writer and photographer Johann Georg Kohl on Manchester in 1844

What makes Manchester Manchester? Its architecture? Its history? Its people? Or just the way it feels? Perhaps there are many Manchesters, as Morag Rose suggests in 'Spirit' – a plurality of versions of the same place that coexist and sometimes bleed one into the other. The sense we get, walking its streets, living our lives among its suburbs and centre, its roads and moorland, parks and museums. As Sean R. Mills shows us in 'Feel', how we experience a place, how we react to its varying atmospheres, has a huge impact on how we act within it, and on the stories we tell

**7** (Opposite) Smoke-stained sunset in Stockport due to moorland fires in the heatwave of July 2018

about it. In Sarah Butler's 'Corridor', a cornucopia of sensations is revealed as we traverse one of Manchester's busiest roads.

As many past visitors to industrial Manchester attest, the city was forged in the Industrial Revolution and became notorious for the smoke and soot that blackened its buildings, fogged its air, and even led to the mutation of its nature – for example, the peppered moth, which changed its speckled pattern to a uniform black to match the darkened walls and trees of the soot-stained city. In his satirical novel *Hard Times* (1854), Charles Dickens portrayed Manchester as 'Coketown', a dark, monotonous 'town of unnatural red and black', from whose chimneys 'interminable serpents of smoke trailed themselves for ever and ever'. In this section, Jonathan Silver takes up the image of Manchester's chimneys, considering their architectural and symbolic importance for the city, as well as their role in climate change.

Today, Manchester is a cleaner, 'smarter' city, energised by technology and creativity rather than belching smoke and the relentless pounding of machines. Still, the city can be overwhelming – a bombardment on the senses. Nick Dunn takes us to the night-time city, where the senses give us a very different set of atmospheres to negotiate; while Cassie Britland in 'Moors' takes us out to the edges of the city, places that often make us feel uneasy. How we relate to specific places, how we imbue them with story and memory, help create their various and varying atmospheres. Manchester's 'spirit' is regularly evoked by those in the business of selling the city – innovative, creative, revolutionary: it is simplified and sanitised in order to attract people and investment. But as the following pieces suggest, Manchester's atmospheres are more varied, complex and challenging than we are often led to believe.

8 Ghost-sign (extract)

# Manchester: Something rich and strange

## *Spirit* – Morag Rose

The spirit is dying, the soul is being lost. I hear this constant lament about Manchester, and occasionally when all I see are constellations of cranes juxtaposed with cries of suffering, I feel it too. There's a growing revulsion at the spectacle, a despair at the narrowing of potentials and the closing down of stories. It's a smoothing, sanitising and suffocating marketing scam of regeneration that is killing *something* special, something somehow authentic. It's fear of powerlessness in a city dominated by capital, every space pure money, privatisation, securitisation – enclosure stealing our common treasury. It's the banshee wail every time a piece of heritage is lost or another dull tower goes up. The litany: Pomona, Turner Street, Library Walk, the Ancoats Dispensary and so very many more.

But what does it really mean? What are we losing? What is the essence of Manchester? Usually given shape in popular culture, it's a swaggering cliche of rain or football or Corrie cobbles or blokes with guitars, rough diamonds, working hard, partying harder. The civic symbol of the bee has unified in times of strife, bringing comfort and solidarity (see 'Bee', p. 285). It's been recovered and co-opted now, so it's mandatory on every bus, fridge magnet and rubbish bin. Repetition can't erase love, but it can warp it when viewed from outside. I've always had my doubts about its multiple meanings anyway; for me our forefathers (and they were fathers) wanted worker drones, not mutual co-operation. I believe the reality is so much more beautiful, chaotic and diverse than a single genius loci can handle. How can there ever be a symbol that encompasses all that?

I've lived here twenty years now and am more convinced than ever that essentialism is a dangerous thing and we need to embrace an openness, a multiplicity of Manchesters that are all particular, none exceptional. We are all interconnected beyond our own

## Atmospheres

narratives, part of a bigger tapestry. The late Doreen Massey, herself a Mancunian, whose ideas help shaped modern geography, articulates this perfectly – her vision of a network of relationships, always attentive to power, always open to change, a multiplicity of stories so far.[1] We can change the outcome of those stories, but we also need to acknowledge how we got to where we are now.

Recently I was walking with a friend and she was telling me how much she loved the red-brick mills and warehouses that characterise the architecture of Manchester's first Industrial Revolution. Her love was ambivalent because she knew they were built on exploitation; she spoke of visions of blood pouring out of the walls, and yet the allure of the city still transfixes. Together we stood on a corner near Shudehill bus station, an accidental confluence of the city's past and present. The Arndale Centre, a wine bar commemorating a brutal Victorian street gang, The Scuttlers, a cherished scrap of wasteland colonised by flowers she could name, a soon-to-be-evicted community space, and the edge of the Northern Quarter. Rambos' tattoos and exotic piercings, its dilapidated signs a source of absurd joy: '*Dare to be different … Take That, Manchester United, The Entire Australian Rugby Team, Stars of Brookside and many more … Fresh needles for every client*'. And of course, to our left, the bus station – people leaving, arriving, the ebb and flow of everyday travel in the networked city. Which of these Manchesters is more real, more true? Where is the city's spirit abiding?

In my kitchen is a bottle of sloe gin, the fruit picked from the green down the road, nourished by the earth; but I don't think the city's spirit is in there, although perhaps it's getting closer: imbibing our *terroir*. The shelf the liquor sits on is in a ramshackle Georgian terrace in a suburb named in The Smiths' song 'Miserable Lie': 'What do we get for our trouble and pain? Just a rented room in Whalley Range.' It's at the heart of my Manchester and its crumbling walls have been central to my intense and ambivalent love affair with the city. When I arrived here I was fleeing from rather than running to; a toss of the coin bought me here, and I didn't imagine staying more than six months. Lost and alone, I stumbled into a housing co-op which became both a sanctuary and incubator: a home. I was luckier than I realised (does anyone really know when fortune shines?) because this house had more heart, more stories than I could have dreamt.

On the wall, above where I sit writing, there's a large enamel sign, salvaged from the cellar, which proclaims this the residence of James Kite, N.A.T.M. It displays a phone number traced to the early twentieth century, and in particular the time between the wars when paranormal phenomena, alternative therapies and spiritualism were fashionable passions. This street had been grand once, a tollbooth at the end remembered in the name of 'Brooks Bar' bus stop. Later, a time of bedsits and bad reputations as fortunes waned and fashions changed and Kite's paraphernalia languished unloved. He boasted of 'lady assistants' and administered wonders such as diathermy, ionisation and sun-ray treatment. Light was the cure for a range of childhood maladies and a restorative cure for many ills. Patients wore goggles and little else as they absorbed the magical rays. Quackery was suspected right from the outset with concerns about the possible carcinogenic affects of direct exposure to sunlight.

A few Christmases ago some women knocked on our front door; they had occupied our house in the 1970s and had stories of squats, placard making and births in my bedroom. They recalled renovating the building to create a community and told us about an object they discovered under the kitchen floorboards. Their preliminary research suggested it was an ectoplasm machine, the kind used during seances to give the illusion of a manifestation or a possession. Perhaps Mr Kite conjured apparitions too, gave comfort to people he also exploited – an entertaining fraudster or dangerous charlatan, depending on your taste. Perhaps his wraiths were as authentic as any other that claim to be the spirit of Manchester.

# Piccadilly

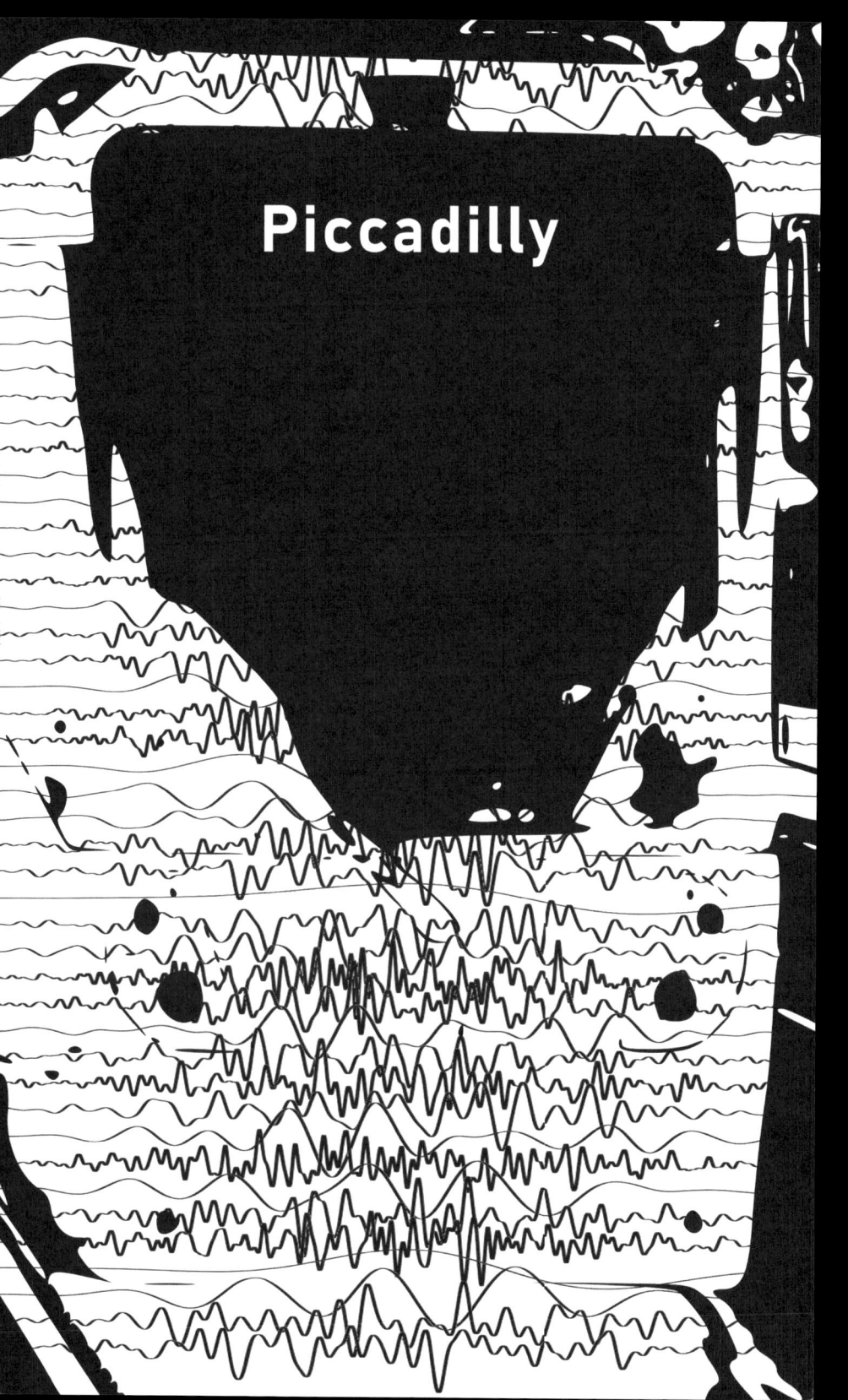

## *Feel* – Sean R. Mills

As the tram approaches Shudehill, you start to feel a change in the line. The smooth, low-intensity vibration begins to throb up through the soles of your shoes. With your fingertips, you can feel the different harmonics travelling through the metal, beating out a staccato rhythm of low-pitch pulses and high-pitch whines that travel through your skin, layering complexly like music. It builds to an astonishing intensity, and you step aside to watch the tram trundle past. As it slides away, the pattern of vibration in the track changes, becoming less intense, smoother, as travelling waves of motion interact and flatten each other. You can feel, if you concentrate, the footsteps of people crossing near you, the bouncing wheels of a bicycle, the rattle of a passing bus.

When you brush your fingertips over a surface, the friction of your skin causes vibrations. Neurons in the skin of your hand have been waiting for this. Their tightly packed bodies are minutely sensitive to indentations of the skin, compressing by just nanometres and screaming out electric signals. They instantly start to construct a coded message: Where is the indentation? How is it moving across the skin? What are the properties of the vibration it's causing? Each tiny bump and ridge in the material – a piece of wood, fabric, glass – induces a corresponding change in the properties of the vibration. The signals travel quickly to your brain. They are picked apart and processed and reconstructed by layer upon layer of computation. Neural codes of dazzling complexity quickly become the quanta of textures – the 'feel' of wood, paper, glass, plastic, concrete, brick and steel.

Your hypersensitivity to vibration serves another purpose: it extends your very sense of self. When you use a tool – a pencil, say

9 (Previous page) A tram transmits vibrations through the streets of Manchester, exciting our tactile sense

## Atmospheres

– the vibrations travelling through the tool allow you to 'feel' what it 'feels'. Through the pencil, you feel the texture of the paper, the grip it feels on the surface as it moves. This is a circular form of feedback, controlling the minuscule muscle movements in your arms and providing information about the motion of the tool – the tiny slips between pencil and surface and tool and hand – that allow you to write. As this happens, your brain begins to think of the tool as part of your body, extending yourself along its length, embodying its form as a part of you.[2]

The vibrations in the city travel through surfaces and into our skin in exactly the same way as the vibrations we create ourselves. Put your fingers on a steel tramline at Shudehill and you feel that it is *textured* by a tram pulling away from the platform. Stay a little longer and realise that the track is a part of you, an enormous metal arm you *embody*.

On Oxford Road, huge black construction hoardings amplify the impact of tools. You can feel the texture of a pile-driver slamming into the ground, hidden away behind the barriers. The feeling arrives a moment after the sound, an echo of motion. Scaffolding – bitterly cold in the morning air – transmits the harsh rattle of an impact wrench from high above. At first, you can feel the waveforms through your fingertips, overlapping frequencies amplified and dampened by the structure and the flex of the steel. After a few seconds your fingers are numb with cold, and you can only feel the vibrations through your arm, dull and blind to the details.

In Manchester Art Gallery, the lift shudders and rattles as it slows, and you can feel the mechanism that moves and lifts you through the building. Under the Mancunian Way, you can brush your fingers against the concrete supports and time the passing of cars, coaches and heavy lorries. The road is enormously loud. The sensation at your fingers is weak, but you can feel how it changes from second to second. The same is true on the twenty-third floor of the Hilton, hot and still and smelling of stale coffee.

## Manchester: Something rich and strange

Your fingertips against the glass can feel the rhythm of the wind rushing above the city, pulsing against the side of the building, silently shaking.

At Piccadilly station, seven soldiers from the First World War limp into the city. They wear tattered greatcoats and peaked caps made of bronze. Their eyes are wrapped tight in bandages, and each holds the shoulder of the man in front, following in his footsteps. They are a memorial – *Victory Over Blindness* – to the thousands of service members who have lost their sight.[3] There are two signs, one of which is in Braille. You move your fingers across the sign, the texture of the letters bursting into clarity. As commuters stream from the doors of the station, a few reach out and touch the statue. When the train engines thrum and leave the station, you can feel the soldiers move.

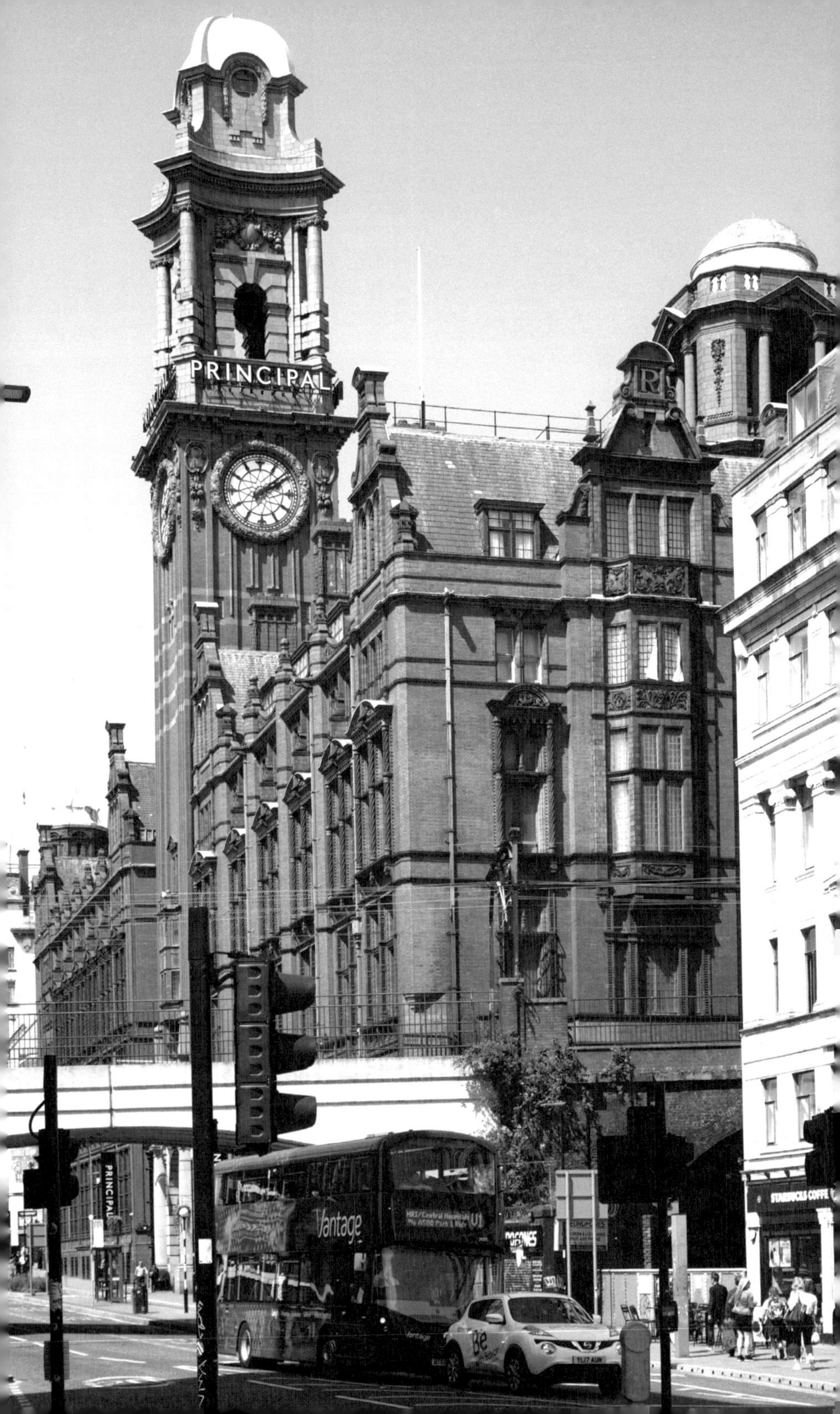
PRINCIPAL
R
PRINCIPAL
Vantage
STARBUCKS COFFEE

## *Corridor*[4] – Sarah Butler

There are no lines telling you where it starts and where it ends. So let's draw them in. Two trails of coloured chalk across the tarmac. Here: from park to shops. Here: from library to hotel.

Let's make them both the beginning. This is, after all, a place where things start: life; adulthood; careers; love affairs; ideas; my own entrance into the world among them – on a snowy Thursday morning, April 1978.

Let's make them both the end. Things come and go, after all: dingy clubs and office blocks, bridges and grand plans – all that dust.

Two beginnings. Two ends. And everything in between lined up one after the other. Except this place doesn't like to stay still. Corridor. *Correre*. A run, rush, hurry part of town.

*write me a line, hold your breath, walk the length of it, as far as you can go without falling off*

The busiest bus route in Europe, they say. Thousands shuttling from stop to stop, forever changing their collection of strangers. Among them, bikes weave their own, solitary patterns along the road. And the cars. And the taxis. And the people who walk. You never step in the same corridor twice.

Corridor. Forget lines of chairs under fluorescent lights, noticeboards crammed with warnings about salt and cigarettes and unprotected sex. Forget swilling crowds of school kids. Forget carpeted non-spaces lined with closed doors. Forget the place where the shoes get left.

**10** (Previous page) The Principal Hotel – where Oxford Road becomes Oxford Street

## Atmospheres

*The thing about lines is that you can
break them.*

Under the bridges, everything is amplified. The slap echo of a manhole, not quite flush with the tarmac. The stink of traffic fumes. The lack of somewhere to sleep. The colour grey.

*Out of line.*
    *Cross the line.*
        *Down the line.*
            *End of the line.*
                *Bottom line.*

Free books. Pizza. Burrito. Noodles. Theatre ticket. Plug adaptor. Memories. Cheap veg. A place to go. Guitar string. Lamb karahi. Family swim. Concerto. Americano. Chameleon. Knowledge. Music. Prayer. Pre-loved jumper. Haircut. Bank loan. Fertility treatment. Contemporary art. Trees.

A line into and out of the city. A place of beginnings and middles and ends. A string of and then, and then, and then. Except nothing will stay in place. In August it sleeps; come September it's frenetic. In the early hours, the night-time stragglers do-si-do with street cleaners, delivery vans, early shift workers.

There are no lines telling you where it starts and where it ends. So let's draw them in. Two trails of coloured chalk across the tarmac. Here: from hotel to library. Here: from shops to park. A beginning and an end. An end and a beginning. All this life and dust in between.

11 The chimney at Royal Mills, Ancoats

## Atmospheres

## *Chimney* – Jonathan Silver

It was 1987, and the chimney somewhere in Bolton looked like it would stand for years longer. Red bricks reached up into the grim sky. This was when tall buildings in the city were a rarity and the skyline was lower, punctuated by these relics of the industrial age. The cordon around the site kept out some of the crowd; I followed the steeplejack inside and across the piles of smashed-up bricks and twisted masonry. Other factories and chimneys surrounded the site, their day of reckoning still to come. Those inside the cordon, which seemed to be more an arbitrary addition than a vital health and safety measure, were making small talk and sipping mugs of tea.

After some time out in the cold, and once more timber, tyres and other flammable debris had been brought in by eager young hands, the steeplejack lit a fire at the base of the chimney and the assembled masses stepped back. The fire became more intense, a horn sounded from the steeplejack to alert everyone it was about to fall, and he started to sprint, perhaps more as performance than from outright concern. And then it came down. It was not a graceful fall; the chimney was gone in a few seconds and a giant dust cloud gathered, while a ripple of excitement, followed by applause, emerged from various parts of the perimeter. The operation itself was one of precision as the chimney fell in the only space that would not cause damage to people or property.

Another chimney in Greater Manchester had fallen and the man responsible was none other than Fred Dibnah. I was on the scene because my grandfather was the director of the BBC Series *A Year with Fred*, following Bolton's well-loved steeplejack. The demolition, later to be shown on the nation's screens, was one that had been played out dozens of times in the 1970s and 1980s as the obdurate built environment of the Industrial Revolution began to be disassembled. Factories, warehouses, industrial buildings of all types – and, of course, entire working-class neighbourhoods – were deemed redundant. Britain's economic power ebbed away, taking hundreds of these vertical structures with it. But not all have disappeared, and a wander around outlying towns such as Oldham, or central neighbourhoods such as Ancoats and Ardwick, remind us that Greater Manchester was once a conurbation of chimneys.

One could argue that the chimney had perhaps the greatest iconic value in the architecture of industrialisation and the topographies of the industrial city. From the single chimney of Arkwright's spinning mill in 1786, to what the journalist Angus Bethune Reach described as 'the dull leaden-coloured sky, tainted by thousands of ever smoking chimneys which broods over the distance'.[5] It was no wonder Sir Charles Napier termed Manchester, 'the chimney of the world … the entrance to hell realised'.[6] By 1843, evidence was brought to the Parliamentary Select Committee on Smoke Prevention of over 500 industrial chimneys in Manchester attached to hundreds of cotton mills across the conurbation, along with row upon row of terraced housing and their attendant chimneys.[7] The city was covered in soot on every one of its surfaces.

There were many notable chimneys that may well have been worth retaining. The chimney at Victoria Mill, where a young Friedrich Engels worked for his family firm, stood in Weaste until around thirty-five years ago. In 2007, the 240-foot chimney associated with the former textile works at Strines, and a landmark across the Goyt Valley, was demolished for new suburban-style housing. In 2015, the 131-foot Durban Mill chimney in Hollinwood suffered a similar fate. The last chimney to receive attention as a result of its demolition was perhaps the 180-foot Boddingtons Brewery chimney that lasted until 2010, when capital deemed it superfluous to the plans to create a new 'vibrant' neighbourhood in Strangeways. Many of these demolitions over recent years have been in the name of clearing brownfield space for housing as the conurbation awakens from its post-industrial slumber. Brick by brick the city has demolished many of these totems of industry; but how should they be remembered?

The emergence of the chimney, as part of the architectural assemblage of the Industrial Revolution, was the result of the energy source underpinning the steam-powered mills – namely coal. Brought from the Lancashire coalfields by barges on canals such as the Bridgewater, or from nearby collieries such as Bradford (mining there only ceased in the late 1960s), the burning of coal powered not only the growth of Manchester but an entire global empire of cotton. If these chimneys have now, in the main, disappeared from Manchester, replaced by a new verticality of skyscrapers, then the legacy of these technologies is profound and long-lasting. Climate change was in effect kick-started by these brick structures bellowing carbon into the atmosphere. What was considered a localised problem of smog, pollution and air quality in Manchester has now become planetary in scope, even as the chimneys stopped smoking and the soot-covered buildings were cleaned. In an era of climate crisis, the Mancunian chimney has much to answer for.

**12** Night-time view of Castlefield's railway viaducts

# Atmospheres

## *Night* – Nick Dunn

What is the Mancunian night? Over the last six years I have spent many hundreds, if not thousands, of hours walking through various cities at night, but by far my most regular city has been that of my home, Manchester. Cities are subject to change, but at night they can appear unfinished somehow and allow our imaginations to create alternatives within their atmospheres and ambiances. Manchester at night offers this possibility. Barely noticeable features of the daytime city's architecture and streets take on completely different aspects in the nocturnal hours. Urban margins and crevices, apparent footnotes to the story of the city's daily routine, now ready to become new narratives. To be on your own in the city at night is not to be alone. The architecture follows you, in close kinship with the streets.

Yet the Mancunian night is disappearing. Not perhaps in the most obvious way either. In 2014, the city announced it would begin the replacement of its 56,000 street lamps with LED lights. The economic rationale for this transformation is clear, but the ecological, spatial and phenomenological implications are far less known. This process has already significantly altered the character of some parts of the city at night. The diversity of different lights and qualities of darkness across Manchester at night is being diminished, and specific experiences of the nocturnal city are lost as a result. This loss is not necessarily permanent, but access to a wider variety of night-time atmospheres is being prevented, or at least impeded, by LED street lighting. Coincidental to my nightwalking have been attempts to record the different ambiances and sensory experience of darkness across Manchester before they change substantially. Unlike the officially sanctioned festivals and displays that form part of the city's cultural tapestry, the locations I discover during my walks are smaller, subtler, and more distributed around the centre and the suburbs. To be clear, I am less interested in the busy, commercially driven aspects of nightlife in places; rather, I'm attracted towards the secret, the hidden and the unknown. What follows are excerpts from this ongoing body of work as I explore the Mancunian night.

Standing before the cathedral, the time is slowly falling beyond midnight, the building's Gothic Perpendicular style accentuated by the interplay between light and dark. Here, the blending of sodium street light, the directional wash of coloured light up the cathedral's tower and the white disc of its illuminated clock enhance its brooding presence. Wandering down to the River Irwell, a molten mirror that both separates and binds Manchester and Salford, there is little activity along the water's edge save for some disembodied laughter and the clinking of bottles. Moving back up Quay Street and then along past the Science and Industry Museum, I am drawn to the slumbering infrastructural beasts of Castlefield. Vast brick arches and iron trusses of the Cornbrook Viaduct run alongside the huge tubular steel Great Northern Viaduct. Their giant forms reaching out into the night beyond, the monumentality of their scale enhanced as the sodium street lamps at the feet of their columns appear tiny.

Heading up Hewitt Street and then taking a right towards that concrete serpent, the Mancunian Way. This is a place of magic as the road escapes from the ground and rises overhead. Underneath its grey and orange-tinged belly the geometry of this elevated motorway undulates between ever-skyward buildings and into the distance, literally disappearing on 14 August 2015 due to a sinkhole, but since fully restored. This award-winning (1968 Concrete Society) behemoth suddenly springs into life as the beams of car lights move above and below it – a dynamic shadow play that brings the curvaceous structure momentarily to life as the vehicles appear and recede with their red and white light traces. Following its arc around the city centre, at ground level my feet follow a similar curve to the motorway above which brings me to the modernist views of UMIST. This complex of buildings and

## Atmospheres

their multilevelled access points is rapidly losing its power as the city's ultimate statement in concrete and glass as the rapacious nature of urban redevelopment is quickly taking large chunks of it away. Dipping under the sinewy curve of Victory House (then Telecom House, now MacDonald Hotel) I arrive at Mayfield Depot. The former railway station, then parcels depot, is now subject to a new promise of urban regeneration. Plans are afoot, but these premises will not be entered by myself tonight. Instead, I walk around the back of Piccadilly Station, moving swiftly across Great Ancoats Street with its industrial estates and cheek-by-jowl apartment blocks. The dark mirror of New Islington Canal Basin lies before me, its surface gently rippled by the resident geese. A perfect place to pause and reflect on the mobile urban cinema I have experienced in the last couple of hours, with its dramatic choreography and nuanced expressions of light and dark.

Away from the pubs, clubs and other nightlife is a very different Mancunian night. It is contemplative, fascinating, eerie and enchanting. For, in the nocturnal hours, the city is somehow less fixed than in the daytime as most of us escape from our daily routines. This otherworldliness is also because at night our vision becomes less dominant and reliable than in the daytime, and we have a greater multisensory experience of places. So, if you think you know Manchester and its many charms, go for a walk around the city at night. To head out at night with nothing more purposeful in mind than a walk is a decisive act. It signals the end of the day and the start of a new time and place to explore. It enables the city to be rediscovered, reimagined and reinvented with each step. Even as more and more construction cranes fill the skies, their red lights forming new constellations in the nocturnal Mancunian sky, the offer of the city at night and the rewards for walking around it remain numerous and wonderful.

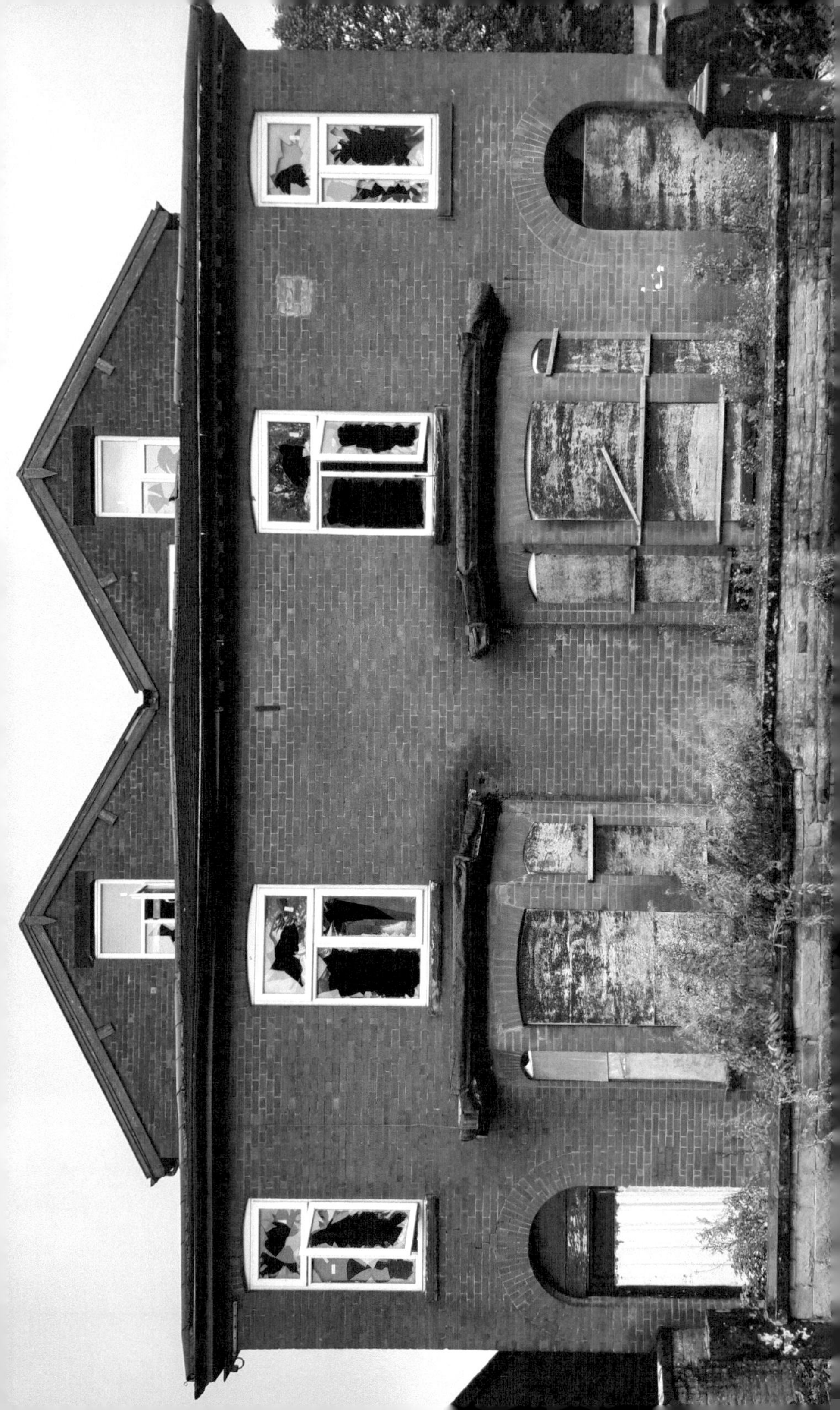

## *Moors* – Cassie Britland

'This place feels stabby.'

That's my friend's way of saying she feels uncomfortable. She's no snob – she herself grew up in a deprived community and has no time for white middle-class paranoia. We're on the same page most of the time – but not today.

'It's just this house', I say, gesturing to the abandoned building we're walking alongside. 'A few smashed windows and a soggy mattress will make anything look bad.'

I feel fine. In fact, I'm having fun. Abandoned buildings mean I can snoop around with impunity. I poke my head over fences and lift up my camera to take photos of spaces I'm not tall enough to see into. But my friend – who's even more interested in this stuff than I am – just can't relax.

We're in Glodwick, on the outskirts of Oldham, looking for the remains of the old Glodwick Road train station. Just over 130 years ago, Mary Ann Britland and Thomas Dixon (the husband of the woman Britland would later be convicted of murdering) were seen leaving a train here and walking towards a street named Bottom O' Th' Moor. We're here to follow in their footsteps – to try to understand where they might have been going and why.

If you're interested in history and urban ruins, the area just south of Bottom O' Th' Moor is fascinating to wander around. It's mostly industrial today, but there are remnants of forgotten structures littered everywhere. Most date back to the nineteenth century, but some are even older. Some, like the bollards on the walking path that branches off Hamilton Street, continue to serve their original purpose. Others, like the old station itself, have been co-opted and absorbed into modern structures. The most obvious example is in a tiny park on the corner of Southlink and Glodwick

**13** (Opposite) Abandoned semi-detached home in Glodwick, Oldham

Road. At the western end of this park, hidden beneath the scrub, there's a ramped brick platform that was once likely part of a train shed; today it's the foundation for a transport yard.

But other ruins are more obvious. On Moorhey Street, across the road from a Westmill noodle manufacturer, there's a row of massive square stones left over from one of Oldham's many old mills and reservoirs. Near the corner of Moorhey and Beckett Meadow streets, there's also part of an old stone wall that runs alongside the path behind the Bridge Inn pub. The top of that lane is a perfect hotchpotch: Victorian red brick, old stone, modern fence palings and overgrown hedges, all vying for the same space.

As we return to Glodwick Road and head towards Bottom O' Th' Moor, my friend reminds me which moor the name refers to. Bottom O' Th' Moor leads to Saddleworth Moor, a place synonymous with tragedy. It is most infamously associated with the Moors Murderers: Ian Brady and Myra Hindley. In the 1960s, Brady and Hindley tortured and murdered five children, burying four of them under Saddleworth Moor. One of those four – Keith Bennett – has yet to be found. It is unlikely he ever will be now that Hindley and Brady themselves have also died.

But Saddleworth's misfortune did not begin or end there. On a misty day in 1949, a British European Airlines plane crashed into one of Saddleworth's hills, killing twenty-four of its twenty-nine passengers. And in 2015, the body of a man with no obvious cause of death was found in the same location. For over a year, the man's identity and reason for coming to Saddleworth were a mystery. Police hypothesised he was one of the two child survivors of the 1949 crash, who had decided to end his life at the scene of his childhood trauma. But in January 2017, the man was finally identified as David Lytton – a former Londoner who had retired to Pakistan in 2006. Lytton had flown into Heathrow on the day before his death. Within twenty-four hours he had caught a train to Manchester, then walked from Greenfield to Wimberry Stones

## Atmospheres

– the site of the crash. To this day, no one knows why he came to Saddleworth Moor to die. But a post-mortem found the cause of his death – a self-administered overdose of strychnine – the same poison Mary Ann Britland was convicted of using to murder Mary Dixon, 130 years earlier.

Events like these can make any place feel grim and threatening (or 'stabby', as my friend would say). But Saddleworth Moor is a good six miles up the road. It feels like we're missing part of the story.

We find it the following day. An acquaintance tells my friend that Glodwick was the site of the Oldham riots. In 2001, some children – Asian and white – had an argument over a game of cricket. When the fight spilled out onto a white woman's doorstep, she called her brother, who was drinking at a pub. Minutes later, two carloads of white men arrived and started attacking Asian people and properties at random. Unsurprisingly, some Asian men retaliated to this treatment, and within hours Glodwick's streets were filled with violence: windows were smashed, pubs were firebombed, and more than a hundred people injured.

Fast-forward eighteen months. Today, at my home in Sydney, I've sat at my laptop for hours, writing and rewriting the final part of this chapter in an attempt to understand why my friend and I had such different reactions to Glodwick. At first I put it down to experience. She lives in Manchester and has a greater personal and historical context from which to create her meanings and interpretations of the city. This context turned an abandoned and abused building into a symbol of rage and violence.

But this conclusion feels like a disservice to both her and me. My friend would be the first to point out that I've actually spent more time in Oldham than she has. That I am not blind to the difficulties of Manchester and its surrounding towns. And that she has since joined me on a second trip to the exact same part of Glodwick with *even more* knowledge of the area's history and felt no discomfort at all (other than being soaked by rain).

## Manchester: Something rich and strange

There are so many factors that influence our individual feelings about places and spaces. When I'm not investigating 130 year-old murder cases I work as a travel writer, and one of my favourite ways to get to know a destination is to ask the locals what they think of it. The variety in personal experiences is always fascinating. Especially when they contradict each other.

## Notes

1. Doreen Massey, *For Space* (London: Sage, 2005).
2. L. Cardinali et al., 'Tool-use induces morphological updating of the body schema', *Current Biology* 19:12 (2009), pp. 478–9.
3. Paul Britton, 'A poignant new statue has been unveiled in Manchester', *Manchester Evening News*, 17 October 2018, available at www.manchestereveningnews.co.uk/news/greater-manchester-news/manchester-piccadilly-blind-veterans-statue-15289155 (accessed 17 June 2020).
4. This piece was originally commissioned by Manchester Urban Institute (University of Manchester) and published as part of *Stories From The Road*. See www.mui.manchester.ac.uk/connect/stories-from-the-road/.
5. A. B. Reach, *Manchester and the Textile Districts in 1849* (Helmshore: Helmshore Local History Society, 1972).
6. See David E. Nye, ed., *Technologies of Landscape: From Reaping to Recycling* (Boston, MA: University of Massachusetts Press, 1999).
7. See Stephen Mosley, *The Chimney of the World: A History of Smoke Pollution in Victorian and Edwardian Manchester* (London: Routledge, 2014), p. 14.

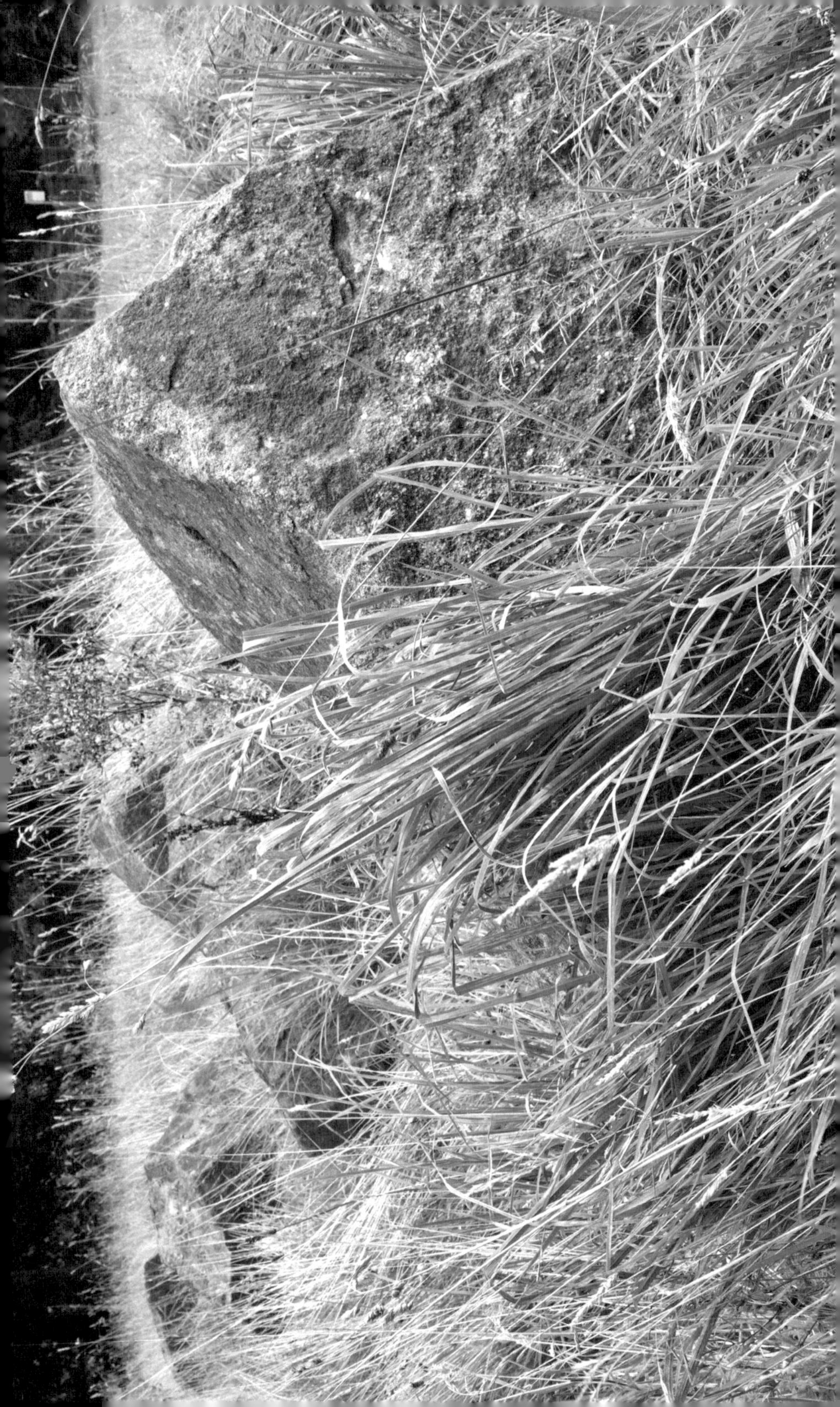

# Monuments

> Manchester is a more interesting city to walk over than London. One can scarcely walk about Manchester without coming across examples of the *grand* in architecture. There has been nothing to equal it since the building of Venice.
>
> *The Building News*, 1861

To compare the architectural beauty of Manchester with that of Venice might seem outlandish, but back in the 1860s it did seem to many as if the industrial city was finally sloughing off its image as an ugly, utilitarian hellhole into a new one of positively Renaissance-inspired splendour. Warehouses inspired by the great Italian cities of the past lined the streets of the city centre as well as colourful new buildings that would indeed have not looked out of place in Venice.

All of us who live in Manchester have an image – or several images – in our minds about what constitutes the city's most important monuments. Some would no doubt cite the Town Hall, Manchester's largest and certainly most impressively Gothic Victorian building, and still the civic heart of the city; others, one or other of the city's museums, flagships of culture that also provide memorable landmarks for navigation, even if, as Jonathan

**14** (Previous page) Former bedding stones for machinery, Upper Monsall Street, Monsall

## Monuments

Silver explores, their collections are sometimes the result of colonialist theft. Other less architectural products of culture might too become monuments: conventionally, the city's statues have always functioned as monuments, mostly to men, as Natalie Bradbury argues, but are increasingly drawing attention to what's previously been neglected, from the suffrage movement to the tragedy of the Peterloo massacre in 1819. And in hidden corners, artistic gems, such as the stained-glass windows in Manchester Cathedral explored by Clare Hartwell, provide enduring monuments to both trauma and hope, the leitmotifs of human existence and, by extension, the life of cities.

For those less culturally inclined, shops may features highly among Manchester's monuments – the 1970s Arndale Centre still the retail heart of the city today, as explained by Martin Dodge. As the core of Manchester, and parts of Salford, are being transformed by new residential and commercial towers, monuments to the present-day dominance of global capitalism are being constructed at a furious pace. Whether these will survive the next financial crisis is anyone's guess. If they don't, they'll become monuments of a very different kind: sad reminders of an age of greed that was only concerned with the most superficial kind of value, namely monetary gain. There will be some who will say it has always been thus in Manchester – a former industrial city after all, founded on exploitation and greed. But there are others who think another kind of future is still possible, one in which the city's monuments will speak of the importance of different values: of equality, ecology, compassion, generosity – all things we can find in the city, if we know where to look.

WORDS

### Monuments

## *Statue* – Natalie Bradbury

*A City Speaks*, Paul Rotha's classic 1947 documentary/propaganda film, was commissioned by the Manchester Corporation to educate citizens about the city's post-war redevelopment, highlight the social issues the city faced, and remind Mancunians of their forebears' achievements in science, industry, politics and culture. It begins by posing the question 'What is the city but the people?'. The first person we see is a young schoolboy in shirt, tie, shorts and long socks, who slowly and apprehensively tiptoes into Manchester Town Hall and through its sculpture hall. Inquisitively, he peers up at an oversized, robed figure, seated seriously and contemplating a model of a scientific instrument clutched in one hand. He's looking at Salford-born scientist James Joule, carved in white marble. Stepping across the ornate mosaic floor, he turns. Behind him is an equally impressive figure – another scientist, John Dalton, book in hand and deep in thought.

The looming figures of such eminent men recur throughout the film. The next statue we see is of the Duke of Wellington, towering over Piccadilly Gardens as ordinary Mancunians bustle about beneath. The camera pans past the statue of Abraham Lincoln to remind viewers of the solidarity shown by working Mancunians during the cotton famine of the 1860s, boycotting slave-produced cotton from the southern United States despite this resulting in significant hardship as employment dried up in Manchester. Back in the Town Hall, committee decisions are overseen by the figure of reformer and politician John Bright, standing sternly in Albert Square outside. Towards the end of the film, the schoolboy leaves the Town Hall and salutes the statues he passed on the way in,

**15** (Opposite) *Rise up, Women*, by Hazel Reeves, a statue commemorating the life of Emmeline Pankhurst and unveiled in St Peter's Square in December 2018

as the voiceover reminds him of the importance, as a citizen, of remaining curious, keeping his eyes open, and playing an active part in the city.

The most memorable moments of *A City Speaks* are provided by an exhilarating sequence which sets Wagner's *Ride of the Valkyries*, played by the Hallé orchestra and conducted by the famous John Barbirolli, to a montage of sporting and pop cultural imagery. A multiheaded Barbirolli later took his place, arms raised as if still conducting the orchestra, among the cast of eminent Mancunians in the sculpture hall.

It would be another seventy years before these figures were joined by a woman. In 2014, Manchester-based 'craftivists' Warp & Weft highlighted the male dominance of the city's statuary in their *Stature* project, a playful temporary intervention which placed crochet masks depicting eminent Mancunian women, such as the social justice campaigner Esther Roper, the mathematician Kathleen Ollerenshaw and Channel swimmer Sunny Lowry, over the faces of the male busts in the Town Hall as part of the city's International Women's Day and LGBT History Month celebrations. It wasn't until 2017 that the first female Mancunian took her proper place in the sculpture hall: Erinma Bell, who campaigned against violence in Moss Side in the early 2000s, and whose likeness is created not from the traditional materials of bronze or marble but from melted down firearms gathered during gun amnesties in Greater Manchester.

There have been efforts to bring more statues of women to the streets of Manchester too. Until 2018, a stately Queen Victoria was the only female celebrated with a statue in the centre of Manchester. In 2015, the public were invited to vote for the woman who would be commemorated in a new statue. From a shortlist of six, including the Labour MP Ellen Wilkinson and the novelist Elizabeth Gaskell, the Manchester-born suffragette Emmeline Pankhurst was chosen by a large majority. *Rise up, Women*, by Hazel Reeves, depicts Pankhurst standing on a chair, one arm outstretched, as if addressing a public meeting. The statue was unveiled to a huge crowd in St Peter's Square on 14 December 2018 – 100 years to the day after some women were first given the vote in Britain.

In recent years, public crowdfunding campaigns have celebrated other figures who otherwise may have been overlooked. In 2001 – twelve years before he finally received a posthumous pardon for a conviction received under outdated homosexuality laws six decades earlier – campaigners raised £16,000 to create a statue of the mathematician and Second World War codebreaker Alan Turing. Sitting on a bench in Sackville Gardens, a quiet spot close to the Gay Village, he holds an apple in a reference to the poisoned fruit which killed him prematurely at the age of 42.

To the roll call of scientists, politicians and other eminent Mancunians have recently been added the entertainers and comedians who have brightened everyday life in the northern city, and exported its humour to a wider audience. After his untimely death from cancer in 2010, fans raised funds not just for comedian Chris Sievey's funeral, but for a statue of his creation Frank Sidebottom – complete with oversized papier-mache head – to be erected on an otherwise unremarkable shopping street in the Altrincham suburb of Timperley, the setting and inspiration for his uniquely surreal brand of silliness. Hundreds of fans, many in fancy dress, turned out for its unveiling in 2013. Appreciators of the comedian Victoria Wood, meanwhile, raised £20,000 for a statue in Library Gardens in her home town of Bury.

Increasingly, Manchester's statues are being elevated beyond silent presences from an earlier time. Several have been brought alive by the Talking Statues project, which gives voice to their histories through smartphone technology. Voiced by famous actors – for example, Prunella Scales narrates Queen Victoria, who she has played on stage several times – these stories encourage us to engage with those who came before us, rather than seeing their lives as distant and unconnected from our own.

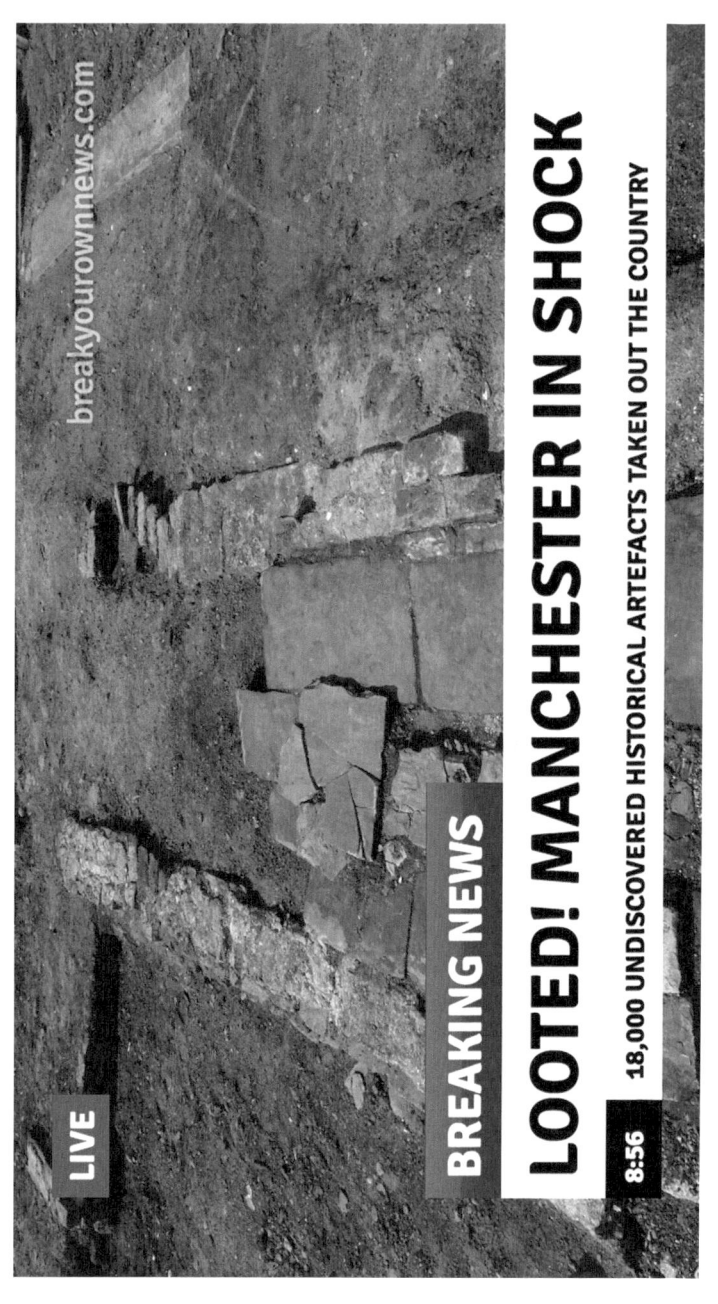

**16** An imagined news headline announcing the theft of historical artefacts from Manchester by a museum in North Africa

## Monuments

## *Museum* – Jonathan Silver

Imagine news emerged that 18,000 undiscovered historical artefacts relating to Manchester had been illegally taken out of the country by a museum in North Africa. We can only think what the response in the city would be in such circumstances. Political leaders would demand the return of the stolen goods, public protests would break out, and commentators would call such an act barbaric, immoral and a cultural crime. If such a scenario seems unlikely, then this is precisely what happened in Egypt at the end of the nineteenth and beginning of the twentieth centuries. It forms the invisible history of the Egyptian collection at the Manchester Museum, housed in the 'Ancient Worlds Galleries' inside Alfred Waterhouse's splendid neo-Gothic building.

These artefacts are best known as a world-leading collection of Egyptian archaeology that has helped to nourish young minds and contributed to global knowledge on the history of ancient civilisation. The collection includes a unique set of ritual objects from a tomb in Thebes, a 3.8-metre-tall pyramid temple column from Herakleopolis Magna, various animal mummies, hundreds of small figurines, gilded mummy masks, jewellery and statues. Perhaps the highlight of the collection are two mummies of the brothers Nakht-Ankh and Khnum-Nakht and numerous associated items, taken en masse from the 'Tomb of Two Brothers' found in the cliffs above the village of Dier Rifa and dating back nearly four millennia to the Middle Kingdom.[1]

The finance for the excavation and subsequent theft of the 'Tomb of Two Brothers' by the famed archaeologist Flinders Petrie was sourced from the wealth of cotton magnates, including Jesse Haworth. Haworth was a partner in the cotton merchant firm, James Dilworth & Son, and the pivotal figure in establishing the museum's collection.[2] The history of such connections and interest in Egypt can be traced back to moves by the Lancashire cotton industry to shift its supply from the American South to Egypt during the US Civil War. This led to the formation, in 1902, of the Manchester-based British Cotton Growing Association.[3] It led to Egypt becoming intricately connected through trade to the city, spurring trips to explore the region's archaeology by figures such as Haworth, inspired by Amelia Edward's 1877 book *A Thousand Miles up the Nile*.

It is this problematic history that suggests the collection is not just a world-leading space for Egyptology, but a historical artefact of imperial violence and its aftermath. It is a reminder of the ways that colonialism lives on in Manchester in forms that demand urgent public debate, and a recognition of the underlying brute force unleashed in the making of Cottonopolis and its prized cultural institutions. We must consider the collection colonial because it was financed through the wealth of the cotton trade and the slavery, later forced labour and natural resource exploitation of British imperialism, often led by the demands of Manchester's cotton capitalists. We can no longer ignore the history of a collection literally financed through the sweat, tears and blood of enslaved Africans. And we should not ignore how the collection was stolen from its home and brought to the city without permission. Like thousands of precious cultural artefacts plundered from Africa over centuries, it represents the violence that the British Empire visited on many parts of the planet. It is a stark reminder of how museums must be understood not just as celebrations of culture, but also through these darker colonial histories.

Debates concerning decolonisation have gathered force over recent years, spurred on by the heroic young people of the 'Rhodes Must Fall' movement in South Africa. The move to bring decolonisation into the cultural and public sphere has generated

**17** (Opposite) Egyptian artefacts in the Manchester Museum

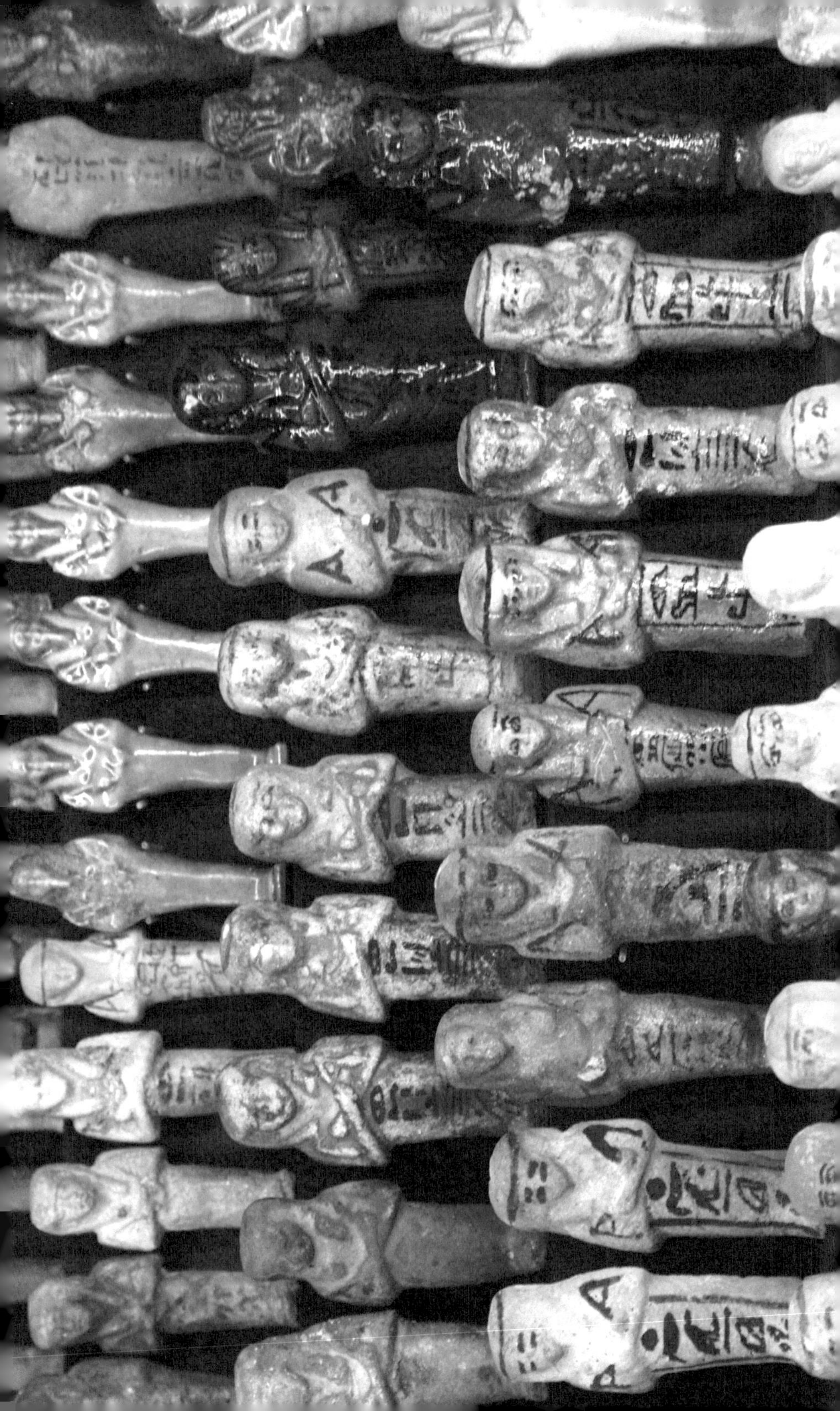

difficult questions about statues, museum collections and national memory. This drive to decolonise is important in the UK in which a 2014 YouGov survey showed an astonishing 59 per cent agreeing that the British Empire is 'something to be proud of'. Our conversations in the UK are beginning, the museum being a good place to start in a city that has chosen to forget so much. Next time we wander down its long, imposing corridors, our questions might revolve less around the fascinating artefacts on display and more on how they have long been an unrepentant symbol of the colonial underpinnings of the city.

I began to think about this task of decolonisation. That the city must recognise this living colonialism on display. That the museum must find ways to be led in its decolonisation by black and minority ethnic communities, and ensure that curators are representative of the city's diverse population. That staff at the museum would need to think about how the practice of curating could be transformed to represent artefacts that were appropriated, and to think more about the ways they are displayed beyond a Eurocentric notion of Western scientific objectivity. And finally, that discussions about what kind of reparations and returns the collection demands; to whom, and how this will be achieved, should not be put off until some undetermined future moment.

Up until the appointment of the current director in early 2018, Manchester Museum had seemingly done little to address these questions, nor confront the colonial history of this cherished (by some) institution. But this has changed quite dramatically. This chapter was initially written with this silence in mind. However, the era of obfuscation came to an end publicly in 2019 as the museum took the important, near-unprecedented decision of repatriating forty-three sacred items to the Gangalidda Garawa and Nyamal Nations in Australia after a century of possession. These inspiring steps, developed through dialogue between the staff and these nations, show how decolonisation as a process of learning and unlearning our histories and presents can transform

## Monuments

how museums operate. It is likely that such moves by Manchester Museum will also encompass the Egyptian collection at some point. The museum has transformed forever. Its decolonisation has begun.

**18** Aerial view of the Arndale Centre in the late 1970s

## Monuments

## *Shopping centre* – Martin Dodge

Since the medieval period, the heart of Manchester and the hub for shopping has been Market Street. At the start of the twentieth century it was regarded as overly congested and an inadequate thoroughfare for the cotton metropolis. Many schemes were advanced to widen it and the surrounding narrow streets to provide space for larger retail premises and easier pedestrian movement.

Yet it was not until the 1950s that serious plans for redevelopment were drawn up by officials in the Town Hall. By the mid 1960s, a Comprehensive Redevelopment Area had been approved by Whitehall for a large plot of land bounded by Corporation Street, High Street, and from Withy Grove to Market Street. It was to be completely cleared. Eventually a massive new structure would be built enclosing over one million square feet of space and providing modern premises for around two hundred shops. It would cost over £15 million, and was reputedly the largest indoor shopping centre in Europe when completed in 1978.

The Manchester Arndale Centre was undertaken by a partnership of the city corporation and specialist developers, Town & City Properties Ltd. They were led by Bradford-based entrepreneurs, Arnold Hagenbach and Sam Chippendale, who amalgamated their first and last names to create the 'Arn'–'dale' moniker that would become synonymous with their big covered shopping centres. Starting with their first shopping centre in Jarrow in 1961, they became successful in city-centre retail developments, particularly in provincial towns and smaller cities, and by end of 1980s had built twenty-four Arndale Centres up and down Britain. The one in the middle of Manchester was very much their flagship development.

The detailed architectural design was by the Hugh Wilson and Lewis Womersley partnership, who were also responsible for several other notable redevelopment projects in Manchester in the

## Manchester: Something rich and strange

1960s, including the Hulme Crescents and the master planning of the Higher Education Precinct around Oxford Road. Begun in the early 1970s, the Arndale Centre was a massive project to realise and brought significant disruption to the heart of Manchester for many years. The main mall was spread over two levels and included a walkway over Market Street to a large new Boots store that was built on the site of the *Guardian* newspaper offices. Also included was an indoor market for small stall holders that was to be managed by the council, an integrated bus station on Cannon Street, and space for around 1,600 cars in a multistorey car park. Rising above the centre was a substantial twenty-one-storey office block. Beneath the public mall was a service level with a roadway for delivery trucks. There was going to be an underground train station on the planned Picc–Vic rail tunnel, a major 1970s transport scheme for Manchester city centre that was never built.

From the late 1970s onwards, Manchester's new Arndale has been a major presence in the centre of the city, impossible to ignore and transformative in its impact on pedestrian circulation and retail commerce. Stores included many of the major names in 1970s retail – particularly those with wide popular appeal to female shoppers – such as C&A, Littlewoods, British Homes Stores and Mothercare. Directly adjacent to the Arndale itself were three big-name department stores – Debenhams and Lewis's on one side and Marks & Spencer on the other. As a retail destination it regularly attracted more than 100,000 shoppers each day, proving popular for many people by offering all the shops they wanted in an enclosed and clean environment, with easy transport links and plentiful car parking.

However, the Arndale was also a rather unloved hulk. Many criticised its 'ugly' architectural design and alienating effects on the surroundings streets. Particularly problematic were the expansive blank facades made from precast concrete panels that were clad in tiles of a distinctly unattractive yellowish hue. The resulting edifice had something of the ceramic tile appearance of a municipal

## Monuments

lavatory, and for evermore the Arndale would be ridiculed for looking like a toilet.

The undoubted scale of the Arndale gave the public of Manchester and wider region the closest thing to an American-style retail mall that the city would see for twenty years. However, the lack of natural light in the interior shopping areas made it feel claustrophobic to some. Wayfinding was also difficult, with multiple dead-end corridors and a monotone design throughout. While the retail on offer was sizeable, it was constricted in scope, favouring the national chains able to pay the high rents. The Arndale also lacked a sense of place and symbolic connection to Manchester's past – it was a typically soulless shopping space, its rows of mass-market identikit stores having little individuality. However, through the 1980s many teenagers' weekends were spent happily 'hanging out' in the Arndale, and for many families and older shoppers in particular the safe indoor environment, with seating and toilets, was a pleasant place to spend a few hours browsing.

On Saturday 15 June 1996, a 1,500 kg lorry bomb was detonated on Corporation Street, right outside the Arndale. Miraculously, no one was killed in this IRA attack, but massive damage was inflicted on surrounding buildings. In the aftermath of the explosion, the southern half of the Arndale required extensive repairs; as part of the renovation most of the reviled yellow tiles were replaced by sandstone and glass cladding. A new glass-bridge link over Corporation Street to the Marks & Spencer was constructed, and the internal bus station on Cannon Street was replaced by a new transport interchange on Shudehill.

Today, the Manchester Arndale continues to thrive despite much competition, particularly from the Trafford Centre, a massive £600m American-style shopping mall which opened in 1998 and is strategically positioned right next to the M60 motorway at Dumplington. Yet the scale of the Arndale development and its positioning were and remain controversial. One can lament

## Manchester: Something rich and strange

what has been lost in terms of the maze of side streets and alleys adjacent to Market Street, and point up the contrast between the sterile corporate feel of the Arndale and the more creative and quirky ambiance of the Northern Quarter area lying just beyond its Withy Grove boundary. Yet the Manchester Arndale remains full, with big-name retail brands and busy with shoppers of all ages.

**19** Fire Window, Manchester Cathedral, designed by Margaret Traherne and installed in 1966

# Manchester: Something rich and strange

## *Stained glass* – Clare Hartwell

Like almost all medieval churches of any size, Manchester Cathedral was once filled with stained glass, but little is known of it, apart from tantalising descriptions and a few fragments taken elsewhere.[4] What survived into the twentieth century, including Victorian as well as ancient glass, was finished off by the Manchester Blitz. The cathedral went on to acquire the major examples of twentieth-century glass which are considered here.

Stained and painted glass was and remains a major strand in ecclesiastical art. Complex resonances and meanings are inherent in the way that daylight, which can be seen as a fundamental aspect of God's creation, is mediated by stained glass. Displays of colour change subtly with each passing cloud and are influenced by the movement of the sun in diurnal and annual cycles, reflecting the liturgical day and year. At night, artificial light from within reverses the effect, so the glass can be seen from outside.

Despite the rich possibilities of expression, stained glass has often been considered as a craft rather than an art form. Manufacture by traditional methods is a laborious task, in which a series of complex processes must be undertaken to produce, colour and decorate the glass before individual pieces are fitted together using pliable lead strips called cames, seen as black lines against the light. Medieval glass was highly influential in the Victorian Gothic Revival, but design generally became completely divorced from production. As new artistic directions emerged in the late nineteenth century, the Arts and Crafts movement promoted involvement in the techniques of manufacture; combining studios with workshops on the same site meant that direct collaboration between artist and craftworker could be realised. This system was fundamental to the operation of the Glass House in Fulham (London) from 1906 until its closure in the 1990s.[5] As a principal centre of stained-glass production, some of the best and most influential glass artists in

## Monuments

Britain worked there, including Margaret Traherne (1919–2006), who designed windows for Coventry and Liverpool cathedrals, and the artist and sculptor Tony Hollaway (1928–2000), who made some of the Manchester Cathedral glass there.

The bombing of Manchester in 1940 badly damaged the east end of the cathedral, including part of the north-east Regimental Chapel. Here the east window commemorates the Blitz and the architect responsible for post-war rebuilding, Sir Hubert Worthington. Known as the Fire Window, it is the work of Margaret Traherne and was made in 1966. In red, vermilion and orange, the window illustrates this artist's interest in colour through use of textured and streaked glass of relatively large, mainly rectilinear panels, in which the leadwork of the frame is subordinate to the character of the glass. Flame-like forms appear, but discontinuities in the way the glass is arranged suggest violence or disruption, while the colours vary in intensity according to light levels outside. In some conditions, the window casts a pool of blood-red light onto the floor of the chapel. Added resonance derives from the fact that it was damaged by the Manchester IRA bomb in 1996, and later repaired under Traherne's supervision.

The five west windows by Tony Hollaway were prepared in consultation with the cathedral architect, Harry Fairhurst. There was a practical, as well as an artistic aim, to reduce glare from the afternoon sun in a building which is otherwise relatively dark. Since all the original glass had been lost, the project created a rare opportunity for a complete west-end scheme, one of very few examples in British cathedrals. The windows, noted for their coherence and artistic integrity, are widely considered to be among Hollaway's finest works. They represent an act of sustained artistic endeavour, started in 1972 and completed over more than twenty years. There is much colour, and pieces of glass interlock in panels of differing sizes. In contrast to Traherne's strictly non-representational programme, there are recognisable symbols and forms. The scheme explores a spiritual journey from beginnings and birth to endings and the afterlife, starting with Genesis and Creation on the south side, concluding with Revelation and the End of Days on the north side. Inner windows refer to St George, the Virgin Mary and St Denys, to whom the cathedral is dedicated. The dedication dates from the reorganisation of the church's administration by royal licence in 1421, when the inclusion of St Denys, a patron saint of France, perhaps reflected the dynastic aims of Henry V. The Creation window suggests form emerging from chaos in the coalescence and crystallisation of shapes, while the St George window is more directly representational, with a red cross and an abstracted dragon.

The central Mary window incorporates a circular motif struck through by shafts in a complex evocation of conception, sacrifice and prophecy, with much blue and jumbled words from the Magnificat. The circular motif is answered, this time in fiery reds and yellows, in the swirling, abstracted forms of the upper part of the St Denys window. The motif contrasts with the representation of St Sernin in Toulouse (France). Manchester Cathedral was twinned with St Sernin in 1973 at the instigation of the then Dean, the Very Reverend Alfred Jowett, who wished to promote links with the church in France. Finally, the Revelation Window is more purely abstract, with angular blocks dissolving upwards into less formal, flickering shapes. Hollaway intended to represent the stones of the Heavenly City, with the blue panel near the centre of the composition evoking the artist Wassily Kandinsky's 'pure and supernatural' colour of eternity. Each window consists of hundreds of pieces of glass, shaped and set within the irregular lead framework. They come in many different sizes, grouped and accumulated so that colour families are created from pieces of varying hues and shades. The leadwork is an integral part of the composition, used to create shape and movement. For these characteristics, Hollaway is surely heir to the Arts and Crafts tradition.

The windows considered here are among the most powerful examples of twentieth-century public art in the city. They reflect

**20** Revelation Window, Manchester Cathedral, designed by Tony Hollaway and installed in 1995

enlightened patronage in a Christian context, but are not exclusive or narrow in the focus of their subjects and concerns. As with all good art, their qualities transcend immediate historical context and invite participation in their visual worlds.

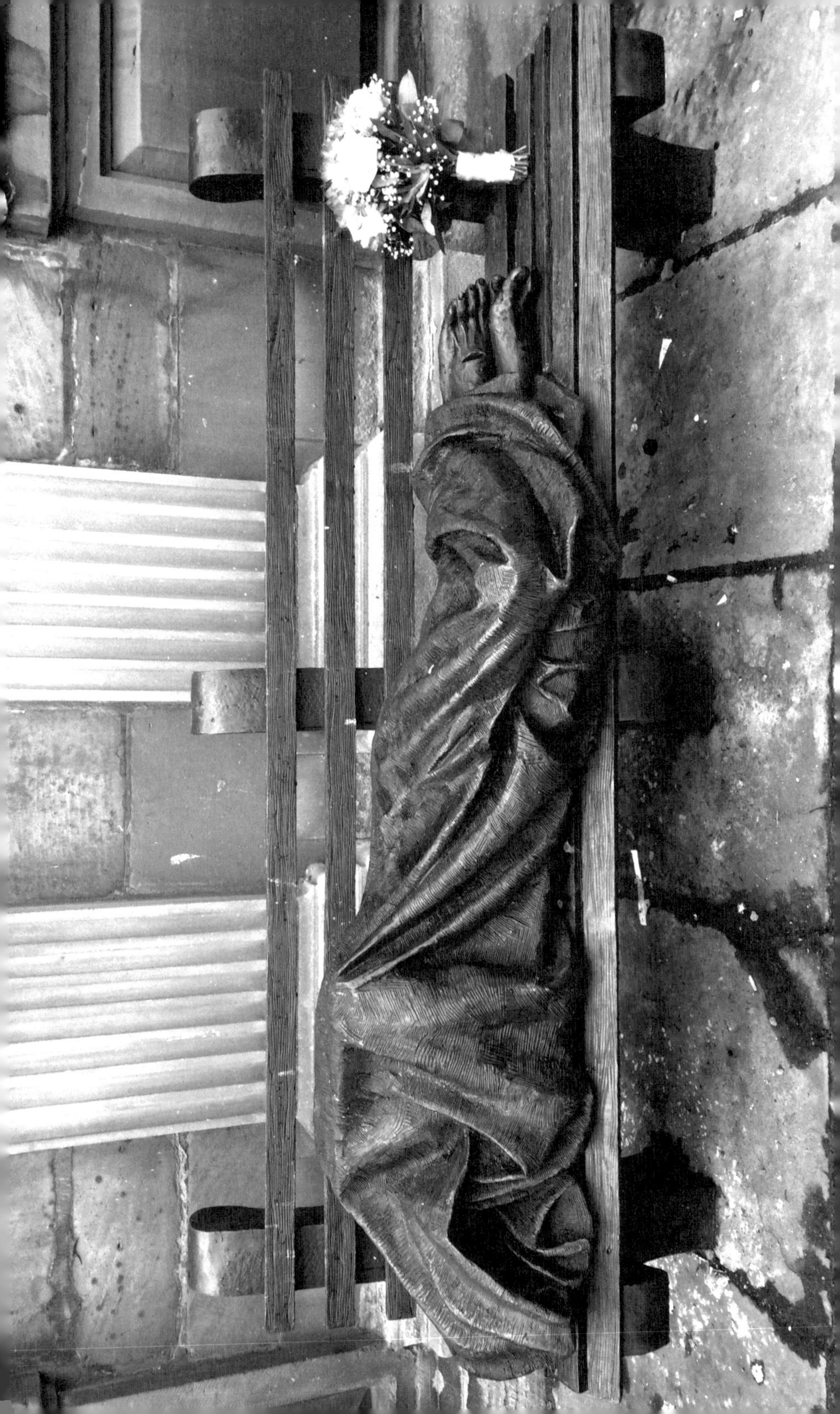

## Manchester: Something rich and strange

## *Sculpture* – Natalie Bradbury

In the summer of 2018, a swarm of giant bees appeared across Manchester. Sponsored by organisations and businesses and decorated by artists, schools and community groups, the *Bee in the City* sculptures took the city symbol of Manchester – newly prominent in the public consciousness in the aftermath of the Manchester Arena bomb attack – and combined it with visual imagery from Manchester's sporting, political and cultural heritage (see 'Bee', p. 285).

For months, social media feeds were full of enthusiastic bee spotters, accumulating photographs from days out to track down each sculpture. The project initiated a giant, city-wide treasure hunt, leading many to comment that they had visited places they had never heard about before, and walked down streets they had never previously visited. Perhaps the impact of the bees lay in their temporariness. Auctioned off for charity at the end of the period, there was no time to get bored of the bees, or become accustomed to their presence.

Conversely, much of Manchester's public sculpture is quietly overlooked. Where sculpture has been noticed, it has often been due to its notoriety. Thomas Heatherwick's ambitious *B of the Bang* translated a quote by sprinter Linford Christie into a sculptural spectacular, installed outside Manchester City's stadium in Beswick, east Manchester, to mark the legacy of the 2002 Commonwealth Games. Composed of large corten steel spikes which flexed and hummed in the wind, the sculpture cast a dramatic silhouette over its bleak, roadside setting. It was on site for only four years before being removed on health and safety grounds, yet its reputation remains – the prospect of impalement by falling spikes captured

**21** (Previous page) *Homeless Jesus*, a sculpture on a bench directly outside St Ann's Church

## Monuments

the imagination far more than the artistic merits of the sculpture. Its replacement by Ryan Gander, paid for by a refund awarded after a protracted legal battle, is far more anodyne. *Dad's Halo Effect* comprises three-metre stainless-steel chess pieces in the checkmate position, outside a new college and leisure centre.

While not all public sculpture attracts such attention, it can still add atmosphere to a place. The former campus of the University of Manchester Institute of Science and Technology (UMIST) is a cluster of high-rise modernist buildings dating from the 1960s, set in leafy, landscaped grounds just south of the city centre. The sense that this was the university's centre for new discovery and innovation is subtly reinforced by a series of public artworks, commissioned in the late 1980s and early 1990s, and inspired by themes such as combustion and insulation; one even depicts a naked Archimedes rising from his bath at the moment of inspiration.

Public art also played a large part in the creation of the trendy area now known as the Northern Quarter, which came into being in the 1990s; artists who worked in the then rundown area, attracted by cheap rents, played an important role in giving the area its name and identity. In 1997, a public art trail was developed around Tib Street. Look up, and you might spot ceramic parrots by the artist Guy Holder, referencing the area's former pet trade. *New Broom*, by George Wylie, was designed to reflect the cleaning up of the area, while *Toy Boy*, a neon sculpture on top of a multistorey car park by Peter Freeman, aimed to reflect the growing vibrancy of the area (ironically, the sculpture was switched off between 2005 and 2010 as an argument took place about who should pay the electricity bill; today its neon lights have been replaced with LEDs, and it is switched on for only a few hours each day). The Irwell Sculpture Trail is more wide-ranging, following the River Irwell thirty-three miles from Salford Quays to Bacup in Pennine Lancashire. While many of the sculptures, developed in collaboration with local communities, reference the history of their localities, the highlight of the trail is the American

## Manchester: Something rich and strange

artist Lawrence Weiner's text work, *Water Made it Wet*, emblazoned boldly on a bright red bridge over the disused Manchester, Bolton & Bury Canal.

Sculpture can be functional as well as ornamental. The concrete Hollaway Wall, built in 1968 and listed in 2011, acts as a sound buffer, screening the UMIST campus from the noise and fumes of the A6, as well as a striking Brutalist structure. Liam Curtin's *Meccano Bridge* in Bolton, made from scaled-up, primary-coloured pieces of the popular construction toy, takes walkers over the Manchester, Bolton & Bury Canal north of the M60.

Sculpture can also bring social and political issues to our attention – such as the scale of Manchester's homelessness problem in recent years. From a distance, *Homeless Jesus*, a bronze figure sleeping wrapped up in a blanket on a bench outside eighteenth-century St Ann's Church, is disturbingly realistic; it's only close up that the stigmata in his feet are visible, and it's apparent that it is an artwork.

Some of the best sculpture in Manchester can be found in the open-air sculpture garden in the grounds of the Whitworth Art Gallery, cleverly subverting our expectations of the types of ornaments we expect to see in a Victorian park. Gustav Metzger's *Flailing Trees* upends willows and places them in a bed of concrete. Cyprien Gaillard's quietly dignified *Whitworth Park Obelisk* uses aggregate in contrasting colours made up of crushed brick from demolished terraces in Moss Side and the notorious Hulme Crescents. Anya Gallaccio's reflective stainless-steel sculpture of a London plane tree twists through the park's greenery, complementing the Whitworth's light-filled extension. In *Bending*, by New Delhi-based Raqs Media Collective, a statue steps down and bows to its plinth.

Unfortunately, several of Manchester's best sculptures, including work by some of Britain's most important twentieth-century artists, have been hidden, lost, neglected or forgotten. Elisabeth Frink's *Flying Man* at Manchester Airport celebrates Alcock and Brown's unprecedented non-stop flight across the Atlantic in

## Monuments

1919, combining a spindly human form with the sleekness of a flying machine. Reportedly disliked by the families of the men it commemorates, it's now relegated to an out-of-the-way corner of Terminal 1.

However, there is some good news. In the early 1960s, a bronze peacock by Gertrude Hermes was commissioned for the new Ordsall Secondary Modern School in Salford. After years in storage following the school's demolition, the *Ordsall Peacock* has at last returned to Ordsall, and is displaying its plumage to the city's people once more.

## Notes

1. Rosalie David, *The Two Brothers: Death and the Afterlife in Middle Kingdom Egypt* (Bolton: Rutherford Press Limited, 2007).
2. Christina Riggs, *Unwrapping Ancient Egypt: The Shroud, the Secret and the Sacred* (London: Bloomsbury, 2014).
3. Sven Beckert, *Empire of Cotton: A Global History* (New York: Vintage, 2015).
4. H. A. Hudson, 'The ancient glass of the Cathedral Church of Manchester', *Transactions of the Lancashire and Cheshire Antiquarian Society* 25 (1907), pp. 119–41.
5. Peter Cormack, *Arts & Crafts Stained Glass* (New Haven, CT: Yale University Press, 2015), pp. 248–53.

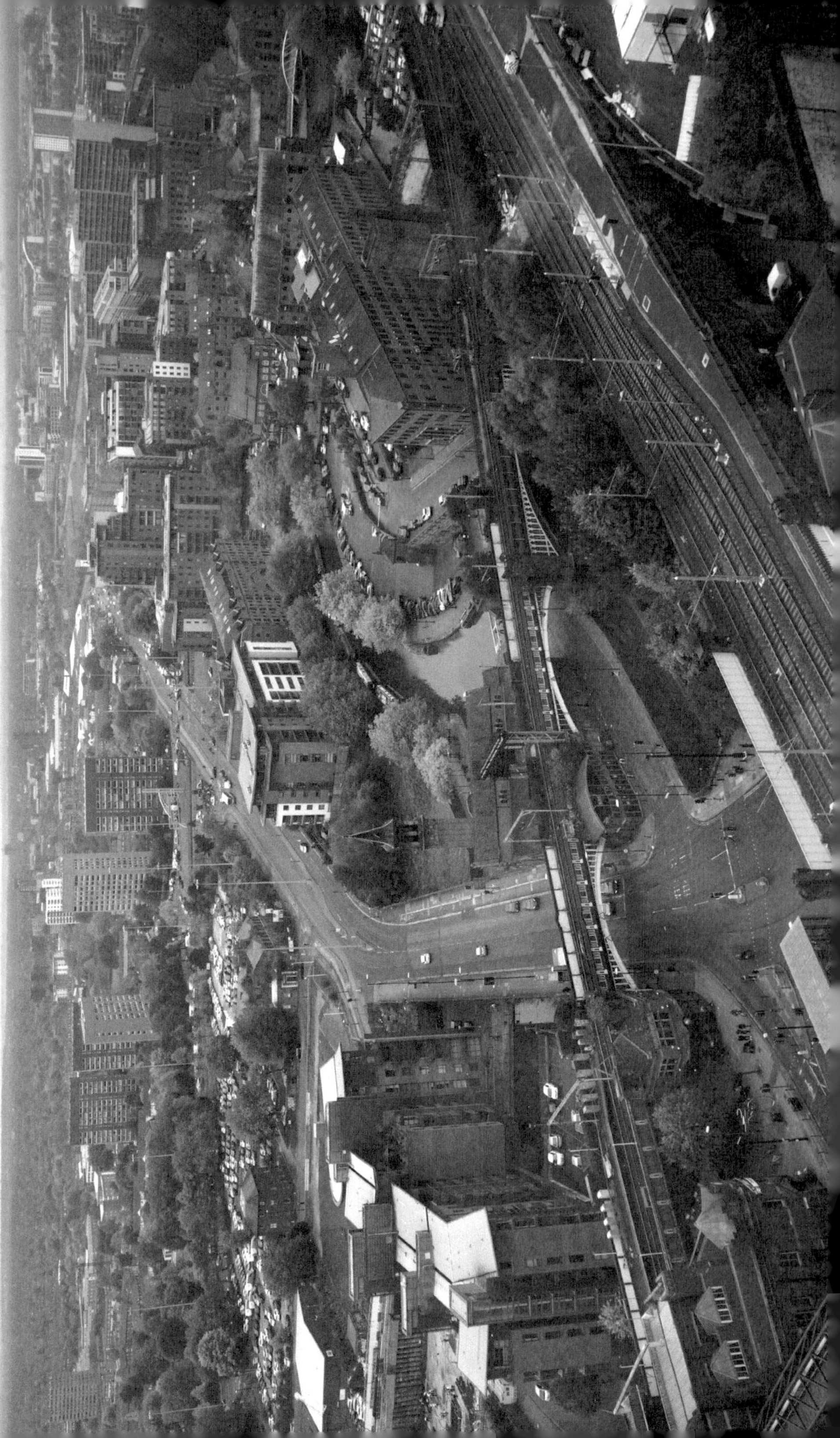

# Movement

> The whole of the factories in Manchester spin threads, in one year, which, tied together, would measure the almost incredible length of 313,385,384 miles!! A length of thread sufficient to wrap round the earth, nearly twelve thousand times.
>
> Joseph Aston, *A Picture of Manchester*, 1816

This extraordinary image of the strung-out and tied-together cotton threads of Manchester wrapped around the earth summons up a powerful picture of world dominance – of a single city exerting a far from benign global influence. It shows us how, above all, industrial Manchester was a place of movement; people and materials constantly travelling in and out of the city to and from far-flung corners of the planet. Incoming materials – by first river and road, then canal and railway – included everything necessary for the concentration of industrial production in one place: raw materials – illustrated here by Tim Edensor's 'Stone'; workers from both the countryside and overseas (mostly notably Ireland); and buyers and sellers. These rhythms of movement in the period of King Cotton were gathered in the successive incarnations of the Cotton Exchange buildings, places where prices were set and deals done, a movement that would eventually evolve into the

**22** (Opposite) View of Castlefield and south Manchester in 2011 from the twenty-third floor of the Beetham Tower

mysterious world of financial stocks and shares, as explored by Steve Hanson.

Movements within the city are no less important – and the history and politics of public transport continues to be a hugely significant part of the city's story, both in the past and projected into the future. Public transport isn't just dry infrastructure; it holds within it millions of stories of how people actually move across the city, what's possible and what isn't, tales of misery and frustration and of joy and freedom. Those possibilities are evocatively opened up in Nick Dunn's meditation on Manchester's orbital motorway, the M60, still the only feasible way of travelling efficiently (some of the time at least) between many areas of the city and its satellite towns. And cars are always difficult to get away from in the city – despite an ambitious plan for new cycle routes across the region, the city remains woefully devoid of anything resembling a coherent cycling network. Rare exceptions include the Fallowfield Loop, described here by Natalie Bradbury, which has used redundancy (of a railway) as an opportunity to promote greener alternatives.

Nearly all of us have experienced the buses of Manchester: a hodgepodge of competing companies vying to make money from what has never been a profitable enterprise. But in some parts of the urban area – much of Salford, for example – that's all there is; and, as Peter Kalu evocatively describes, long waits for late-night buses home continue to be part and parcel of how some of us experience the city. And, should we need reminding, Morag Rose shows us how movement in the city is a far from equitable activity. Choosing to walk the streets might seem an option open to everyone, but for those with disabilities or who stand out in other ways, it can be a frightening prospect, full of barriers and dangers that remain invisible to those with more privilege or confidence.

**23** The Corn Exchange in 2018 after its remodelling into a hotel and restaurant space

Manchester: Something rich and strange

## *Exchange* – Steve Hanson

There are three Manchester exchanges. The first two exist in architectural form, but their uses have altered. These are the former Corn Exchange and former Cotton Exchange, and they emerged as spaces to trade cotton, material and goods. The third exchange is a form of transaction that has become taken for granted globally as a natural fact since the early twentieth century – the Stock Exchange.

Marx wrote about the rise of the banknote, and of the ways in which forms of exchange became abstracted as the global economy grew. The high abstractions of complex financial instruments that evaporated under the noses of their owners across the 2007–8 period – the great crash – emerge from the logic of this third exchange: stock market capitalism.

Manchester was a key driver of these processes. Described as the first 'shock city', Engels noted – outside the Cotton Exchange – how the muck and the brass in Manchester are directly related, but politically riven apart. At that point, Engels could see the link between the abstract numbers and the *labour* those numbers were tied to, from the steps of the Cotton Exchange. This is more difficult now, but Manchester – contra the cliches surrounding the city – was a forerunner in *alienation*.

Of course, bonds and shares do not emerge directly from Manchester; they have a much longer history, in the form of loan certification to pay for wars and other urgencies. But the high abstractions of contemporary finance, the ways in which economics, people – labour – and social life, become viewed instrumentally and thus divorced from each other, is very particularly Mancunian. Manchester's bee symbol, viewed from this perspective, looks like an alibi. What Marx did was to explore how money becomes 'more money' via the exploitation of labour. This exploitation couldn't be achieved without the abstractions inherent to exchange mechanisms. The point at which workers have reproduced their own upkeep, and the outlay of the capitalist, and are now working for free, tipping 'surplus' into the capitalist's hoard, couldn't be concealed if the worker were paid the exact, correct amount for her or his work, on the hour, every hour. The exploitation of the exchange is obfuscated by the system of exchange.

The first two exchanges, in architectural form, have interesting afterlives. One is the site of middle-class chattering and leisure, the Royal Exchange Theatre; the other, the Corn Exchange, became a site of mass consumption – a shopping mall – which saw its more informal traders socially cleansed after the 1996 IRA bomb. The former Corn Exchange is now a hotel as well as a shopping space, mirroring the other contemporary Mancunian process, of public spaces shifting to private ones (see 'Facade', p. 226) and, of course, 'gentrification'.

Manchester's much touted 'radicalism' is in fact the radicalism of the right. It is a capitalist, laissez-faire radicalism. Factory Records flirted with Thatcherism in the 1980s and the zeitgeist of postmodernism. In postmodernism, the meaning is sacrificed to the message. Similarly, in Manchester the meaning of 'exchange' has been sacrificed to money. These are the qualities of 'The Exchange' in Manchester.

24 Blocks of sandstone in the former Collyhurst Quarry

## Movement

### *Stone* – Tim Edensor

Lying a mile from the city centre is the densely populated suburb of Collyhurst, a former site of industry with coal mines, brickworks, paper mills and chemical works, and now a mix of tram depots, wastelands, railway tracks and viaducts, high-rise and terraced housing, and retail parks. Yet lurking in its complex topography is an older industrial site: the quarry that provided much of the stone for the city's pre-industrial buildings. Now located in the country park of Sandhills, an aged cobbled road leads away from the quarry's jagged faces that erupt through grassy banks. The Binney Sandstone, as geologists call it, was carted along this road to the nearby River Irk, where it was transported on barges until it arrived at the city centre where the Irk merged with the Irwell. The sandstone was created from large windblown dunes in the Early Permian era, which were subsequently compressed over many millennia to form sedimentary formations; it is sobering to consider that Manchester is situated on an area that was once a hot desert. The stone quarried at Collyhurst remains present, notably in the city's most venerable buildings – the cathedral, Chetham's School of Music, and St Ann's Church – and it is amply evident on the facades of the latter two buildings.

The quality of this locally sourced stone was poor, and it dissolved, cracked and fragmented in Manchester's wet climate. The quarry closed down over 200 years ago because, during the Industrial Revolution, other sources of stone became available as canals, and subsequently railways, opened up transport links to more remote quarries. The massive growth of the industrial cities of the North and Midlands generated a huge increase in stone quarrying as rural localities sought to supply the building material that was essential for this vast urban development. The use of better, easier-to-work, cheap and more durable stone was now accessible and heralded the start of a process whereby Manchester

## Manchester: Something rich and strange

would be constituted out of stony material from further afield. More resilient stone was first sourced from nearby Derbyshire following the opening of the Peak Forest Canal in 1796, and in the same year, the Peak Forest Tramway that created a connection with the limestone quarry at Dove Holes near Buxton. As canals and railways extended further outwards, a greater diversity of building stone became accessible, changing central Manchester's fabric.

Certain preferred stone reoccurs across the city, including the fine-grained, yellow-grey sandstone – or Millstone Grit – from Darley Dale in the Peak District; the deep-red Runcorn sandstone, sourced from what was once the UK's largest quarry; and the pinkish-yellow sandstone from the still extant Hollington quarries in Staffordshire. All these stones remain as part of the variegated mosaic of St Ann's Church. Yet others among Manchester's signature buildings have their own particular constitution: the solidity of the Town Hall is provided by 500,000 feet of Spinkwell sandstone from Bradford; the ornate design of John Rylands Library is wrought out of distinctive red Permian sandstone from Penrith, Cumbria; and, like many prestigious buildings in the UK and abroad, the Central Library is clad in resplendent Portland limestone.

These stones bestow on Manchester a particular colour palette, now visible after the almost universally soot-covered buildings of the 1950s were cleansed. Despite its reputation, Manchester is not a grey city. Its stony polychromatic appearance is being supplemented by the multiple hues of more contemporary building materials to create an ever-changing kaleidoscope of colour. This stony fabric also testifies to the multiple connections that the city has forged with numerous sites of stone supply over the past 300 years. This reveals that like all cities, Manchester is ceaselessly reproduced by innumerable networks of material supply, as well as of people, transport, money, information, energy and commodities. No city is an island. A city requires a continuous flow

## Movement

of matter from elsewhere: stone, concrete, brick, wood, clay, tiles, plaster, glass, plastic, iron and steel. Decisions about which building stone should be imported to facilitate urban expansion and restoration depends on a host of factors, including architectural fads and preferences, availability and cost, financial deals between key players, and changing stone-cutting, transport and building technologies.

Such decisions might mean that sources of supply are suddenly dropped, perhaps with catastrophic consequences for quarrying communities. The unequal relations that existed between the economic powerhouse of Manchester and the rural quarries that supplied it invariably created significant impacts upon local economies beyond the city. In fact, while some connections between sites of stone supply and Manchester may have endured for decades, ultimately all have withered. The evidence of these prior associations is found in the old transport routes that, like the long-disused cobbled byway in Collyhurst, are no longer plied by carts, horses, trucks and rail wagons. The Peak Forest Tramway, closed in 1925, is today a heritage attraction and cycle path; the road that leads away from Runcorn Quarry is disused. Runcorn Quarry itself closed down over a hundred years ago, and Darley Dale Quarry lies abandoned.

Nowadays, building stone is typically shaped into thin veneers and used to clad facades, conveying an impression of solidity that belies the existence of the less attractive but structurally important concrete behind. And in contemporary times, Manchester rarely obtains the stone used in large building projects from local, or even British, sources. The Arndale extension, which opened in stages between 2003 and 2006, is adorned with stone from a variety of foreign sources: grey Sardinian granite; grey limestone from Solnhofen in Germany; streaky grey-green Brazilian migmatite; and black South African basalt. Spinningfields Square is covered with silver granite from Jinjiang, China. This seems to signify an era in which Manchester has become detached from its region, rejecting local stone sources in favour of cheaper imports from all over the world. Yet concrete, that most ubiquitous of building materials, is used in much greater quantities than stone, and although it seems to bear little visible trace of its place of origin, is invariably composed of sand and stony aggregates quarried from local and regional sites.

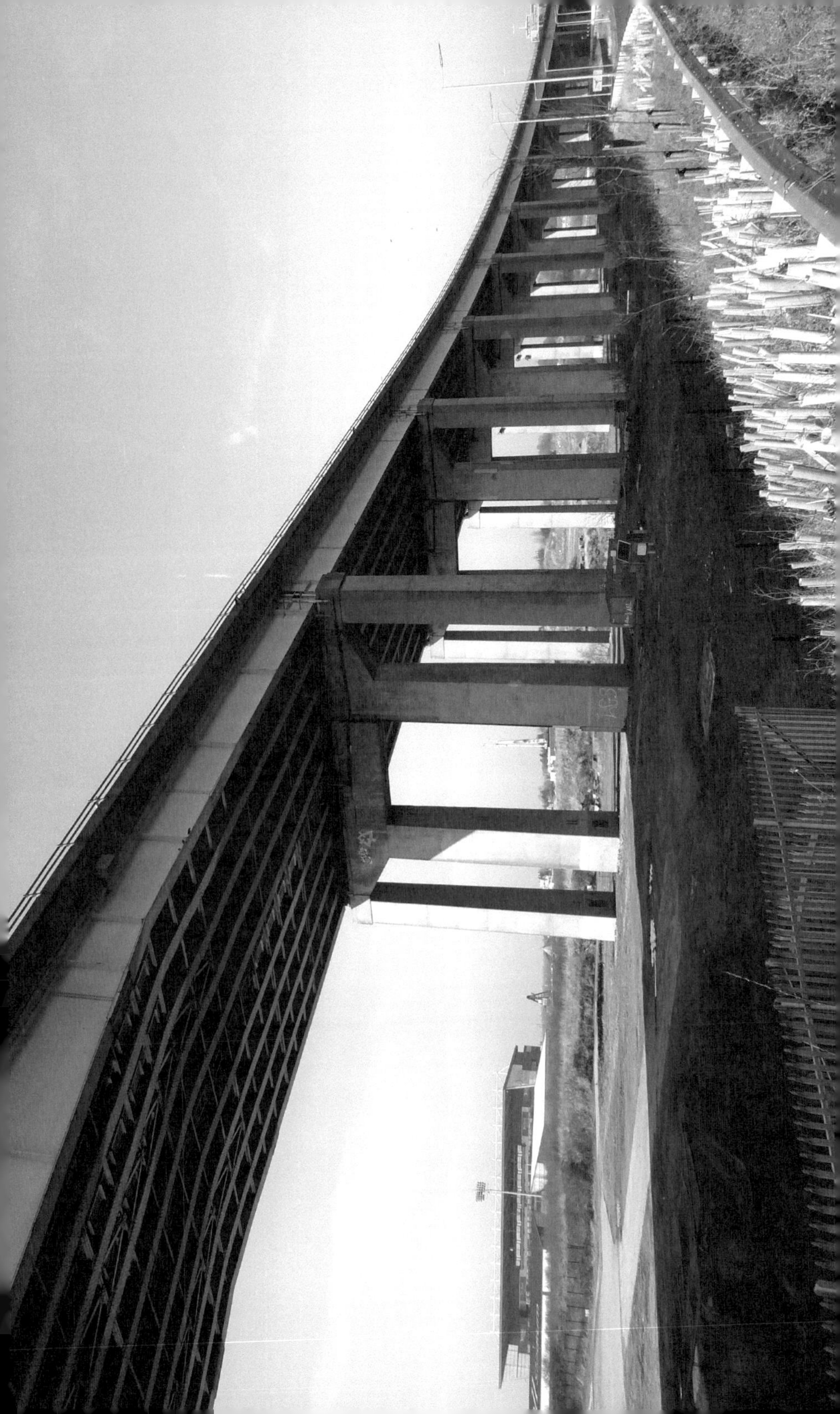

## Manchester: Something rich and strange

## *Ring road* – Nick Dunn

The M60, the Manchester outer ring road, is a thing of wonder. Thirty-six miles of tarmac and concrete that form the UK's only circular motorway that, were it not for its twenty-seven junctions, could be an infinite loop of Ballardian lust for drivers. An orbital motorway that stitches together the various districts and communities within its concrete ring, and provides a significant forcefield for those beyond it. I was one of those. Born in Salford, but quickly dispatched to Boothstown then Tyldesley, the respective postcodes of M28 and M29 seeming to echo the increasing distance from the centre of things. Formative memories were visiting my paternal grandparents in Urmston, who happened to be called Jack and Vera. Being the same names as Manchester's then most famous couple from the TV soap *Coronation Street* has always seemed to raise a wry smile whenever they are mentioned in conversation. The journey was particularly spectacular from the backseat of the car. Joining at Junction 13 in Worsley, heading southbound, our family car suddenly elevated from the humdrum 30-miles-per-hour limits of suburbia into the fast flow of the motorway.

As the lanes to the left quickly peeled away, providing exits for the M602 and the M62, our two-lane (subsequently widened) ribbon of infrastructure shot forward and up in the air like a whip crack of asphalt. Ascending the Barton High Level Bridge, the bonnet of my dad's gold Ford Cortina became resplendent even in the Dumplington murk, as the anticipation of being briefly above everything – a highway in the sky – was giddying. Then the descent. This is arguably the most epic part of the M60 which, like the city itself, has been brought together from a patchwork

**25** (Previous page) Underneath the Barton High Level Bridge on the M60 motorway

## Movement

of different elements and identities. Manchester tells a great story about itself, forming a coherent narrative from disjointed bits and pieces. But here, especially on a sunny day, Manchester briefly becomes Los Angeles as sleek concrete curves take you into the sky and towards the city of dreams. However, rather like those who seek their destiny in Hollywood, the M60 can never take you to Manchester, but instead enables you to circumnavigate it – always full of promise, but somehow always in the distance too.

During my youth, this landscape was populated very differently from how it is now. With the Davyhulme Sewage Works on one side, its UFO-saucer settling tanks forever earthbound, and light industrial sheds and works on the other. The sheer scale and height of the ring road at this section creates significant indifference to architecture. Make no mistake, when you travel over the Barton High Level Bridge you are very high indeed. It was designed to give clearance of around 100 feet to enable waterborne traffic on the Manchester Ship Canal to pass freely underneath. However, with the arrival of the Trafford Centre and its neighbouring developments, this challenge is assailed with the bizarre, gargantuan bric-a-brac of indoor ski slopes, postmodern retail offer, and, most recently, a dinosaur-themed adventure golf park. Rather than diminish the Californian imaginary, these Americana accoutrements simply serve to reinforce the cinematic experience of the journey.

That so many people drive over this grand concrete-and-steel serpent each day without really thinking about it keeps this outstanding piece of infrastructure in the background of everyday life, consigning it to the banal. It is anything but. My dad still vividly recalls walking over the bridge before it was opened to traffic. He remembers it being exciting and somewhat frightening being up above everything the eye could see, apart from hills in the distance. It certainly would have been an incredible experience, not least for a 12 year-old and his friend, walking over the landscape at such a height, arcing around the city and having those spectacular views from a vantage point designed for much higher speeds than walking legs.

Opening in October 1960, the Barton High Level Bridge was originally part of the M62 and known as the Stretford–Eccles Bypass. This was the very first stretch of motorway built and maintained by a local authority, in those days Lancashire County Council. In addition, the first construction work on a UK motorway happened right here, before the Preston Bypass section or the M6 or the M1/M10/M45 combination. The local authority acquired a vast amount of landfill and used it to build up the embankments for the bridge. This was a bold move given the motorway had not been given the go-ahead at this point. Prior to its completion, all the traffic in the area was forced to cross the Manchester Ship Canal using the Barton Road Swing Bridge, or further upstream using the Trafford Road Swing Bridge. Six decades ago, the Manchester Ship Canal was a very busy route with waterborne traffic at all hours of the day and night. Therefore, every time either one of these bridges was swung open, it often resulted in long queues of road traffic.

Such heroic infrastructure does not always go unacknowledged. Today, somewhat covered with dirt, lichen and vehicle-exhaust pollution, the commemorative stone marking the opening of the M62 Stretford–Eccles Bypass still stands at the southbound entry of Junction 13 of the M60. Officially opened by Sir Andrew Smith CBE, JP, Chairman of the County Council, on 21 March 1961, the stone also confirms the bypass' receipt of a Civic Trust Award in 1962. The significance of the M60 outer ring road, especially this particular section of it, like so many of Manchester's lesser-known achievements, weaves into the fabric of daily routines. In character it is monumental, yet in use it is unassuming – a poetic mix of qualities that define so much that is latent or forgotten in the city. But stretching out at either end of the Barton High Level Bridge is the ceaseless thrum of traffic on the M60 outer ring road, audible to many within its circumference and beyond, reminding Mancunians that their circulation system is very much alive.

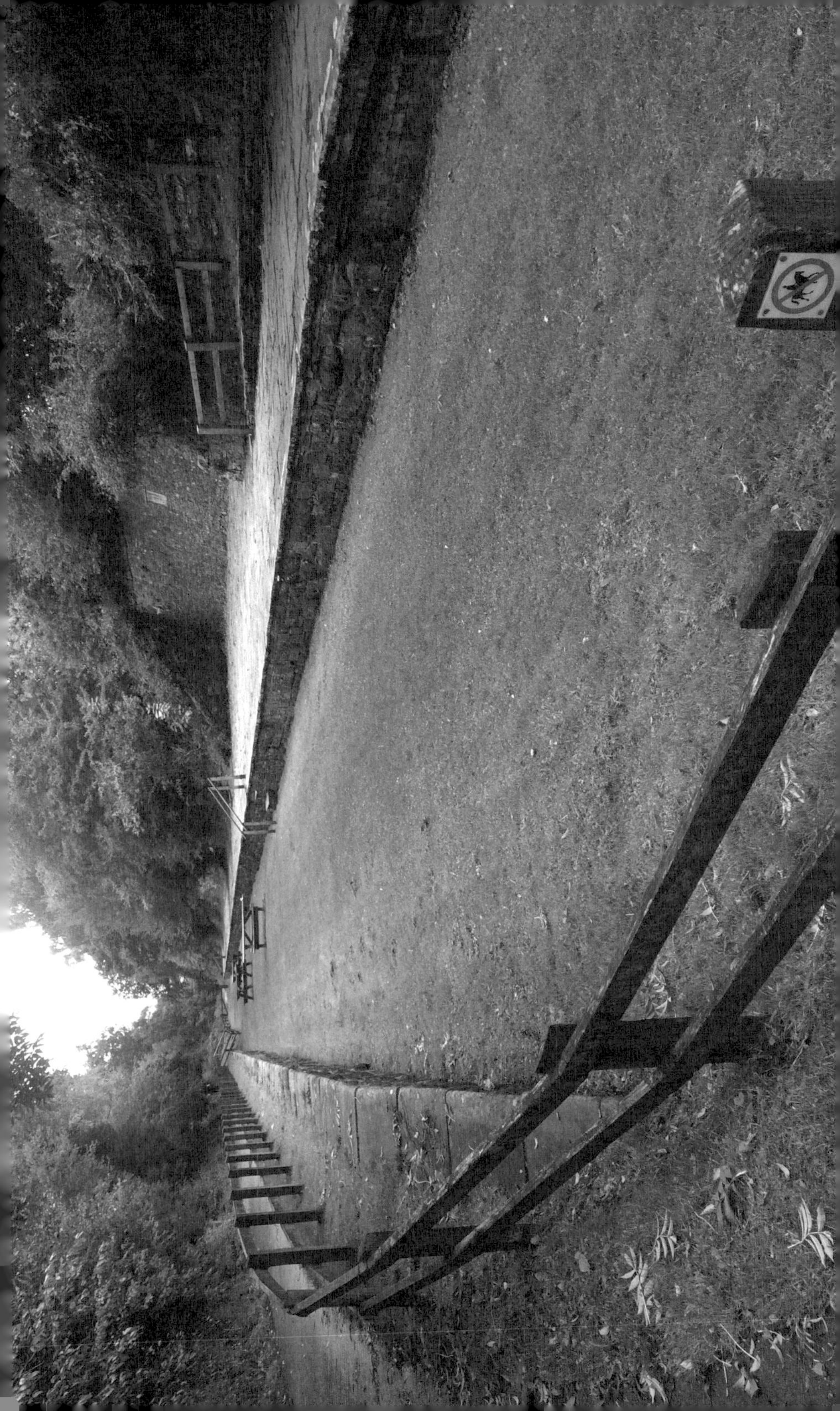

# Manchester: Something rich and strange

## *Loop* – Natalie Bradbury

In the 1960s, Dr Beeching paved the way for the reduction of the British railway network, closing small village stations and branch lines across the country and catalysing the ascendancy of the motorcar as the dominant mode of transport in Britain.

Some of these long-closed lines are now reopening, after decades lying dormant. Others have had their tracks removed permanently. In some cases, station buildings have now been converted into shops and supermarket cafes, as is the case with the former Fallowfield station in the heart of the student district in south Manchester. Another suburban station, meanwhile, Levenshulme South, is being reborn as Station South, a community-run cafe and bike hub, following crowdfunding by local people.[1] The venue will cater for cyclists who use the former train tracks below, which have been paved over to provide miles of dedicated bike path free from the traffic and aggressive motoring that increasingly chokes our towns and cities.

Greater Manchester benefits from several such suburban 'loop lines', which offer routes through and out of the city for both the commuter and the leisure cyclist. The best-known is the Fallowfield Loop, which stretches eight miles from inner-city Openshaw west and southwards to Chorlton, undulating through the former industrial suburbs of Gorton and Levenshulme, passing through picturesque Debdale Reservoir, skirting the boundary of Stockport at Reddish, and finally cutting through Fallowfield and leafy Whalley Range.

The Fallowfield Loop has the feel of a linear park, offering a backdoor view of the city and its patchwork of official and unofficial green spaces. The Loop itself is an underacknowledged green

**26** (Previous page) Former railway station platform on the Fallowfield Loop cycleway

## Movement

space. In spring and summer it's overgrown with leafy branches, forming a green tunnel. When the leaves drop in autumn the slipperiness of the accumulated layers can be treacherous. In winter, the foliage is stripped bare to reveal numerous back gardens, allotments, recreation grounds, school playing fields, overgrown brownfield sites and industrial land reclaimed as country parks.

It's also a fruitful place for the urban forager. Depending on the season, edible mushrooms, horseradish, strawberries, raspberries, cherries, plums, damsons, sloes and apples can all be found along the Loop, while in late summer individuals and groups of people of all ages appear with an assortment of receptacles, from large yoghurt tubs to seaside buckets, tupperware tubs and carrier bags, to gather blackberries, and offer hints on the best picking spots.

The Fallowfield Loop has become a place of community activism and voluntary litter-picking; riders have mobilised en masse to draw attention to a spate of bike muggings on the route, arguing for mounted police to increase their patrols. However, it's also a place for creativity, from street-art murals celebrating the city's architecture, to handwritten personal declarations. It's a place to encounter culture, from bicycle theatre troupes performing Shakespeare plays, to public artworks sponsored by the cycle charity Sustrans, which document and draw attention to the flora and fauna of the route.

Salford, too, has the Roe Green Loop Line, which begins in the village suburb of Monton, near the orange-hued Bridgewater Canal, passes through the affluent area of Worsley with its acres of woodland, and ends on the outskirts of the city in down-at-heel Little Hulton. The Roe Green Loop Line starts at a higher level than the Fallowfield Loop, looking onto fields of cows and expanses of open grassland, before passing through grand Victorian parks such as Walkden's Parr Fold Park. Here, the line's infrastructural past remains apparent: the former station platforms still stand, although nothing will stop there now other than the weary cyclist seeking a rest on a bench. The development of the Manchester

## Manchester: Something rich and strange

to Leigh guided busway, which runs through Salford's outer suburbs on into the borough of Wigan, provided a catalyst for the provision of cycle infrastructure: the area has also benefited from the Tyldesley and Ellenbrook Looplines, which have been newly resurfaced, partially with recycled bike tyres.

Out on the edges of Stockport, the Middlewood Way strikes out into deepest Cheshire. Running almost parallel to the Macclesfield Canal, this former train line was part of the Macclesfield, Bollington and Marple Railway, which carried stone and coal from quarries and mines into Manchester and surrounding towns. It shut in the 1970s, and a huge stone viaduct in the quaint village of Bollington was nearly demolished before it was saved by the community and purchased by the local council for just £1. The Middlewood Trail was created using a government grant and opened in 1985, running twenty miles between the market towns of Marple and Macclesfield. It passes near local landmarks such as White Nancy, offering views of the Cheshire Plain from its verdant former track lines.

To the west, the former Altrincham to Warrington route has been converted to the Lymm Railway Line, which heads out past the Dunham Massey estate into picturesque farmland. Another former train line, from Altrincham to the town of Irlam on the outskirts of Salford, could be reopened as a heritage railway line and bike path under plans proposed by local businessman and philanthropist, Neil McArthur from the Hamilton Davies Trust. These Loop Lines link up with other traffic-free routes, too – from the Ashton Canal, with its miles of recently resurfaced towpath, to former branch canals such as the Stockport canal, and rivers such as the Mersey.

Loops are places for learning and instruction, for small children to gain confidence and practise their bike skills away from the road. They're also places of conviviality and sharing: if a cyclist stops at the side of the path, the next one to pass will stop to see if all's okay, and offer help fixing a chain or a spare inner tube.

## Movement

They are well used by walkers, joggers, dog walkers, students, and children on their way to and from school, as well as shoppers and pedestrians just getting from A to B.

In spite of their myriad uses, perhaps cyclists benefit most of all from a safe cycling environment, not just free from traffic and pollution, but uninterrupted by the frequent stops and starts of traffic lights – and the unpredictability of the road.

ZERO FRIZZ
GIVEN.

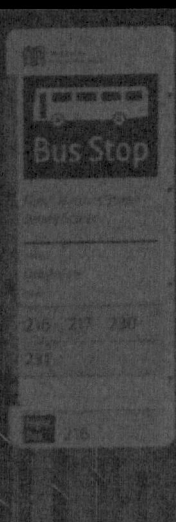

GREAT HAIR
THOUGH.

AUSSIE

## Movement

### *Bus stop* – Peter Kalu

We are the exhausted, the deluded, the drunk, the disappointed, the iced, the dishevelled and the disorientated. We assemble at this urban installation of folded metal and sheet perspex in a collective act of summoning through the midnight mesh of supervening events – crashes, no shows, roadblocks, breakdowns, other emergencies – the last late bus out of the city centre.

Cooks still in their filthed-up whites, exhausted by shifts in baking heat, are now shuffling stiffly in the cool slap of winter air, curdled eyes avoiding everybody. Aged, bleached, shrouded office cleaners, their empty purses and full heads stuffed with thoughts of a better life at least for their grandchildren, headphones plugged in and nodding to a steady bassline of syncopated dub. Young clubbers in their minimal threads. Three of them clustered in a nearby doorway in a swirl of joking, hugging, heat and phone-screen sharing. Now I notice at their feet the brown-skinned girl slumped in the lap of the white boy; that this is no bother to anybody at the bus stop is the beauty of this moment in the time–space of the Mancunian universe.

Above, the starless, joke sky, revealing itself as it never can do by daytime, in twists and flips of chugging colour, doing kaleidoscopic variations on Degas, Chagall, Sokanu; now sunken omni-blue, now aubergine black, a drink-everything sky that taps you on your shoulder with its benign indifference.

Passing along in the middle of the road to the taxi-rank queue go a fist of garrulous, argumentative, Rocky Horror Show devotees, loaded on goth eyeliner, lager and lyrics. This is the liminal space, if liminal admits the possibility of some bare-chested youth coming around the corner twirling a scaffolding pole, left, as, right and at the same time, a distraught, blonde-wigged woman in a

**27** (Opposite) Bus stop on Great Ancoats Street

## Manchester: Something rich and strange

pink cocktail dress stumbles, clutching a pair of Cinderella ballroom shoes.

Pity the rich, I suddenly find myself thinking. Those who can afford taxis might never experience this cinema of the street. We are social animals, and to be social in these circumstances, in these extremes of night of exhaustion of temperature is to be in the rare crucible that creates perfect storms, one-off movies without a plot.

A beetroot-faced, wide-mouthed, crop-haired man sways up, and after a moment of uncanny steadiness in a failed attempt to decipher the various limbs of the loved-up couple entwined at his feet by the shop doorway, lifts a hand up to me.

'Who you looking at?'

I move not away but towards him, until I'm alongside him, and he's puzzled. His outstretched hand had tried and failed to track me round, his moment for swinging at me long gone. 'I don't know', I tell him, gently, 'but I'm guessing you're going to tell me?'

He sees me up close; I flick one eyelid up and stare cockeyed with him at the world. His hand lowers, the violence sinks from his shoulders. A wet sparkle enters his eyes and with it the story of a job in Newcastle, a beach in Barbados, a divorce, a missing lottery ticket and his mother's last lover. He intersperses these narrative riddles with verses from what I take to be Royal Navy drinking songs.

'We', he concludes, 'are brothers. Now do you have a cigarette, pal?'

Someone holds one out and he goes in the direction of that hand and is soon started on another story. A bus comes along. Hope rises, but the sober among us see the bus has only headlights on and no house lights – it's a ghost bus heading for the mythical depot. Folk struggle up, gather bottles, hats, purses, shoes, only to see it refuse to pull in. There are jeers, groans, a clamour of 'fucks' and hand signals. The white-shirted driver is nonplussed. She has tunnel-vision eyes, steering through and on and out.

## Movement

Time stretches. We are soon in the witching hour, the time when all the pep and zing of club chuck-out has fizzled as flat as the crushed plastic beer cups in the road, and some serious distance-cost ratios are having to be made. Slowly the queue of expensive taxis starts to look a decent bet, their diesel chug alluring. Taxi-sharing starts to blink up as a solution in minds, and we eye one another up.

Still there is hope of a bus. The oracle of the bus timetable maintains its prediction. I'm waiting in the chill, wanting blankets if not a lover's arms. Micro sleeps. Over by the slanted, granite-floored fountain of Piccadilly, a soup kitchen is folding its tables for the night and street dwellers disperse slowly from the last steam of their urns. The borders of consciousness are fraying and I'm unable to separate hallucination and dream from what's out there. The huddled lovers slink tighter into each other's arms. The shimmering gold robes and kissing finger timpani of parading Hare Krishnas, the petit-bourgeois suits of the canvassing Jehovah's Witness pair puffed up by their sign saying 'God Loves You' in Xhosa. A memory of where I was earlier in the evening – watching the film *Moonlight* in all its saturated blues and heartbreak. This civic sky slowing as CCTV pods swivel less, tracking only the odd movement from their lofty poles. The streets are empty. The sleep lag tugging at my eyelids. Someone sobs, one of those mewling grumbles rather than a fully fledged exhalation – a grizzling that chews at the edges of my mind, crawls around my middle ear. Then a howl and a scatter of feet. We all turn to see a bloodstained figure emerge from a back street. His eyes are rolling with the satiated satisfaction of the just-revenged. He walks quickly into the middle of the road, head swung right up to the cameras in defiance, giving them the V.

I'm slumped down admiring the efficiency of the ride-on billy-goat litter-scrubbing vehicle, its tight turns and sharp weaves, when the night bus hoves into glorious technicolour view. The miracle has occurred. The oracle is proven true. In a flick of cigarettes and

### Manchester: Something rich and strange

blink-up of phone screens, in a haul of limbs untwisting, of clothes and lips untangling, in a hazard of pressed shoulders, in a cloud of nicotine, kebab sweat, motley perfume and fresh slash of lipstick, we, the chosen ones, get ready to board.

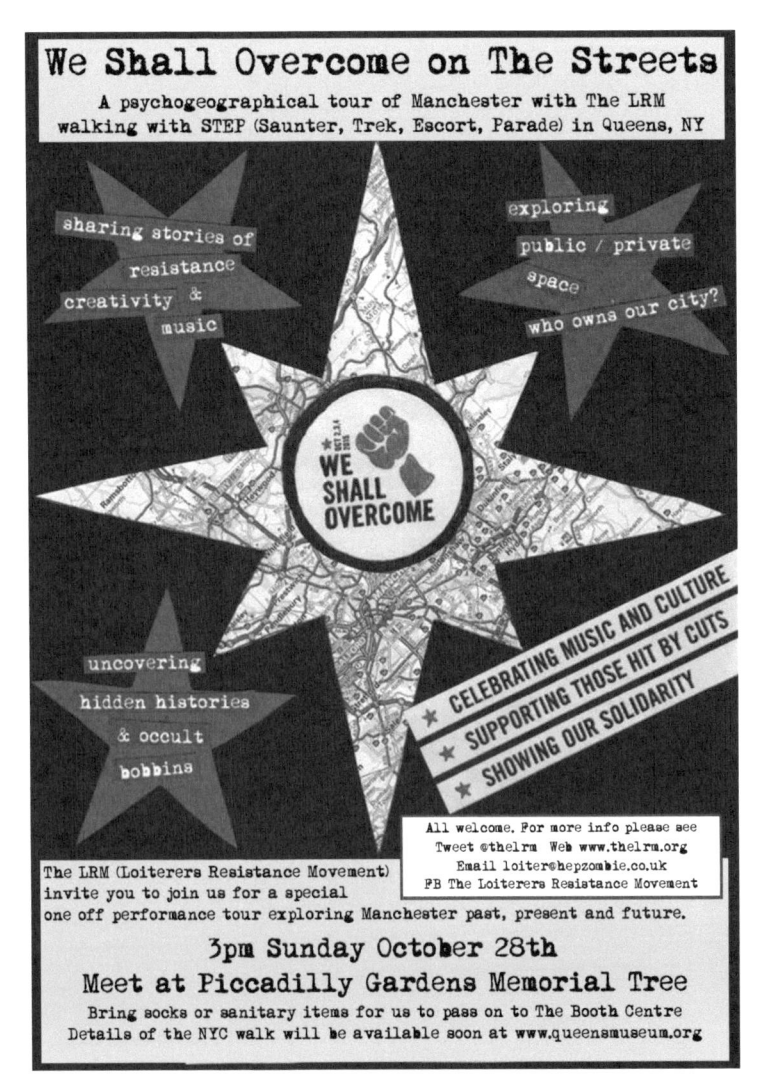

28  Flier for the Loiterers Resistance Movement

# Manchester: Something rich and strange

## *Walk* – Morag Rose

A walk can exist like an invisible object in a complex world.
Hamish Fulton

I believe that the streets belong to everyone and we all have the right to be in, (re)create, (re)claim and coexist in public space.[2] We must cherish and protect that right. Pavements are sites of encounter, serendipity, diversity, vernacular creativity and concrete poetry. Walking is more than pedestrian; it is an assertion that we are here and we can, and will, take up space. This should not be radical or naive, but sadly it sounds like both sometimes. I should have said I fantasise that 'the streets belong to everyone' because they don't, of course: but they should. I know they don't. I feel it in my bones with every heckle, every glare, the long-form background hum of invisible barriers and warnings, cacophonies of 'smile love', 'show us yer tits' and 'look at the fucking state of that'. When my legs ache and my body feels broken there are the tuts too, hurry ups and sighs and pushes and the sense that everyone else is entitled to be here, but I am not. I am reminded of this sensation when I listen to heartbreaking stories, generously shared, of racism, transphobia and other prejudices; so many bullies working to control space and erase dissent. I rage at the fear and abuse that limits so many of us in so many ways. This is not a criticism of those who stay inside for their own safety. It is valid and true and awful to feel scared, and I regret that; despite my beliefs, it restricts me too sometimes. As ever, the personal is political.[3]

One particular incident has really haunted me. I'd been to a house party just a bit too close to home to justify the price of a cab, and of course I'd missed the last bus. It was a clear night. I felt effervescent, incandescent, king of a world of stars and shadows – no one but the local cats to witness my delight. I was aware that a man was behind me and I hated myself for feeling a prick of

## Movement

fear. Nothing to worry about really, just another dirty stop-out waltzing home late. Still, I crossed the road, felt for the keys in my pocket. He followed. I adopted a stance familiar to the designated vulnerable everywhere, walked confident, away from the shadows, shoulders back, striding on. As my pace quickened so did his, and suddenly I was wide awake, calculating escape strategies. I was holding my phone, called the friend still at the party, paused for a second as I did so – and then he touched me. The phone rang and rang and the voicemail message I left was a strangulated, squeaky voice I scarcely recognised as my own. He began to talk, to cajole, and then to threaten; at this point he was gripping me tightly and guiding me to a patch of wasteland, the bushes an anti-sanctuary in the dark. A scrap of grass somewhere I had passed a thousand times without ever registering its potential peril. The details as to what happened next don't matter, but I was lucky – he was spooked by a passing police car. The car didn't stop even as I jumped and screamed, but it caused befuddlement in my attacker and gave me time to run.

Some walks change us. They cannot be forgotten, but are assimilated, and so we carry on. And I did. I didn't involve the police for obvious reasons, not least like many friends they would have asked why I was out, on my own, at that time of night. If my general resolve to walk on was strengthened, that specific place haunted me and I avoided it for years. It's not far from where I live, so I wandered its periphery, passed on a bus, in a car, but could not, would not, set foot there. It's amazing how easily a place can vanish from your cognitive map of viable routes through the city. Recently I had to confront my fear. No, not had to – I could have taken a ridiculously long detour or declined a wonderful invitation which coincidentally necessitated a return to that street. But I chose to confront my pavement nemesis. Even after all this time I felt sick and shaky, surprised how visceral the sensation was; but I took a deep breath, blinked away my tears, put my head up and best foot forward, and just kept walking. Nothing happened. No

## Manchester: Something rich and strange

big epiphany or ghostbusting or flashbacks; just an everyday stroll on a mundane street in Manchester. A cyclist said 'hi'; I mumbled a greeting back, and life went on. I rang a doorbell, hugged a friend, made a cup of tea. A minor triumph and a huge exhale of breath. One small fear vanquished and another path remapped.

### Notes

1 See http://stationsouth.co.uk/ for plans and background information.
2 I am a walking artist and pedestrian activist, among other things. In 2006 I co-founded the Loiterers Resistance Movement (LRM), a Manchester-based psychogeographical collective. Together we drift through our city, exploring public space, hidden histories, alternative map-making, and the collegiate pleasures of walking and talking together. Our manifesto says 'We can't agree on what psychogeography means but … Gentrification, advertising and blandness make us sad. We believe there is magick in the Mancunian rain. Our city is wonderful and made for more than shopping. The streets belong to everyone and we want to reclaim them for play and revolutionary fun.' On the first Sunday of every month we embark on some form of exploration or creative mischief. Events are free and open to everyone – readers are very welcome to join us.
3 It's material too, of course. As well as harassment, architecture and design can limit our freedom to walk in space too. There are issues around tactile paving, potholes, lack of public toilets, privatisation of space etc, which also need addressing.

danced
Like Leaves
under glittery moon
across
childhood
Shadowed
Steel
heartbeats
Silver
CLOUD
T. BROOME & SON
UNDERTAKERS
MANCHESTER FREE LIBRARY
MITRE INN
MILTON ST
330
299
STRETFORD ROAD
TOMLINSON
MULBERRY
HUP-2002

# Work

> Dark and smoky from the coal vapours, it resembles a huge forge or workshop. Work, profit and greed seem to be the only thoughts here. The clatter of the cotton mills and the looms can be heard everywhere. One reads figures, nothing but figures on all the faces here.
>
> German novelist Johanna Schopenhauer on Manchester in 1813

Few cities in the world can claim to have a history so dominated by just one type of work. Manchester's nineteenth-century title 'Cottonopolis' says it all. From the late eighteenth century until the end of the 1920s, the world's supplies of cotton converged on Manchester – whether transported to the city via Liverpool from American growing fields; sorted, spun and woven in thousands of purpose-built mills that both dominated and surrounded Manchester; bleached or dyed in chemical factories; or, as explored by Martin Dodge, sold and packaged as textiles in the city's hundreds of centrally located warehouses. Of course, this global industry needed many other kinds of work to feed it – for example, coal mining, iron forging, brickmaking (see James Thorp's 'Brick') and transportation – but nearly all of these were in service of the industrial behemoth of King Cotton. As Natalie Bradbury shows

**29** (Previous page) Hulme mural, Stretford Road, Hulme, completed in 2002 and made by the Hulme Urban Potters

in 'Newspaper', it also needed its own media, one that reflected the cotton magnate's celebration of free trade and social reform for workers: the *Guardian* seeing its birth in the city in 1821.

Once that industry went into decline – at first during the Second World War, and then terminally from the late 1960s onwards – the fate of Manchester was sealed. Commentators in the late 1970s spoke of a city emptied of purpose and meaning and, to a certain extent, of people too. Out of this post-industrial wasteland, new kinds of work emerged. On the one hand, periodic waves of office building saw the rise of the financial industries of stockbroking, insurance, pensions and other mysterious assets – and service-orientated industries like cafes, shops, and nightclubs. On the other, young people taking advantage of cheap rents – even zero in the case of the condemned Hulme Crescents – saw opportunities to avoid conventional work and instead make various forms of art, Manchester's now legendary music scene of the 1980s and 1990s emerging as a result.

But other kinds of work remain somewhat neglected in Manchester's history and everyday life. As explored in 'Co-operative', a grassroots-initiated way of buying and selling emerged alongside the mass production of the Victorian factory system. Spawning dozens of buildings in the Greater Manchester region, and eventually a global movement, co-operative societies gave industrialisation a counter-history of bottom-up social organisation that had at its heart the tenet of mutual aid – the workers supported and nurtured by each other. Today, most of these old co-operative buildings have either been abandoned or repurposed; but their role as everyday places of mutual aid lives on in other forms of work in the city – and even the city region's first mayor, Andy Burnham, is talking about co-operatives as the way forward. Finally, Peter Kalu sees a different kind of work in the city's numerous car washes: unskilled labour that nevertheless demonstrates how Manchester's most marginal residents can find a place to belong.

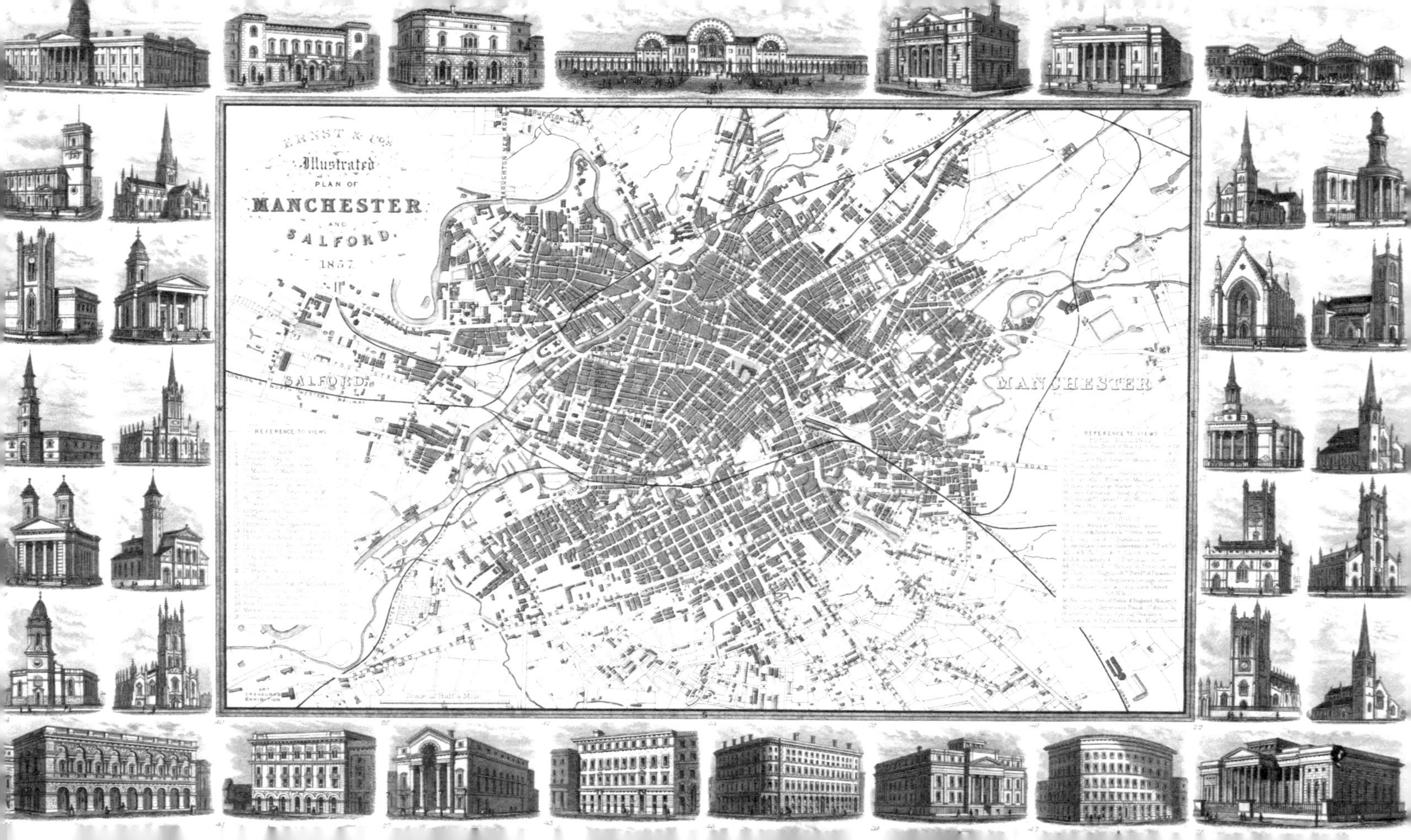

# Work

## *Cotton* – Martin Dodge

Manchester had a long involvement in textiles before it grew into a manufacturing powerhouse in the late eighteenth century. This growth was driven by technical developments in cotton spinning and the emergence of factory system production, the enrolment of steam power, accompanied by improved transport through the building of canals. In the first half of the nineteenth century, through cyclical economic booms and slumps, the large town of Manchester was transformed into a major commercial city funded by a worldwide trade in cotton goods. It was fed by many fast-growing surrounding towns that started specialising in particular phases of production, from spinning to weaving to finishing (including bleaching, dying and calico printing). Other important allied industries included mining, chemicals and, above all, machinery with a growing prowess in engineering.

How did cotton come to be so important to the Manchester region? The origins and value of cotton were described by Andrew Ure in 1836:

> The wool-bearing shrub, called *Gossypium* by botanists, would be universally regarded as a miracle of vegetation … This singular class of [cotton] plants has been largely distributed all over the torrid zone, a conspicuous gift of Providence to its inhabitants, destined to afford them, in its fleecy pods, a spontaneous and inexhaustible supply of the clothing material best adapted to screen their swarthy bodies from the scorching sunbeam, and to favour the cooling influence of the breeze, as well as cutaneous exhalation.[1]

Of course cotton does not grow in Lancashire, and the requirement to import raw materials meant that Manchester was drawn into complex trading relations with distant places of production, and,

**30** (Opposite) Map of Manchester published by Ernst & Co. in 1857

along with Liverpool, bound into the responsibility for fostering slavery, a shameful history that still remains rarely acknowledged.

The ways in which fibrous wool, gathered from cotton seed pods, could be spun and weaved into a 'web of exquisite beauty' unleashed economic forces that transformed the physical landscape of much of North West England. While Manchester was the centre of the international trade in textiles, its role was also essential to the economic dominance of Britain as it became a global empire. For most of the nineteenth century, raw cotton was the single largest import into the country and finished cotton textiles one of its more profitable exports.

Manchester was built – and rebuilt – on the money that flowed from cotton, with whole streets and impressive commercial buildings serving the textile trade coming to symbolise its success. Maps of the city from this period – such as the Ernst & Co. publication from 1857 – illustrate the grandeur of Victorian Manchester. With its combination of a detailed street map and surrounding elevations of key buildings, it was aimed at visitors to the Art Treasures Exhibition held at Old Trafford in that year (illustrated as the central engraving on the map's cartouche). The buildings shown include an array of fine churches – the seat of pre-industrial power and still influential in Victorian Britain – but the rest were really a celebration of the wealth flowing from commercial activity. Ten textile warehouses are pictured along with impressive banks, commercial exchanges, and important cultural and education facilities endowed by the merchant class – architectural icons recently built reflecting the fact that Manchester was now a modern, sophisticated place. The population of the borough itself, according to the 1851 census, was over 303,000 – more than double what it had been twenty years previously. And in 1853, partly in recognition of the growth, Manchester was designated a city by Queen Victoria.

The large commercial warehouses built in the mid nineteenth century occupied prime locations in the centre of Manchester.

## Work

Drawing influences from the Italian palazzos of the Renaissance era, these warehouses symbolise, in architectural terms, something of the tremendous scale of the cotton economy and its huge impact on the social and material landscape of south Lancashire. They were specialised retail spaces, not merely vast storage sheds. In many ways they operated like department stores for wholesale buyers – places to inspect the goods, feel the quality of cloth, and choose from myriad available patterns and print designs. These warehouses also often included the business offices that facilitated trade, as well as accounting and finance. They were located a few minutes' walk from the Royal Exchange and the leading banks – buildings also illustrated on Ernst & Co.'s map.

The first palazzo-style warehouse was Richard Cobden's building on Mosley Street, completed in 1839; but the apogee of this trend was the one built for S. & J. Watts on Portland Street (number 38 at the top-left corner of the map). Designed by the architects Travis and Mangnall, it was ostentatious enough to attract the attention of the *Illustrated London News* at the time of its construction in the early 1850s. The newspaper described it as a

> superb pile, the largest warehouse in Manchester ... It has seven storeys, which, in aggregate, measure 110 feet in height. The style of architecture is Venetian; and the distinctive features consist of four pavilions or tower-like erections, which extend at intervals across the building from front to rear. This arrangement has been adopted partly for architectural effect, but more particularly for the purpose of obtaining rooms lighted only by windows with north aspect – this being an important consideration in the display of certain goods.[2]

The global textile trade continued to evolve and, in fits and starts through the first half of the twentieth century, Manchester experienced a slow and painful decline of the cotton industry, with the last significant manufacturing mills closing down in the 1960s. The fading Cottonopolis was, in some respects, a foreshadowing of the de-industrialisation that would see dramatic changes to Lancashire and the industrial North through the 1970s and 1980s.

## Manchester: Something rich and strange

Much material evidence of cotton was swept away in subsequent decades, but Watts Warehouse survived and remains one of Manchester's Victorian heritage gems. It was converted into the Britannia Hotel in the early 1980s and is now part of the leisure economy that has grown up since the 1990s, a component of the post-industrial renaissance of Manchester's city centre.

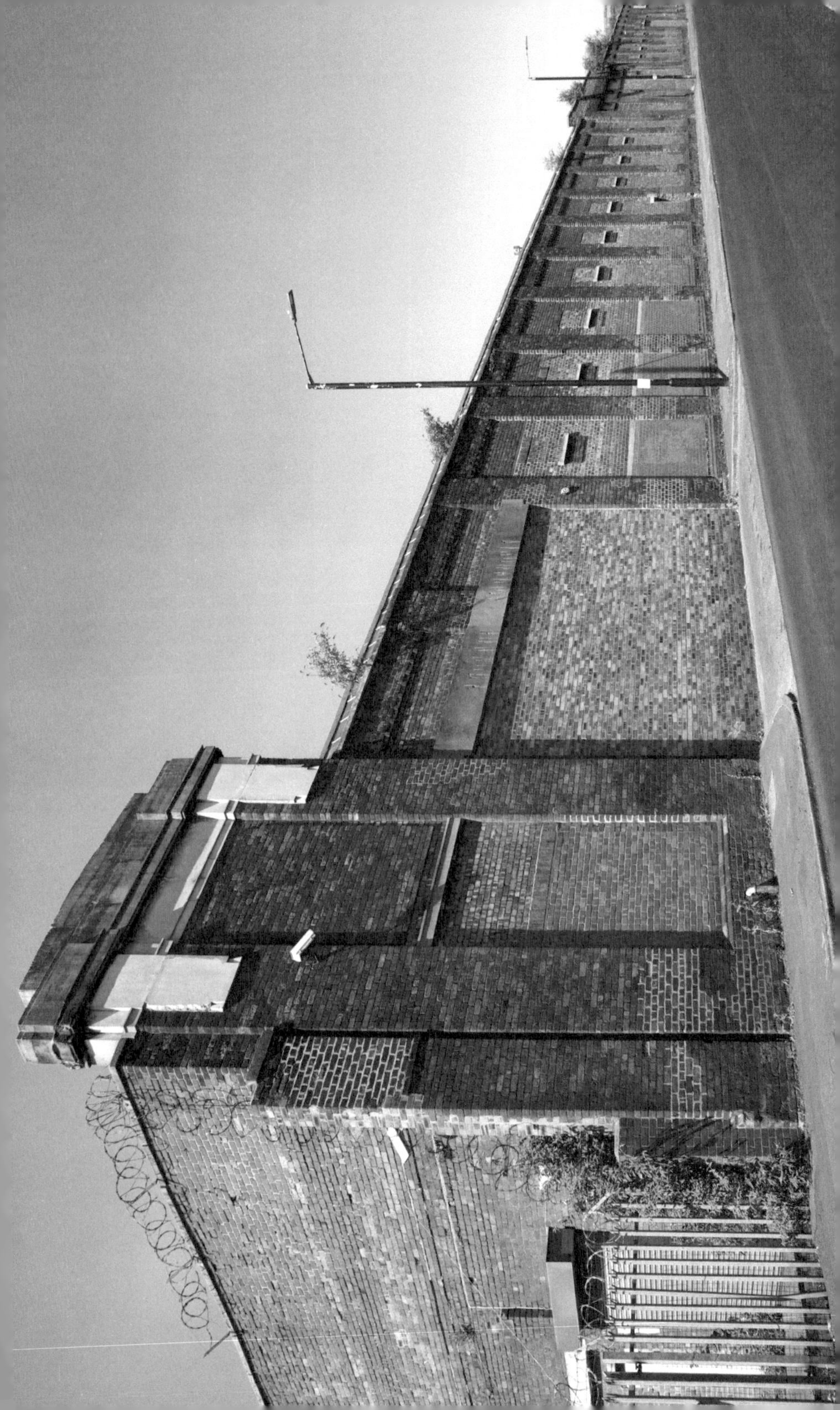

## Brick – James Thorp

Manchester is peppered with voids: sites of former industry that have long since fallen silent. Our subject is the site of Jackson's Brickworks in Newton Heath, one of nine brickworks owned by the same company in the Manchester area. The brickworks' useful life was shorter than that of the average person, going from establishment to disuse in the first seventy years of the twentieth century. Sites like this have legacies – both positive and negative – that outspan their working lives. In the case of the Hardman & Holden factory explored in 'Dye' (p. 195), the presence of chemical manufacturing has created a physically challenging environment for reuse. In the case of Jackson's Brickworks, economic challenges have been more significant for the continued presence of this void in the inner city.

There is little recorded history of Jackson's Brickworks. Nearby pioneering industrial firms like Mather & Platt, A.V. Roe, and Tootal, Broadhurst and Lee are extensively documented and remembered with pride. You'll find their products have pride of place at Manchester's Science and Industry Museum. The brickworks complex itself was not as architecturally impressive as the adjacent Park Engineering Works (home of Mather & Platt), with maps showing clay pits accompanied by modest kilns. Bricks made at Jackson's would have been used to build Manchester's factories and housing, making it an important component of the area's industrial heyday, if not a celebrated enterprise. Brickmaking perhaps isn't as exciting for industrial historians as the engineering, aviation and textile industries. The word 'brick' is often used pejoratively to describe sensations of fear ('bricking it'), an unintelligent person ('thick as a brick'), an ungainly device (e.g. a large

**31** (Previous page) Former industrial building on Ten Acres Lane, Newton Heath

mobile phone), and a device made defunct ('bricked'). Jackson's Brickworks closed in the 1970s economic recession. The company survived and amalgamated with multinational brickmaking companies, but the site in Newton Heath was left as a redundant, bricked void in the urban landscape.

In the half century since the site was abandoned, nature has reclaimed it to create a verdant mixture of grassland, scrub, hedgerow and woodland. Slow-worms have been found during ecological investigations – a protected reptile in the UK.[3] Other wildlife at the brickworks includes palmate newts, frogs and bats, along with birds including blackcap, bullfinch and dunnock – all species of conservation concern. Rewilding of the site happened entirely without human intervention or intent. The flora and fauna that has made its home in the scarred yet peaceful landscape left by the clay pits is a welcome respite from the surrounding arterial routes, industrial and residential estates. Together with the Rochdale Canal, Clayton Vale, Philips Park and Moston Brook, this site, if linked with the others, would form a network of post-industrial green space in east Manchester. Exploring the site at present is mildly hazardous thanks to its misuse and lack of management. Paths have been worn – desire lines of locals taking shortcuts or walking their dogs, often revealing crushed brick rubble underfoot. Fly-tipping presents the most obvious hazard to visitors. Nike trainers, barely worn, lie strewn among festering domestic waste in split polythene bags. A Mobike, minus saddle and one of its wheels, stands as an ironic memorial to the brief period of the Mancunian 'sharing' economy. Burned-out and rusty skeletons of stolen motorcycles can be found peppered along the paths. Deep crimson dogwood thickets suggest an alien post-apocalyptic backdrop.

If the antisocial behaviour and environmental crime didn't give the brickworks enough of a menacing air, the added association with the so-called 'Beast of Manchester' might put potential visitors off. In the mid 1970s, Trevor Hardy murdered three young women in the surrounding areas of Moston, Harpurhey and Failsworth. Being active at the same time as the Yorkshire Ripper meant his notoriety was overshadowed and his infamy has remained localised. The Rochdale Canal that bounds the brickworks was Hardy's preferred stalking route, making the brickworks a convenient void to conceal evidence. The killer led police to a pond at the brickworks when searching for remains, according to newspaper reports. Documents from Trevor Hardy's cell surfaced after his death in 2012 revealing further details of his heinous crimes.[4] A hand-drawn map shows six locations at the brickworks where he buried the remains of Lesley Stewart. If this map is accurate, then the remains are very likely to still be on the site, and there is a case for these to be respectfully and appropriately treated.

Economic recessions have been significant in Jackson's Brickworks remaining undeveloped, despite regular schemes drawn up by enthusiastic property developers. As decades have passed, the site has amassed a catalogue of unrealised proposals. Early schemes for housing didn't materialise as a result of the same poor economy that led to the closure of the brickworks. The void, metaphorically and literally, was filled by waste disposal – a short-sighted 'meanwhile' use that adds to the negative legacy of the site. The site was licensed for landfill operations in the late 1970s, but tipping has likely occurred since the 1950s. Buried detritus includes industrial and construction waste, ash, foundry sand, and boiler and flue cleanings.[5] Raised levels of methane and carbon dioxide have been measured, indicating active decomposition. Local residents voiced concerns over disturbing the waste, especially asbestos material. Tipping would have been haphazard prior to modern sanitary landfill practices. Similar dump sites in the area have been repurposed as green infrastructure, including Clayton Vale and Moston Brook. With suitable capping, landscaping and pollution control, these sites are now valuable assets and green space in the city. These places could have been termed 'brownfield' land for development, but instead have become vital green lungs of the city, while minimising the environmental health risks of former tips.

No buyer has been found to date, so the brickworks void seems likely to remain in much the same form for years to come – another reprieve for the rewilding of the site. The most recent planning application describes the brickworks as 'underutilised, derelict, vacant and overgrown', understating its value as habitat and informal amenity space. But building on the site won't improve Newton Heath's fortunes – just those of the property speculators and armies of consultants currently dominating Manchester's redevelopment. Far better that this site, with its physical and emotional baggage, and beautifully diverse ecology, becomes a designated green space properly managed to limit the blight of antisocial behaviour. Such a green space could become the catalyst for a better environment in Newton Heath, replacing a post-industrial void with something truly meaningful and worthwhile.

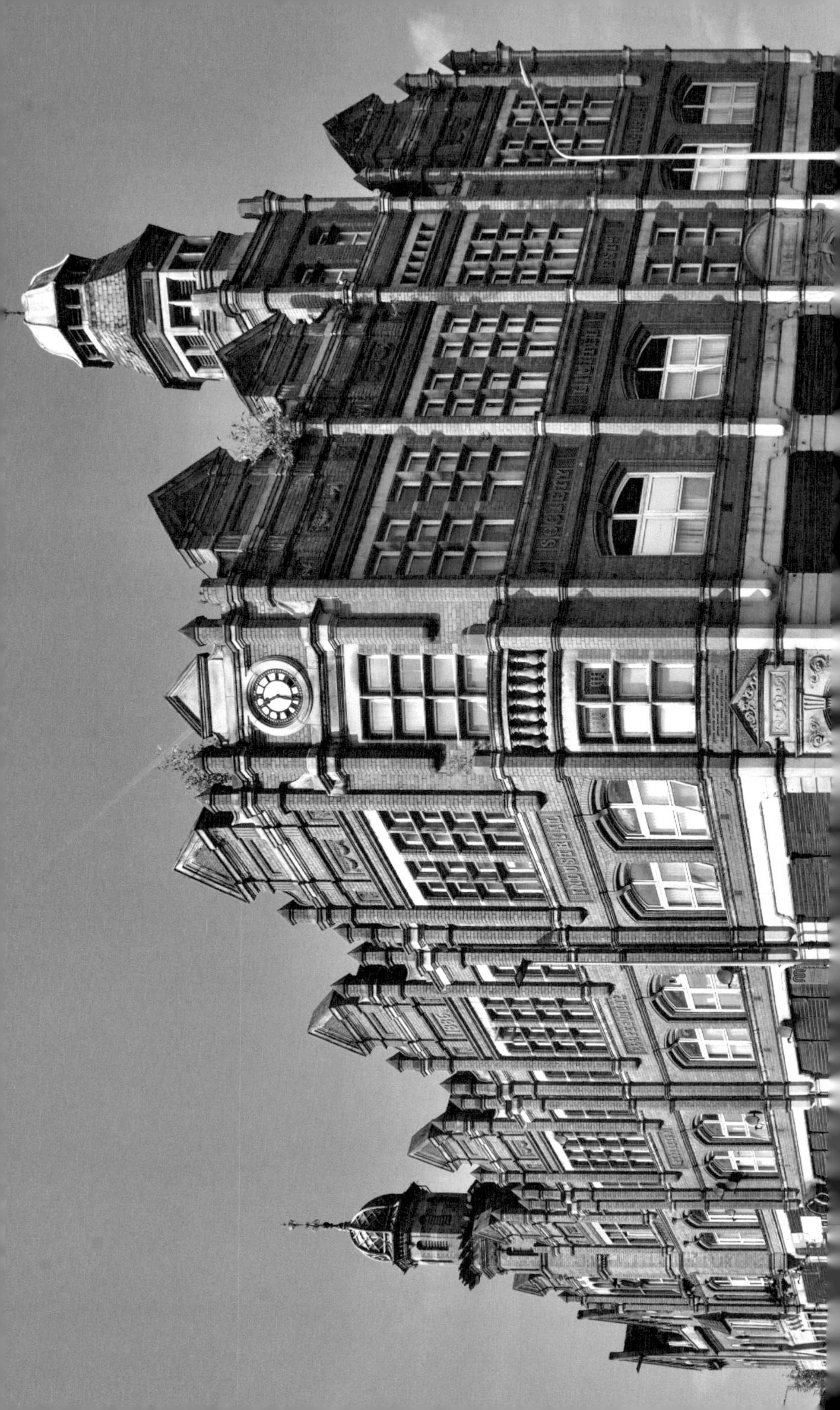

## Co-op – Natalie Bradbury

Like many cities, Manchester markets itself to investors, developers and visitors as a series of brands. Whole areas of the city are labelled, packaged and sold in ways that signpost their designation for city living, leisure, entertainment, consumption or business. In a city already containing an improbably large number of 'quarters' and 'villages', the latest destination is sold simply as NOMA. Referring to a small geographical area adjacent to Victoria train station and Shudehill bus interchange, and bordering the existing 'Northern Quarter' and Ancoats locales, the initials snappily indicate its geographical location: NOrth of MAnchester city centre.

For all its blandness, NOMA belies a more interesting identity, and one that is far more important to the history of the city and its social, cultural, political and architectural development than just a series of initials. In fact, the area could more accurately be branded the 'Co-operative Quarter', largely comprising the former estate of the Co-operative Group, the largest co-operative society in the UK, a major local employer, and an important developer of significant buildings from the nineteenth century to the present.

The co-operative movement as we now know it actually began in the mill town of Rochdale, around ten miles to the north of NOMA, in a small shop on a cobbled street called Toad Lane. It aimed to offer a radical alternative to the existing capitalist model, which relied on the exploitation and subjugation of its workers. Instead, the Rochdale model was based on worker ownership and empowerment, and eventually control of the means of production and distribution. On 21 December 1844, the 'Rochdale Pioneers', the name given to twenty-eight working people who comprised

**32** (Opposite) Pendleton Co-operative Industrial building, Broughton Road, Pendleton, Salford. Completed in 1887 and designed by F. Smith.

the original investors in the business, opened shop for the first time to sell affordable and quality foodstuffs to their fellow weavers and textile workers, who suffered from poor housing, difficult working conditions and the unscrupulousness and monopolisation of the local shopkeepers. From this humble building, which today remains open as a museum, the co-operative movement grew to encompass not just retailing but multiple aspects of life and business – from wholesale and manufacture to housing and education.

Indeed, from Rochdale grew a global movement, with co-operatives across the world tracing their roots back to the town. Today, drivers into Rochdale are greeted by the slogan boldly emblazoned over the railway bridge that crosses Kingsway: 'Rochdale – birthplace of co-operation'. Rochdale has become a place of pilgrimage for members of the international co-operative movement, and there is even an oversized replica of the Pioneers' shop building in Kobe, Japan.

The success of the Rochdale Society of Equitable Pioneers inspired the development of other co-operative societies in villages, towns, suburbs and cities around the UK. Today, few of these independent societies remain – many have merged into larger organisations, or become part of the Co-op brand as we now know it. However, their existence lives on architecturally, in former shopfronts still bearing the names of these local societies. With motifs such as wheatsheafs and beehives incorporated into the stone or brickwork, they are a visible reminder of the values on which the co-operative movement was built: industriousness, co-operation, unity and hard work.

In 1863, the Rochdale Society of Equitable Pioneers expanded to form the Co-operative Wholesale Society (CWS), the forerunner of 'the Co-op' that trades today, which supplied the numerous

**33** (Opposite) Co-operative Group headquarters, One Angel Square, Angel Meadow. Built from 2010–13 and designed by 3DReid.

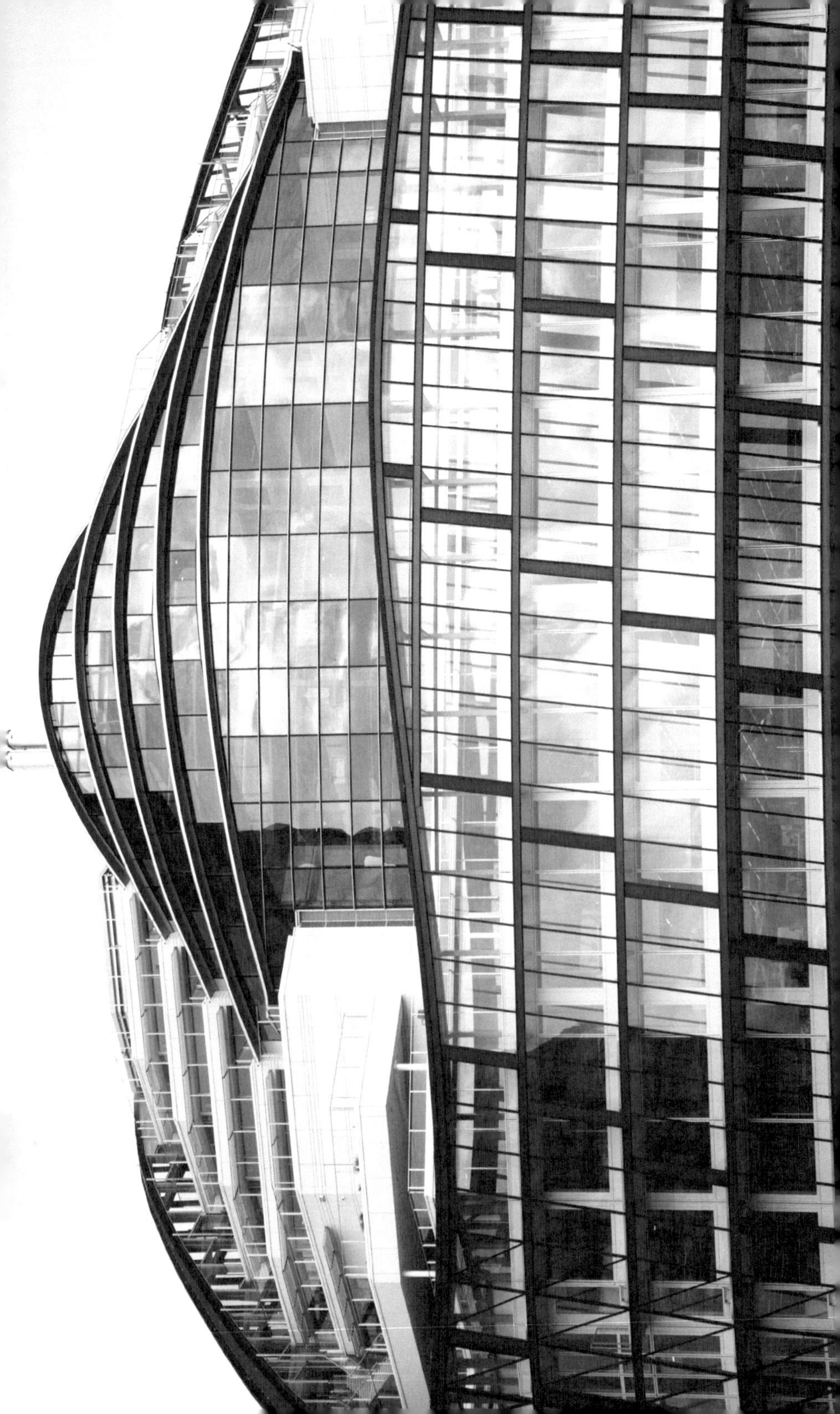

regional co-operative societies around the UK. The CWS's activities required the development of large sites across Greater Manchester, including a soap works in Irlam, on the outskirts of Salford, a biscuit factory in Crumpsall, north Manchester, and a printers in the inner-city district of Longsight. Few of these buildings now remain and, where they do, have been converted for other uses such as housing – a good example is the handsome CWS tobacco factory just north of the area now encompassing NOMA.

At one time the reach of the movement was such that the CWS had its own architects' department, with offices in London, Manchester and Newcastle. The CWS embraced new styles: wandering around the small group of streets that constitute NOMA is to see some of the key trends in architecture over the past century. Federation House, the Hanover Building and E Block are fine early twentieth-century red-brick warehouses: decorative lettering indicates the networks of international trade in which the CWS was engaged. The Old Bank Building, dating from 1928, incorporates an impressive memorial to the fallen of the First World War. The yellow brick Dantzic and Redfern buildings are Streamline Moderne in style, with decorative brick detailing that places them unmistakably in the 1930s. In the 1960s, when the city was moving away from its provincial Victorian heritage to look outwards and upwards, the CWS embraced international-style modernism and followed the trend of incorporating large-scale public artworks, such as murals, into its premises. When it opened, in 1962, the CIS Tower was one of the tallest buildings in Europe, and remained the tallest building in Manchester until the Beetham Tower was completed in 2006.

These buildings tell the story of the expansion of the co-operative movement, from trading to funerals to insurance to banking. A network of underground tunnels shows the interconnectedness of these businesses. These buildings also tell of the decline and contraction of the co-operative movement in the latter part of the twentieth century: when the area was vacated by the Co-op in 2012, it was discovered that whole blocks had been abandoned – in some cases, tinned consumables decades old were found in storage.

In 2013, the Co-operative Group moved into new headquarters at One Angel Square. The striking glass building references co-operative history in its resemblance to a beehive. At the same time, it embraces the paperless, open-plan working environment of the modern office, aiming to set new standards in environmental sustainability.

The move was overshadowed by scandal and a series of crises that culminated in the Co-operative Group relinquishing its stake in the Co-operative Bank. The CIS Tower has since been sold, and the former Co-operative campus of buildings is becoming part of the commercial city that surrounds it, aiming to draw people in with upmarket housing, cafes and bars. As with many aspects of Manchester's history, the once-radical ideas that underpin the development of the area have become another marketing tool, reduced to vintage posters, slogans and retro-branding on the walls.

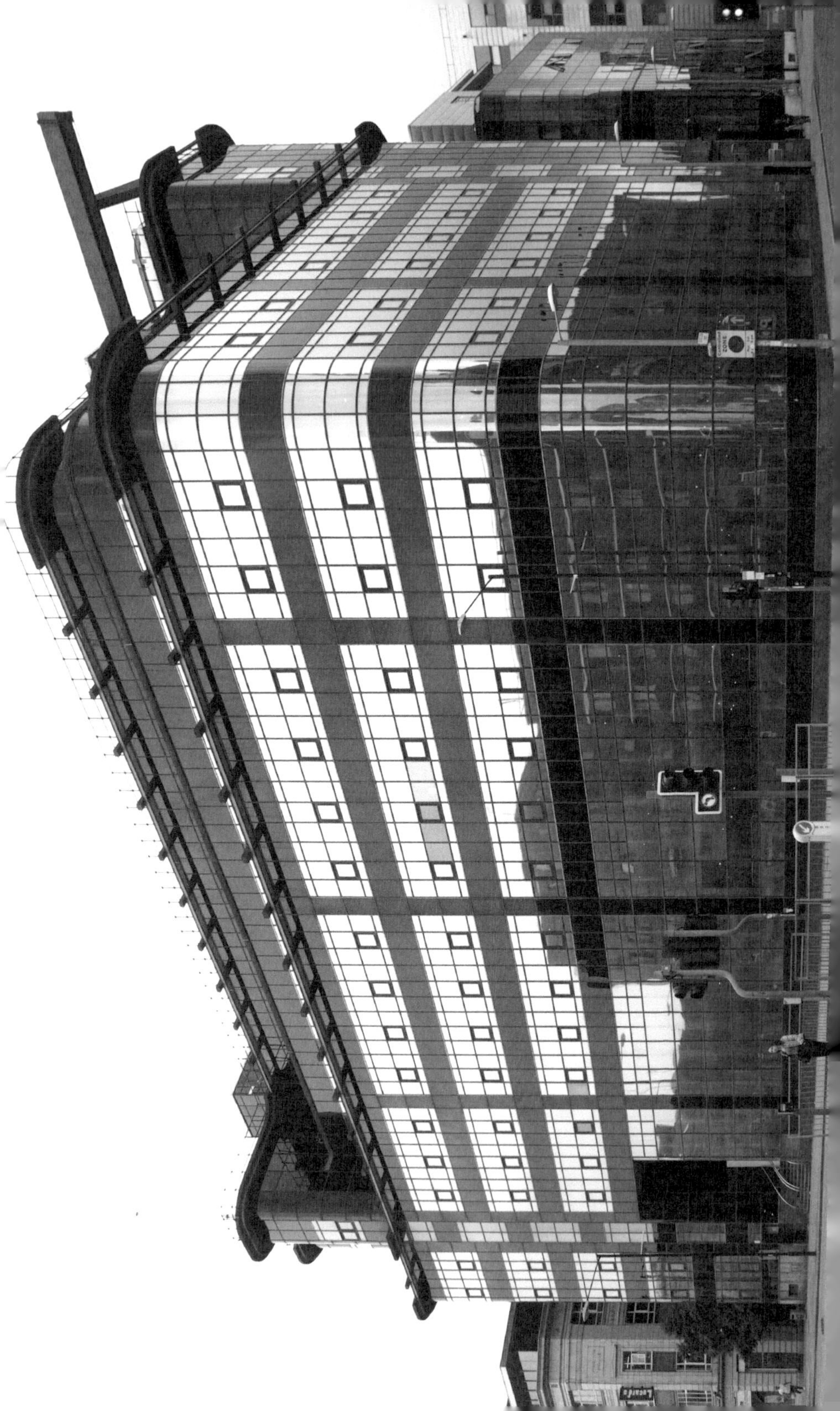

## Work

## *Newspaper* – Natalie Bradbury

In 2011, in a bid to redress an imbalance in regional reporting, the BBC moved thousands of its staff from London to Salford Quays. A purpose-built complex, three miles from Manchester city centre, created a new area known as MediaCity. Sports and children's programming moved wholesale, and the famous Blue Peter Garden was recreated on the banks of the Manchester Ship Canal. Hundreds of acres of former dockland were rebuilt with not just broadcast facilities and studios, but also apartments, restaurants and bars to serve the new workforce, alongside a dedicated tramline and a new campus for the University of Salford. Sleek but soulless, the architecture is dominated by high-rises clad in corporate black and grey; the complex was awarded the Carbuncle Cup in 2011.

Long before Salford's association with media production, Manchester had its own reputation as 'the other Fleet Street', or the 'Fleet Street of the North'. For over a century, it was a centre for the production and distribution of national, regional and local newspapers. Most famously, the *Manchester Guardian* was founded in the city in 1821, in response to the Peterloo massacre of 1819. It dropped 'Manchester' from its name in 1959, before moving to London in 1964.

Manchester's own daily newspaper, the *Manchester Evening News*, marked its centenary in 1968 by commissioning a short film, *Here is the News*. The film goes behind the scenes at the paper and places it at the heart of the city. The tone is optimistic, admiring Manchester's new, modernist architecture of the 1960s. Another documentary, *The Voice of a Region*, made in the early 1970s, visits the *Manchester Evening News*' premises, purpose-built by the

**34** (Opposite) Daily Express Building on Great Ancoats Street, completed in 1939 and designed by Sir Owen Williams

architects Leach Rhodes Walker next to the John Rylands Library on Deansgate, praising the 'striking modern building' surrounded by courtyards and squares where the public could relax, 'soothed by the sight of flowers'. Today, the site of the old offices has been replaced by the shiny office blocks, upmarket shops and restaurants that characterise the Spinningfields district. Like many regional newspapers, which were hit hard by the financial crash of 2008 and changing habits in media consumption, the *Manchester Evening News* left its city-centre location in 2010, centralising its operations at one out-of-town site next to the M60 motorway in Oldham.

Manchester also had a long tradition of alternative and radical publications. *The Clarion*, a weekly socialist newspaper founded by the journalist Robert Blatchford, began in the City Buildings near Victoria railway station in 1891; derelict for many years, the building has now been restored as a boutique hotel as part of the NOMA development. Clarion Cycling Clubs, riding around the countryside, helped distribute *The Clarion* and spread its message of socialism and brotherhood. Until its closure in 1936, supporters could meet at the Clarion Cafe on Market Street, decorated with propagandistic slogans and murals by the arts-and-crafts illustrator Walter Crane.

The co-operative movement, too, had its own newspapers, each aimed at different groups. Large lettering on the exterior of its now demolished red-brick premises on Long Millgate, close to Victoria station, announced that *Millgate Monthly*, *Woman's Outlook*, *Sunshine Stories* and *Our Circle* (for children) were produced there, along with the *Co-operative News*, the world's oldest co-operative newspaper. The Co-operative Press remained on Long Millgate until it moved to the imposing Art Deco former Veno's medicine factory in Old Trafford in the 1950s, now derelict and awaiting redevelopment into apartments. Much reduced in size, the Co-operative Press moved back to the city centre in the 2000s, where it continues to produce the *Co-operative News* today, surrounded by other co-operative organisations in the area now rebranded as NOMA.

In the nineteenth and twentieth centuries, Manchester's newspaper industry was centred around Withy Grove and Shudehill. The most dominant building, Thomson House, dating from 1873, occupied a huge corner plot on Withy Grove. Once home to the largest composing room in Europe, the printworks housed thousands of workers and produced millions of newspapers every week, including the *Telegraph*, *Times* and *Mirror*. Such was the scale of operations that the building once had its own internal railway and turntable for transporting newspapers.

In 1985, the complex was bought by press baron Robert Maxwell for £1. The amateur film, *The Way It Was* (1985), sets grainy, jerky footage of massive machinery which has come to rest, interspersed with close-ups of contemporary headlines and announcements of redundancies, to maudlin classical music. Another short film, *New Newspaper Premises* (1983), shows former staff who had been made redundant being guided around the new computerised facilities which replaced them.

The complex stood empty for over a decade, before being redeveloped as the Printworks entertainment centre in 2000. Today, where once there were neon signs advertising the scores of titles that were published there, there are garish logos for chain restaurants, gyms and bars. Some of the building's features have been preserved; stepping over polished stones, and walking past vintage adverts and shopfronts, it feels like an industrial theme park. The building is embracing trends towards inner-city gardening, though: it's home to a roof garden with beehives.

By far the most impressive legacy of Manchester's newspaper heritage is the *Daily Express* building on Great Ancoats Street, which was designed by Owen Williams as a sister to the *Express*'s buildings on London's Fleet Street, and in Glasgow. Built in 1939, it is one of the city's few early modernist buildings. Clad in black glass and Vitrolite, its modernity and glamour are made all the more striking by its location on a busy, polluted inner-city ring road, adjacent to the once dark, satanic mills of Ancoats. The *Daily Express* left the building in the 1980s and it was converted into offices and apartments, although newspaper production continued in the building until the second decade of the twenty-first century – if you can call the semi-pornographic *Daily Sport* a newspaper. The *Express* building's influence reaches far beyond Manchester: it inspired Norman Foster – later to make his name with 'hi-tech' buildings around the world – when he was a young boy growing up in the suburb of Levenshulme.

## Manchester: Something rich and strange

### *Car wash* – Peter Kalu

I drive in softly … and am semaphored to the outer concrete lip of the old petrol station hangar by a gaunt, rough-bearded, mid-twenties bloke with a huge smile and an excessively nodding, well-coiffed head. The hand signal for *stop*. I drop my window and ask for the five pounds basic wash. He nods, refuses money. I get that double-palm *stop* sign again. Another car has come in behind me; he returns, bending the fingers of both hands to *come hither, come hither, come hither*, now *stop* again. The thumbs up. I'm good. He's away in a swift walk to the phalanx of portable pressure washers lining the patch of land.

Roll back the decades and his job might have been in a clothing sweatshop or taxiing, or digging up the roads. Go sideways, time and genderwise, and it's the nail bars. But it's here. By the old mill chimney, not far from my home. The buckets, spray and polish business. On this patch of tarmac. Car washes sprout like wild seed blown across the urban landscape. Their cumbersome evolutionary predecessors were/are the Imo Automatics, Imo's flying rollers and entire circus of flailing automation worth the entry fee simply for the drama. When I was a Saturday dad, if I found myself ten minutes ahead of schedule for returning the child to her mother, I'd soak up that time by driving us into an Imo. My daughter's 5 year-old soul loved the roller clunking, water jetting spray through the window when it's not hermetically sealed shut, can't see nothing through the windscreen, getting dragged along clunk thunk lash, scratch squeal, lurch haul wild-animal-at-your-window effect – a soapy-water-fight-with-a-troop-of-baboons drama. All for a couple of pounds, and now and then a wiper or wing-mirror gone. Pretty similar to Knowsley Safari, but only five pounds. 'Let's do it again, Daddy, let's do it again!'

**35** (Previous page) Soapsuds on a windscreen

## Work

He's squirted foam on my wheels and wants me to inch the car forward. A double-palm *stop* again.

Car washes have minimal set-up costs, no regulation, and I presume it is easy for owners, if they get into scrapes with licensing, tax or other regulators, to dissolve, disappear, fly. They are a fording point to other things, a wonky, sometimes treacherous ladder to economic first base for immigrants, especially those of shaky status, the down on their luck, the can't make ends meet, the almost homeless. The entry point used to be taxi drivers, but now taxi drivers take their cars to the car wash, making the car washers the subaltern's subaltern.

The new guy who is hosing the car bonnet down has a cigarette in his mouth, boss-like among all this water. I like his style. I imagine he has a *Scarface* poster on his bedsit wall and plans to become somebody in this New World. Mainly they scurry. With buckets, sprays, jets then cloths. Suddenly two of my car doors are flung open at once. This only happens in police hard stops and crime serials. Two of them duck in. They are cleaning the door sills, *oga*, all smiles.

Somehow, as people, we became precious over our cars, yet unwilling to get out with the buckets and sponges and do the job ourselves. I remember the money I earned as a kid washing cars, crunching up posh driveways, knocking on random doors in Didsbury. It paid as well as any paper delivery round; I built regular customers who supplied the equipment, so I carried nothing but the pounds I earned. Easy money if you were happy to slog it out in sun and rain on a Sunday morning.

Yes, we love our cars too much. They are our second skin. The valet clean means the hoses go inside the cockpit like a colonoscopy. Turfed-out owners wander the forecourt, hands stuffed in pockets affecting nonchalance, but uneasy – tortoises prized from their shells.

Far to the left is a keeling shipping container holding stacks of used tyres. The car washes often have ancillary services. There is

HAND CAR WASH
FULL VALET BY APPOINTMENT
mob: 0778 468 0832
£2.99
£2.99
FULL VALET
WASH
Open 7 Days Gleam & Go Hand Car Wash
£2.99
Gleam & Go
Hand Car Wash
PARTS
AST AUTOS
DIAGNOSTICS · CLUTCHES
EXHAUST CHANGE & WELDING
& TRACKING
NEW & PART
WORN TYRES
OPEN 7 DAYS
TEL: 0161
224 2333
Eclipse Auto
SK55 WVU

## Work

some hollering between employees. From the gesticulations I work out the lines are not moving fast enough: cars are backing up. The languages spoken vary. I've heard English, Punjabi, Roma, Czech, Polish, French Creole; but the workers are never conversationalists. This is a world of work below minimum wage, undertaken by the undocumented, those without National Insurance numbers, *sans papiers*. They get cash in hand at the end of the day, if they're lucky.

The skill required is minimal. Eyesight. Basic physical handling skills. Very occasionally, the ability to drive a car fifty yards from one place to the next and park it up until the owner returns. The neighbour's kid is 14 years old and from the Czech Republic, and he's dawdling here. He speaks English, Roma and Czech. He has a cigarette in his mouth and can't smoke it without coughing. A team of three are drying my car with chamois leather when he spots me and comes over. 'I can drive cars you know', he tells me, 'I can make them go backwards.'

'You know where to find the reverse gear?'

'Yeh backwards. Do you want me to move your car?'

'Nah, I'm good', I say.

'Yeh, I can drive. I'm working here tomorrow.' He stubs out his cigarette.

They're done. I pay the five pounds to a guy I never saw till now who pushes the neighbour's boy playfully on his forehead. Driving off, I slide past the banks of perspex sheeting that keeps the wash works from accidentally spraying passing pedestrians, then nudge down the exit ramp. I'm soon on a big arterial road. We're not that far out of the city centre, but in a zone where the rent plummets. In my rear-view mirror the tall red-brick mill chimney, all that is left of a once proud mill; ahead of me a McDonalds. I test the wipers, the brakes, keeping the car on the road.

**36** (Opposite) Gleam & Go hand car wash, Longsight

# Manchester: Something rich and strange

## Notes

1  Andrew Ure, *The Cotton Manufacture of Great Britain* (London: Charles Knight, 1836), p. 1.
2  *Illustrated London News*, 6 December 1856, p. 571.
3  G. L. Hearn, 'Planning application for former Jackson Brickworks site'. Planning Application 098689/OO/2012/N1. Manchester: Manchester City Council.
4  *Britain's Forgotten Serial Killer: Trevor Hardy* (video: Josh Whitehead, 2018). Available at https://vimeo.com/253239705 (accessed 17 June 2020).
5  Hearn, 'Planning application'.

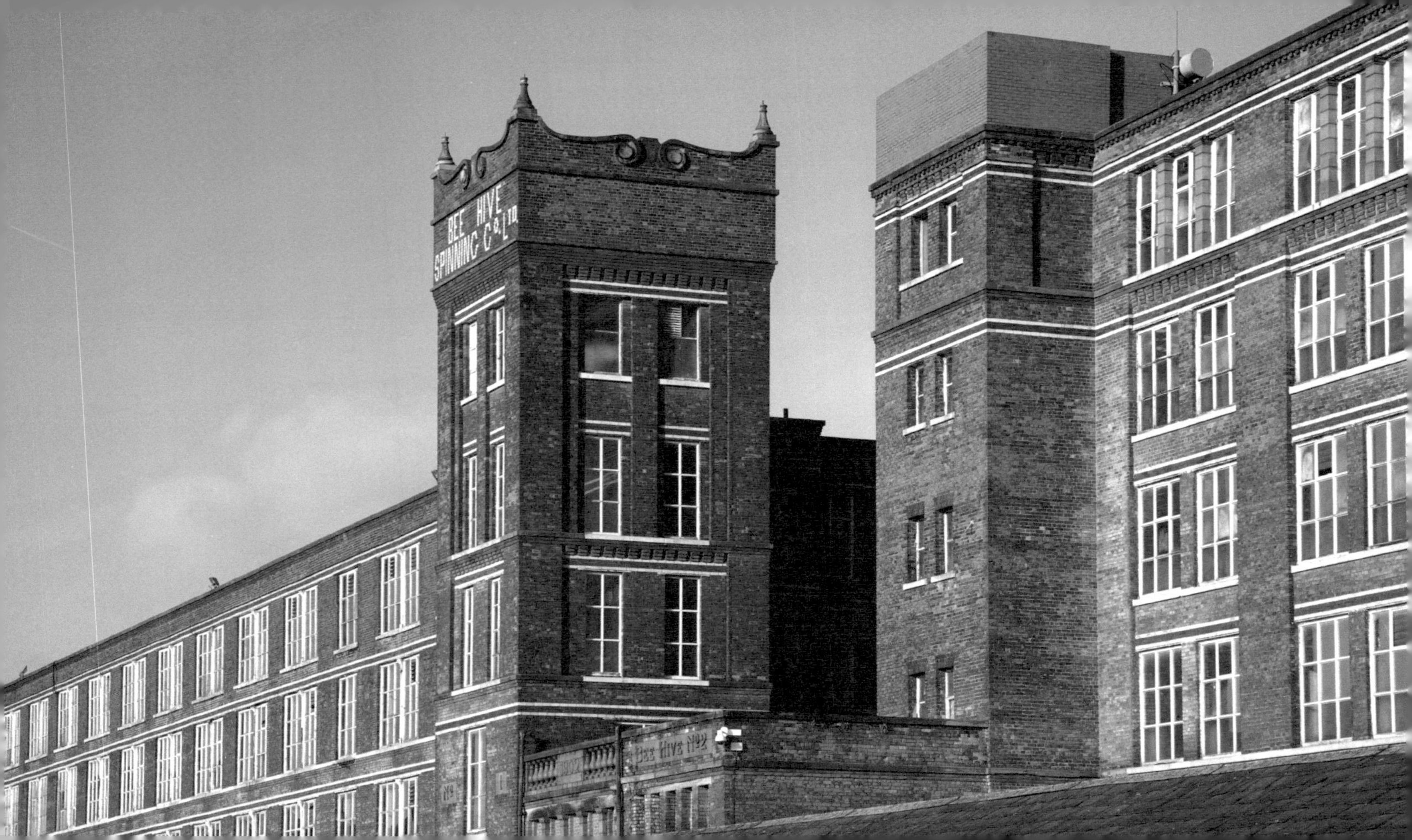

# Relics

> In a short stroll which only lasted fifteen minutes I counted over sixty spinning mills in Manchester. I could well have arrived in Egypt since so many factory chimneys – which are needed because steam engines are used – stretch up into the sky like obelisks.
>
> Johannes Caspar Escher, a Swiss industrialist who visited Manchester in 1814

A city's relics can be both positive and negative. Things that survive from an earlier time are often valued more highly than what is new or recently outmoded; yet relics can also be reminders of anachronous things that now embarrass us: slavery being perhaps the most obvious example, and one extremely pertinent to Manchester's cotton industry in the early part of the Industrial Revolution. Whatever their perceived value, relics force us into an awareness of both history and its ongoing relevance in some material form. Thus, Manchester's relics are generally held up as its buildings of most historic significance: from its medieval cathedral and adjacent Chetham's college and library, to its hundreds of brick-built cotton mills and warehouses, now either abandoned, demolished, or adapted for other uses. Of course, these relics speak of very different periods of history, but they're similar in the way

**37** (Previous page) Beehive mill, Crescent Road, Great Lever, Bolton, built from 1895–1902 and demolished in 2019 to make way for new houses

# Relics

in which they seem to sum up the city at a particular time – both symbols and literal remains of a past we can only imagine, but which still fascinates us.

There are, of course, those kinds of relics here: Clare Hartwell's 'Medieval' expands the meaning of this word in Manchester beyond its conventional understanding, while Brian Rosa explores another symbol of the city's industrial might – the magnificent railway viaducts that are layered one above the other in Castlefield. But there are relics that are much more embedded into the everyday life of the city: the histories of Manchester's greatest sporting asset – football – traced through the displacement of its centres of worship in Tim Edensor's 'Stadium'. And relics that are valuable for the stories they hold: through a lock of hair, Jenna Ashton takes us to an archive – a repository of relics like no other – and unfurls a tale of hardship and hope straddling the world. Finally, there are things that we would rather not turn into relics, but which nevertheless are in danger of becoming so. Thus, Matthew Steele tells a story of private benevolence and municipal neglect of the city's once rich abundance of swimming pools.

There's a melancholy pleasure in contemplating the city's relics: invariably, we imagine a time when things were better, more vibrant and interesting than the present day. Designating things as relics is always a matter of choice – a way in which we hold onto the past as somehow connected with the present. The question remains: what will be Manchester's relics of tomorrow? It would be hard to find a Mancunian who would be so bold as to cast its new apartment and office towers as possible contenders for this title, even as they are, today, the city's most obvious landmarks of the future. Surely, relics need to symbolise something that draws us into lives and times other than our own, rather than monuments to the private, the enclosed and the soulless?

WELLINGTON
OLD WELLINGTON
Sinclairs Oyster Bar
Sinclair ter Bar
SINCLAIR'S OYSTER BAR
ARENA?

## *Medieval* – Clare Hartwell

By the early nineteenth century, Manchester had already established itself as a prodigy of industrial and mercantile power; as an unimaginably different future took shape, it was also an age of re-evaluation of the past. There was growing national interest in native traditions, as romantic notions of a medieval past were developed in Walter Scott's novels, in Romantic poetry, and with the scholarly study of English medieval architecture. Appreciation of a home-grown Gothic style was popularised and validated by the decision in 1836 to rebuild the new Houses of Parliament in English Perpendicular style, to designs by Charles Barry and A. W. N. Pugin. As Victoria's reign unfolded, change was accompanied by often alarming and unpredictable social and physical transformations, while evidence of the past disappeared at an unprecedented rate. In such circumstances, the vacuum could be filled with recreated and invented traditions. Arguably there was nowhere of this time which experienced change more acutely than Manchester, where dislocation with the past was particularly rapid and particularly stark.

Even as the appearance of the pre-industrial city was fading from memory, it was recreated in a remarkable way as part of Manchester's Royal Jubilee exhibition of 1887, held in Old Trafford, where an extensive area was dedicated to scenes of 'Olde Manchester and Salford'. Visitors could stroll along streets populated with life-sized buildings, in facsimile medieval streetscapes, mostly based on lost buildings of the town centre. The scenes, which included Georgian buildings and a 'Roman' archway, were peopled by attendants in costume and animated by demonstrations of traditional handicrafts. The ambitious set was built to carefully researched designs by the architect and theatre specialist

**38** (Opposite) Shambles Square with the reconstituted Old Wellington Inn and Sinclair's Oyster Bar

## Manchester: Something rich and strange

Alfred Darbyshire, whose *A Book of Olde Manchester and Salford* was published in the same year. Just as the city's Art Treasures exhibition of 1857 established its cultural credentials, the celebration of history and architectural heritage in 1887 challenged popular characterisation of the town as a recent phenomenon, a place without significant history, dedicated solely to profit, industry and trade. In short, it embodied a desire to reinvent Manchester's history in an impressive and scholarly manner, as well as in an accessible, unthreatening and picturesque way.[1]

A similar interest was demonstrated in the commissioning of Ford Madox Brown's murals for Manchester's new Town Hall (Alfred Waterhouse, 1867–77), a building stylistically referential to thirteenth-century Northern European Gothic, with highly picturesque interior spaces. The artist wanted his work 'to be the most comprehensive epitome of the rise and progress of Manchester that can be compressed into twelve pictures'.[2] He proposed 'typical' scenes to evoke ideas and ideals, rather than 'documentary' pictures, as he was at pains to explain to his critics, who rightly felt that some subjects, especially the medieval ones, had at best tenuous connections with actual Manchester history. This debate was of course as much about the meaning and uses of art as those of history, but it too was part of the process in which Manchester sought to acquire and celebrate historic identity.

Despite the losses, remarkable fifteenth-century structures do survive in the city centre: Manchester Cathedral and the old buildings of Chetham's School and Library, originally the lodgings of priests. Recreation of the medieval past is traceable in both buildings, in the historicising repairs and reinstatement of lost medieval form, although both incorporate substantial original work. The nave (western part) of the cathedral was largely rebuilt during the nineteenth century, most comprehensively by the architect Joseph Crowther. It had been found (by the standards of the day) to be fatally compromised by age, decay and previous alteration. Almost everything, except medieval carvings from the ceiling and the battered inner face of the tower, was replaced in facsimile, or restored to a medieval appearance. More of the medieval chancel (eastern end with altar) survives, but this was much restored following serious damage in the Manchester Blitz of 1940.

Photographs documenting the aftermath of the bombings show other medieval buildings nearby among the ruins, which had narrowly escaped the devastation. These are the timber-framed Old Wellington Inn (probably seventeenth century) and adjoining Sinclair's Oyster Bar (which has fictive timber framing painted on brick external walls). Collectively known as the Shambles, they originated in possibly the least appealing part of the medieval market place, where meat was sold. Altered and restored in 1925, and patched up after the war, they remained on the site until the 1970s redevelopment of the centre. As the Arndale Centre took shape (see 'Shopping centre', p. 65), a shopping area was planned nearby on the medieval market site. It was decided to keep the two buildings, which, reinforced with steelwork, were jacked up to a completely different, much higher level, in an area christened Shambles Square.

This was not, however, to be their final resting place. The 1996 IRA bomb resulted in the demolition of several buildings nearby and reconfiguration of the whole neighbourhood. In an enormously painstaking and costly exercise, Sinclair's and the Wellington were dismantled and rebuilt in a different position, closer to and on the same level as Manchester Cathedral, in an area designated the 'Medieval Quarter'. They can be seen as talismans or icons, embodying a story of 'miraculous' delivery from the depredations of violence, modernity and commercial pressure. Medieval architecture is a great deal rarer than Victorian and later architecture, but there is no consensus that it is inherently superior, as many Victorian architects and thinkers believed. The buildings we have considered are physical manifestations of something more complex, with significance in ways which concern meaning and collective identity as part of Manchester's continuing and changing relationship with the past.

SITE ACCESS
KEEP CLEAR

## *Railway* – Brian Rosa

Castlefield – the meeting point of some of the oldest industrial canals and railways in the world – is undoubtedly one of the most important sites in Manchester to help us understand the relationship between the Industrial Revolution and urban infrastructure. During the 1970s, a grass-roots campaign to save the abandoned Liverpool Road Station – built in 1830, it's the oldest railway station in the world – led to Castlefield becoming a showcase for industrial heritage and, in turn, driving Manchester's regeneration strategies from the 1980s to the turn of the millennium. In 1980, Castlefield was designated a Conservation Area and, in 1982, Britain's first Urban Heritage Park. Liverpool Road Station itself, along with surrounding Victorian-era buildings, were eventually transformed into the Science and Industry Museum. In 2005, a World Heritage Site bid was drafted; but, by then, investment in heritage was on the wane as the city authorities saw high-rise development as a more valuable mode of regeneration. The result was the abandonment of the World Heritage Site bid in favour of the construction of the hypermodern Beetham Tower, a luxury high-rise completed in 2006 that now dominates the area.

Back in the 1830s, of course, the builders of Manchester's railways also paid little regard to Castlefield's history. Bestriding rivers and canals and ploughing through anything in their path, the railways obliterated the fort of the Roman settlement Mamucium: the 'Castle in the Field' that gave the area its name, as well as the remains of the old town of Aldport. Railways, like urban transport infrastructures that followed, were anti-preservation incarnate.

Castlefield is unique not only as one of the most important sites in the world for the study of transport and industrial heritage, but

**39** (Opposite) Part of the Ordsall Chord railway viaduct spanning Trinity Way, Salford

also because it has raised difficult questions about whether, and how, to treat infrastructure as heritage. Railway viaducts were among the last Victorian structures to be listed by English Heritage (now Historic England) as worthy of protection, attesting to their historical value but also their perception as merely engineered structures, many still in use today. At the same time, as a conglomeration of successive infrastructures that placed Manchester at the centre of the Industrial Revolution, Castlefield's viaducts collectively represent a built artefact of worldwide importance. How much value do we place on historical infrastructure, and should it be treated as a monument, thus potentially limiting its future use for expanding public transport?

Interest in Castlefield's transport heritage was recently reawakened with the proposal to construct a new railway link through the district: the 300-metre Ordsall Chord connecting two railway lines with a viaduct, which would allow, for the first time, direct travel between Manchester Victoria and Oxford Road stations. This was highly controversial because the planned route of the new railway link, crossing the River Irwell between Manchester and Salford, would require the dismantling and modification of listed railway structures, as well as cutting off the historic railway link between Liverpool Road Station and the original route of the Liverpool and Manchester Railway, in place since 1830.

Prominent objectors included English Heritage, the local resident group Castlefield Forum, and, initially, the Science and Industry Museum. English Heritage, responding to the public inquiry into the scheme, advised that they considered Castlefield 'the Stonehenge of railway history' and that the Ordsall Chord would be 'so exceptionally damaging to the historic environment' that it was without precedent. However, upon a £3 million donation by Network Rail to the Science and Industry Museum, they promptly withdrew their objection, which deflated the alliance between dissenters. In an episode that seems to have been largely forgotten, the construction of the Chord was delayed by nine months due to an objection by engineer Mark Whitby, focused specifically on the destruction of infrastructural heritage in Castlefield. Whitby, who had been invited to review the scheme, had identified a route that was less damaging to the transport heritage, but more expensive and disruptive to redevelopment schemes in Salford. After resigning from the review panel, Whitby filed a lawsuit which he ultimately lost.

The so-called 'rusty bridge' constructed over the River Irwell – built with corten steel and completed in 2017 – is the most visible element of the Ordsall Chord project – 'a ribbon of weathering steel, connecting and unifying visually the adjoining structures'. Its engineers described the bridge as one that will 'satisfy the aspiration for a landmark … that will mark the regeneration of the particular site and at the same time show respect to the history of the area'.[3] As the first asymmetrical network arched bridge in the world, the project has won numerous engineering and architectural awards for its design.

When we see such a large, engineered structure, especially as time passes, it is hard to imagine that it once might not have been there. Yet its existence, the physical form it takes, and even its location, were all the result of deliberation and contestation. The arguments for and against the Ordsall Chord and its potential routes have already been forgotten as minor events. However, they represent a rare moment when the civil engineering profession had to reckon with debates around the value of their own predecessors' work as heritage, and when the value of transport heritage came, for a short time, into the forefront of public debate around the future of the city.

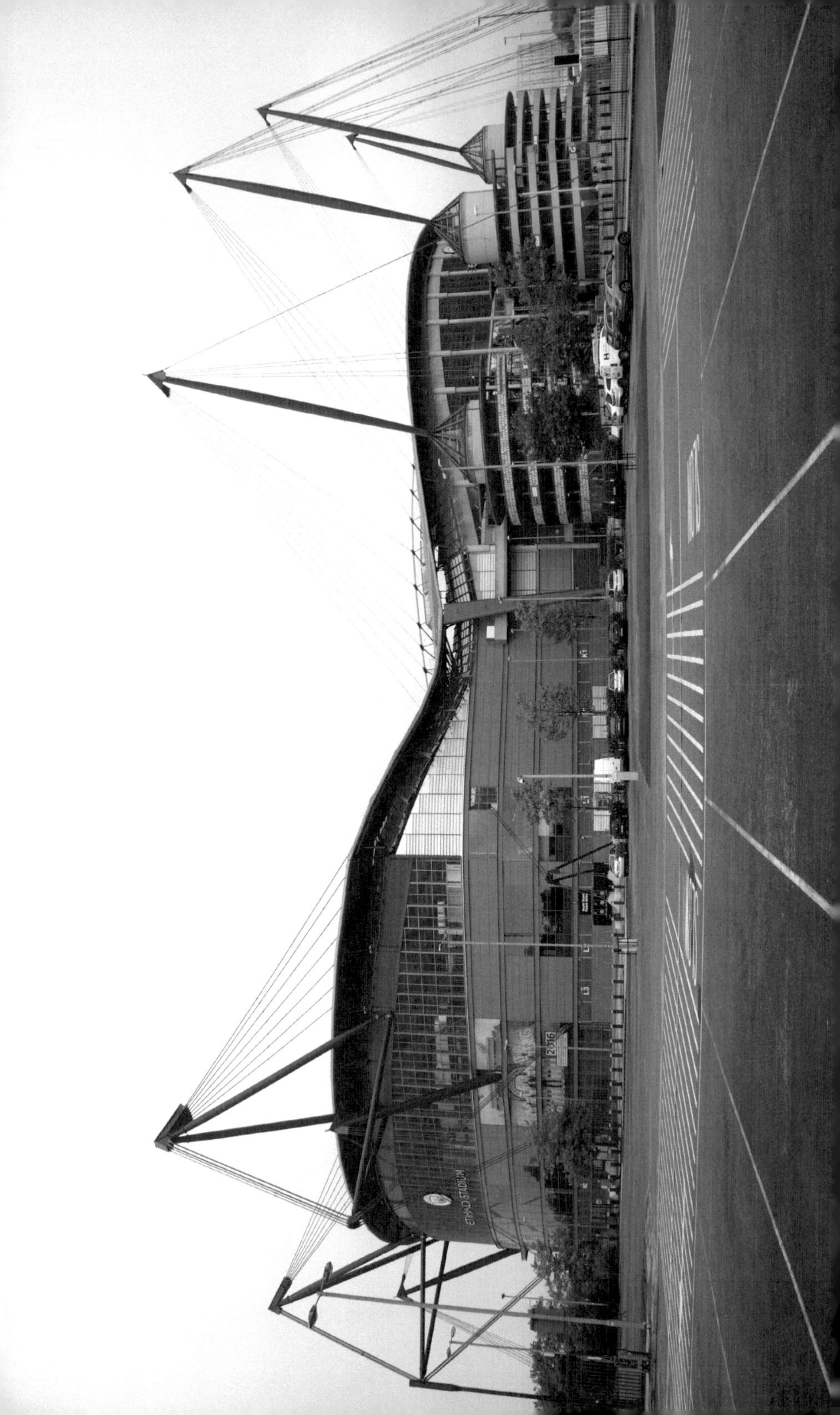

Relics

## *Stadium* – Tim Edensor

In 2003, Manchester City Football Club moved lock, stock and barrel from Maine Road, the stadium they had occupied since 1923, to what was then known as the City of Manchester Stadium, in Beswick, east of the city centre. This large, modern sporting arena was originally designed to stage the 2002 Commonwealth Games that the city had successfully lobbied to hold, and following this mega-event was customised to serve as a football ground. The stadium was constructed as the centrepiece of an ambitious urban regeneration scheme in east Manchester. The strategic intention was to transform a depressed, ex-industrial community into a regenerated area, while simultaneously fuelling the re-imaging of Manchester as an international cultural and sporting destination. At the same time, this sought to fulfil contemporary demands that stadia should be comfortable, safe and accessible, while also catering to the demands of executives who desired facilities in which to entertain their clients – hospitality suites and corporate boxes – and commercial and media interests. The venue was also designed as a multi-use site that could host tourism, shopping, conferences and popular music concerts.

In contrast to Maine Road, the stadium stands grandly apart from surrounding housing and can be seen from far away, notably at night when blue lighting creates an impressive aura akin to a massive extraterrestrial spacecraft. In 2008, the ownership of the club transferred to the vastly wealthy rulers of Abu Dhabi, and the ground was renamed the Etihad Stadium. Since then, the club have endeavoured to make the site homelier, deploying such measures as cladding the exterior and concourse with spectacular visuals, creating a fan zone with bars and food outlets, and building

**40** (Opposite) Etihad Stadium, Beswick, completed in 2002 and designed by ArupSport

a state-of-the-art training complex nearby. Nevertheless, the shift to the Etihad is an archetypal example of how the experience of travelling to and from the match has been transformed in recent years.

Maine Road, built in 1923, was located in a densely populated working-class neighbourhood of Moss Side, in which shifting waves of migrants and long-standing supporters lived and worked over the eight decades of its existence. Built by the doyen of stadium design, Scottish architect Archibald Leitch, stadia such as City's were typically hemmed in by row upon row of small terraced houses. The layout of this realm remains somewhat labyrinthine, cut across with numerous streets and cobbled alleys, and was interspersed with corner shops, fast-food eateries and pubs, with larger spaces occupied by schools and community centres. Accordingly, Maine Road could be accessed via a myriad of different routes from all directions. The Old Trafford stadium of cross-town rivals, Manchester United, was also designed by Leitch, but was surrounded by a different kind of urban landscape, being situated between railways and canals and among diverse industrial units, as well as some housing. This has allowed the club to expand their original stadium while remaining in place.

For City supporters, the experience of going to the match at Maine Road was shaped by the architecture and textures of the streets, and the pubs, shops, takeaways, bookmakers and food stands that became busy before kick-off. Most fans, coming in from Rusholme, Moss Side or Fallowfield, tended to follow distinctive pre-match routines, walking the same route to and from the stadium, and stopping at their favourite hostelries, curry houses and stores. These often long-established routines would have been intimately known, their contours and surfaces offering familiar sensations, cajoling bodies into particular movements, and these sensations became mingled with those of the cigarette smoke and the scent of the chippy that pervaded the air, the dense hubbub of fans, and the occasional galloping police horses who, stirred by their riders, were off to quell an outbreak of trouble between rival fans. Nearing the stadium, footsteps, once singular, would merge in a sea of noise, amplified by the rising cacophony from the ground, the surges of chants, and the utterances of the programme sellers and vendors of cheap fan paraphernalia. The heightened sense of anticipation that coalesced in the mingling of intensified sounds, movements and smells could be further accentuated by the channelling of bodies through narrow alleyways and their sudden exiting to confront the looming presence of the huge grandstands that towered over the houses. These variegated sensations cannot be experienced while walking to the Etihad Stadium: the much smoother materialities, well-maintained shrubbery and the segregated spatialities of the houses, roads and streets, not to mention the dearth of pubs, shops and food outlets, diminish the supercharged apprehension solicited by the environs of Rusholme and Moss Side.

The last game at the old stadium – a narrow defeat to Southampton – culminated in an outpouring of emotion at the loss of this home from home, and the laments that followed the demolition of the ground still resound. Fans were disoriented as they made their way to what seemed like a soulless new stadium and missed their old rituals and habits. For a while, the traces of the catalysing energies of the crowd on match days, and the enterprises that sustained them, lingered on in the fabric of the area. Though the ground had been demolished, there was a vast, muddy, fenced-off area for several years. Burger joints and chip shops closed down, but remained derelict for some time. Numerous small traces of graffiti endured on walls. The Claremont pub on Lloyd Street ceased trading and was converted into upmarket flats, but recognisably maintained the architecture of a pub. Eventually though, the developers who had purchased the site built a large housing complex, filled with modish dwellings, street furniture and green spaces that bore no similarity to the red-brick homes that surrounded them. Initially, it was planned to commemorate the location of the old centre spot on the pitch with a large sculpted ball, but this never materialised.

As time slips by, it might seem that the evidence that this area was once transformed every two weeks by tens of thousands of football fans has been erased – that this quiet residential space is no longer haunted by traces of its former function. However, a closer look reveals this not to be so. An aerial view of the site reveals the big, stadium-shaped space that contains the new housing complex, utterly distinguished from the lines of red-brick abodes that bound it. Moreover, Maine Road itself remains, as does Kippax Street, after which the huge terrace that ran parallel to this byway was named. And nearby lies the 240-unit low-cost Footballers Estate, constructed in the early 1970s and revamped and upgraded recently. Here are a series of closes and streets named after renowned players who graced the old stadium before the Second World War: Tommy Browell, Eric Broom, Fred Tilson, Sam Cowan, Tommy Johnson, Horace Barnes and Sammy Cookson. At the new estate that now covers the site of the old stadium, this tradition has continued with a close there named after Bert Trautmann, and another street designated Blue Moon Way after the club song. The centre spot was also commemorated, but by a more modest memorial: a flat steel plaque to a former groundsman was installed to mark this position, on a stretch of turf that was subsequently named Gibson's Green in his honour.

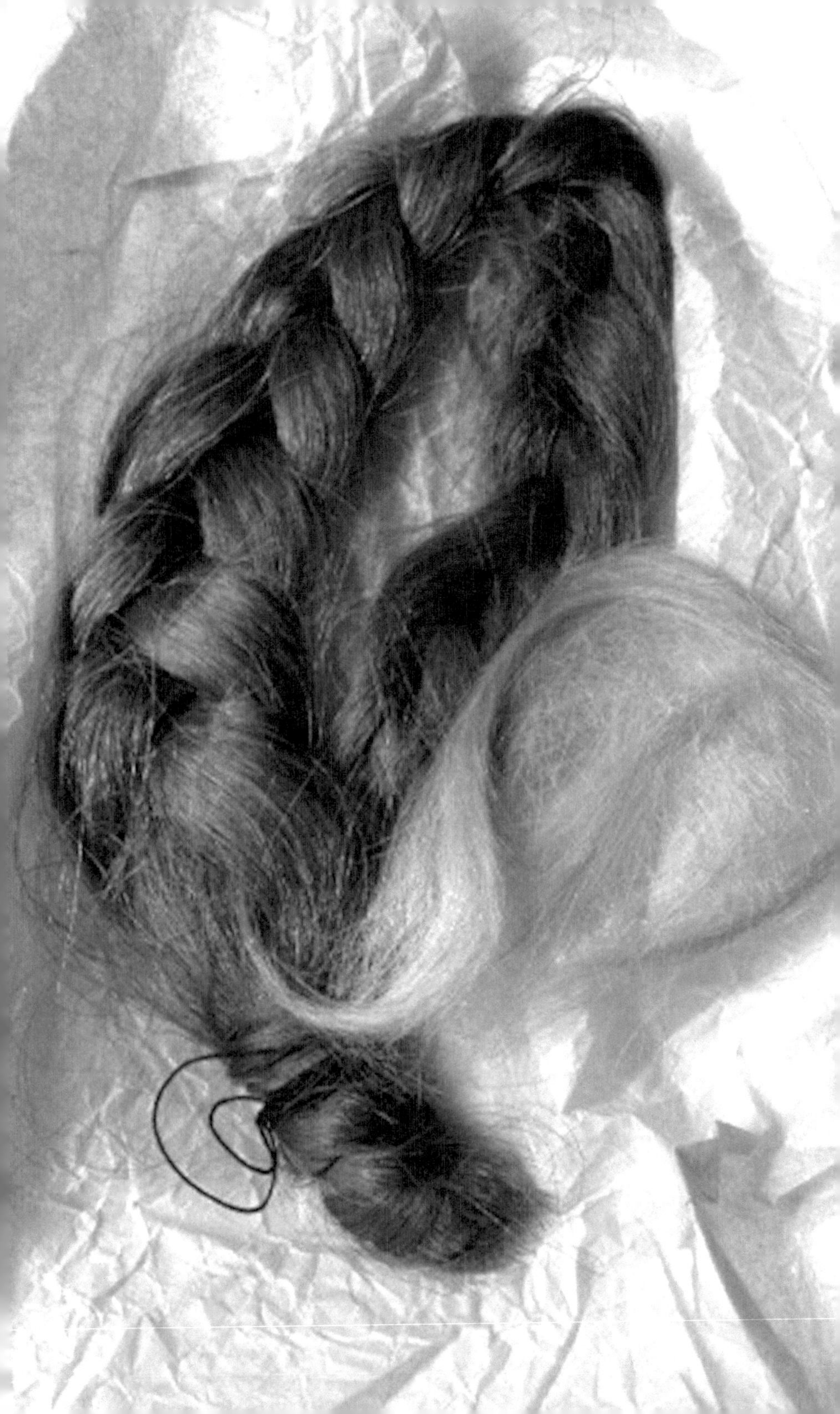

## Hair – Jenna C. Ashton

Can things be, or tell, stories?[4]

I ponder this question as I open the long envelope passed to me by the archivist at the Royal Northern College of Music on Oxford Road. I am in search of an evocative object, a souvenir of longing. I know it resides here.

Whose story do I wish to tell? Can the dead speak through their things? Are we simply clumsy translators looking for meaning to validate our own interests? I suspect it is the latter; but never mind – I find it, I feel it. A brown packet, *Mother's hair & mine* in italicised blue ink. The contents are soft, and well blanketed; I pull out two more packages of crumpled but untorn tissue paper.

The first smaller package reads *My Alice's hair, 5yrs old*; the faded lead scrawl still visible. The second package has no inscription, but I know this to be Alice's mother's hair. *Mother's hair & mine*. A golden curl, an auburn plait. Daughter and mother, at once both present, yet so obviously absent. The golden curl is a duller tone, and is coarser, but I am surprised at the continued vibrancy of the auburn plait. The cuticles still glint and throb with a depth of pigmentation, as if it were cut only yesterday. It is weighty and warm.

The problem with this kind of object is that is falls between the cracks. It is a singular entity; it has no movement, no agency, and no role in grander historical narratives. Thus, it remains hidden. Unimportant. Skin, hair, dust are the detritus of human existence in the domestic sphere. This detritus does not feature in our ideas of the city.

The archive of the Royal Northern College of Music holds a rich collection of records, compositions and personal papers,

**41** (Previous page) A lock of hair found in the Alice Pitfield archive at the Royal Northern College of Music

## Relics

spanning the college's forty-year history and dating back to the days of the Northern School of Music and the Royal Manchester College of Music which came before. Some women, many men; a packet of hair is tucked away among the artefacts of Alice Pitfield (née Astbury; 1903–2000), which exists to accompany her husband's archive, Bolton-born composer, poet and artist, and strict vegetarian and pacifist, Thomas Pitfield (1903–99).

In the archive, Thomas rubs shoulders with the great and the good of the music world, but his own creativity was (is) often negated. His influences of craft, folk customs, nature, speech and dialect have fallen foul of the curse of regionality.

Alice's own story is one of Lancashire mill owners, a Russian childhood and escape from revolution to England. She offers us her own teenage stories in typed script: 'With the help of a diary I kept as a girl in Russia, I have put together some recollections of those days.' Her remembrances are domestic – mealtimes, local woods, nearby peasants, school, pets – and an underlying fear due to the threat of disease, lack of food, and a growing sense of revolution. These limited written reflections emerge in retrospect as Alice-as-adult. The archive holds no earlier writings from Alice or her family.

The locks of hair; we have not yet deciphered their significance. Let me offer an interpretation.

In 1908, Moscow suffers a hard winter. In that same year, still living close to Moscow, Alice's mother cuts a curl from her young daughter's blonde hair. Perhaps she cuts her own plait at that moment. Strands from mother and daughter intertwined and kept together, in case either should part from the other. They are wrapped in soft tissue paper, and Alice's mother scrawls on one of the packets in soft lead pencil, *My Alice's hair, 5yrs old*. Processes of cutting, wrapping, storing, akin to swaddling, caring, and now conserving, ensure the continuous presence of that first lost object – the mother. The kept hair signifies an intimacy between female subjects: mother and daughter – moments of exchange between bodies, between spaces, generations. The act of seeking out the packet, of touching, caressing, placing and photographing, continues that process of material dialogues between women: Alice, her mother and me. New stories may emerge. We are thinking through our mothers.

On an evening in 2016, as part of International Women's Day celebrations, in the foyer of Manchester Art Gallery, I invited women to tell me their hair-stories. I collected forty-six beautiful Polaroid images and a total of seventy-three narratives. The women left written tokens reflecting on sexuality, identity, the body, representation and self-worth.

They talked often of their mothers.

In the gallery space we are building a visible archive. Writing their short responses on a luggage tag and pinning it to standing board, the women who were willing then posed for a Polaroid. The space soon buzzed with humour, anger, frustration, sadness, excitement, coyness and celebration of what hair meant to these different women of all ages, ethnicities and sexualities. This was participatory archival storytelling at its most immediate and unedited. The boards soon became a sea of tags, while the Polaroids came to life in their dark box. Women, men and children loitered to read the comments and stories, and started weaving their own interpretations in response to the slides on display. All the stories are anonymous; the images have no catalogue identifying the women. Yet, each of the women became connected to the next through that act of anonymous writing, of making a statement or thought public and pinning it next to or on top of another woman's tag. Hair-stories enabled Mancunian women, in that short moment, to participate in a collaborative process of writing about their bodies in archiving something as seemingly insignificant as a story about hair.

Hair – 51 per cent carbon, 21 per cent oxygen, 17 per cent nitrogen, 6 per cent hydrogen, and 5 per cent sulphur – is a repository of stories that are continuing to unfold. That cultural heritage women and girls carry with them, in their everyday spaces, experiences, expectations, creative practices, discussions, gossip, relationships and thoughts.

Alice's curl and her mother's plait, alongside the hair-stories of other women, offer us a different type of Manchester. Manchester-as-woman, mother, sister. Manchester as domestic, playful, tender, corporeal and vulnerable. These stories of Manchester have been marginalised, kept in their archival boxes and brown packets, for they are not the 'radical' Manchester of protest. The bolshie Manc bravado that seeps out of every marketing brochure is not the story of hair. *Mother's hair & mine*. These are the stories I seek out, and roll around my tongue to savour them.

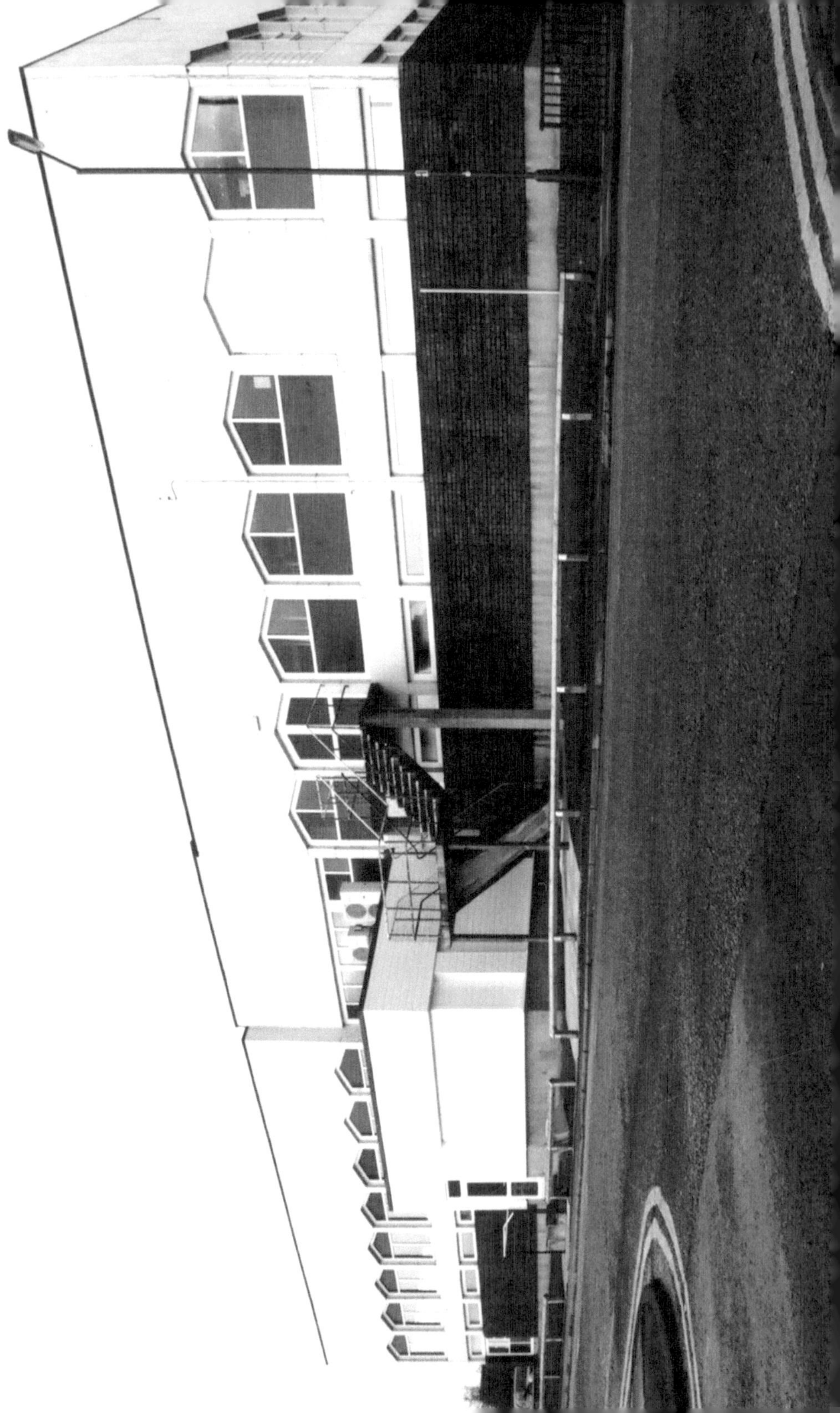

## *Baths* – Matthew Steele

Ever since the Romans established the spa town of Aquae Sulis (later, the city of Bath) in AD 60, there has been a preoccupation with public bathing in Britain. In the early period of public bathing in the eighteenth century, the emphasis was on the reputed restorative powers of natural springs, and was a leisure activity mostly pursued by the gentry and aristocracy. However, the passing of the 1846 Public Baths and Wash-houses Act, which allowed local authorities to raise funds for the construction of municipally run facilities, shifted the emphasis from leisure to hygiene. The impact was most notable in industrialised urban centres such as Liverpool and Birmingham, but in Manchester public baths and wash houses continued to be funded by local philanthropists – indicative of the liberal presence among the city's middle classes. Sir Benjamin Heywood, founder of the Manchester Mechanics' Institute and a prominent Unitarian, paid for a modest bath and wash house on Sycamore Street, Miles Platting (1850), while the charitable organisation known as the Manchester and Salford Baths and Laundries Company built Greengate Baths, Salford (1856), Mayfield Baths, Ardwick (1858), and Leaf Street Baths, Hulme (1860). Evidence of such philanthropic endeavour is now all but lost; only the shell of Greengate Baths on Collier Street remains.

The involvement of Manchester's local authority in the provision of public baths changed with the revised Baths and Wash-houses Act of 1878. Permitted to erect public baths for the sole purpose of swimming, many new facilities were built including baths on Baker Street, Ancoats (1880), Axle Street, Red Bank (1896), Hyde Road, Ardwick (1911), and Manchester Road,

**42** (Opposite) Radcliffe Baths, designed by William Gower in 1968 and demolished in 2016

## Manchester: Something rich and strange

Chorlton-cum-Hardy (1929). Added to those acquired from the Manchester and Salford Baths and Laundries Company in 1877, by 1930 Manchester Corporation was responsible for thirty-five facilities across the city.

Manchester's enthusiasm for municipal baths persisted well into the second half of the twentieth century, partly in response to the Wolfenden Committee on Sport, whose 1960 report was concerned with the provision of physical recreation outside of schools. With wash houses mostly rendered obsolete by fully equipped modern homes, dedicated swimming pools opened across the wider Manchester conurbation, including the Olympic-sized Sharston Baths (1961) in Wythenshawe and Wigan International Baths (1966). Yet while these suburban and out-of-town municipal baths hold important memories for recent generations, memories are often all that remain. Sharston was demolished in the mid 1990s, and Wigan followed in 2009.

For many growing up in the suburbs of Manchester in the 1970s and 1980s, a trip to the baths was a very different experience to that once offered at the now partially restored Victoria Baths (1906) on Hathersage Road, close to the city centre. Walking into the reception of a post-1945 municipal baths, faience tiling and terrazzo floors typically gave way to painted white walls and floors of brown quarry tile, while white suspended ceilings replaced garishly coloured coffered ones. And beyond the brushed stainless steel turnstiles, rectangular wooden handrails mounted on black metal posts snaked their way upwards leading to a canteen or spectator gallery. Materially and visually, these baths offered a taste of modernity no longer fashionable in the 1980s home.

My first experience of this modernity came at Radcliffe Baths, which opened in 1968 and was designed by William Gower; an archetypal modernist cube clad in white mosaic tiling, and with a facade described in Nikolaus Pevsner's architectural guide as being 'faintly Moorish-looking'. As a child, in the warmth of the 'little pool', I resisted my father's best efforts to teach me how

## Relics

**43** Broughton Baths, designed by Scott, Brownrigg and Turner in 1967 and still in use today

to swim – each failure quickly forgotten as the post-swim hot chocolate or vegetable soup washed away the taste of swallowed chlorinated water. It would be a couple of years, and numerous weekly school lessons, before I was able to progress to the 'big pool' and take my badges.

Occasionally, for reasons unknown, these school trips to the baths took us further afield – one alternative venue being Broughton Baths on Great Cheetham Street West. Designed by

## Manchester: Something rich and strange

Scott Brownrigg & Turner, and opened in 1967, Broughton Baths was impressively modern too. Topped by ten glazed pyramid roof lights (sadly, removed in 2015), access to the entrance lobby was via an upper-level gantry which, in turn, led to a spectator gallery overlooking the main pool area. It was spectator galleries such as these that, in later years, provided an unexpected social dimension to the baths: a friend recently commented how he met his first girlfriend while 'hanging around' Sharston Baths on a Saturday afternoon.

In May 2013, storm damage forced the temporary closure of Radcliffe Baths pending remedial works. Alas, with the discovery of significant structural decay, the closure was made permanent and the baths were demolished in October 2016. To the sad list of Manchester's lost post-1945 municipal baths, one can add Miles Platting (1978, demolished in 2015) and Oldham Swimming Stadium (1975, demolished in 2016). How long before Dukinfield's William Andrew Swimming Baths (1965, closed in 2016) suffers a similar fate? If you like your baths modern, don your swimming costume and head to Broughton Baths while you still can.

### Notes

1. Alan Kidd, 'The industrial city and its pre-industrial past: the Manchester Royal Jubilee Exhibition of 1887', *Transactions of the Lancashire and Cheshire Antiquarian Society* 89:61 (1993), pp. 54–73.
2. Quoted in Julian Treuherz, 'The Manchester Murals', in John H. Archer, ed., *Art and Architecture in Victorian Manchester* (Manchester: Manchester University Press, 1985), p. 172.
3. See A. Bistolas, T. Abbott and R. Rusev, 'The Ordsall Chord network arch bridge – addressing complex demands through collaboration', paper presented at the 8th International Conference on Arch Bridges, 5–7 October 2016, Wrocław, Poland.
4. Mieke Bal, 'Telling objects: a narrative perspective on collecting', in Roger Cardinal and John Elsner, eds, *The Cultures of Collecting* (London: Reaktion, 1997), p. 121.

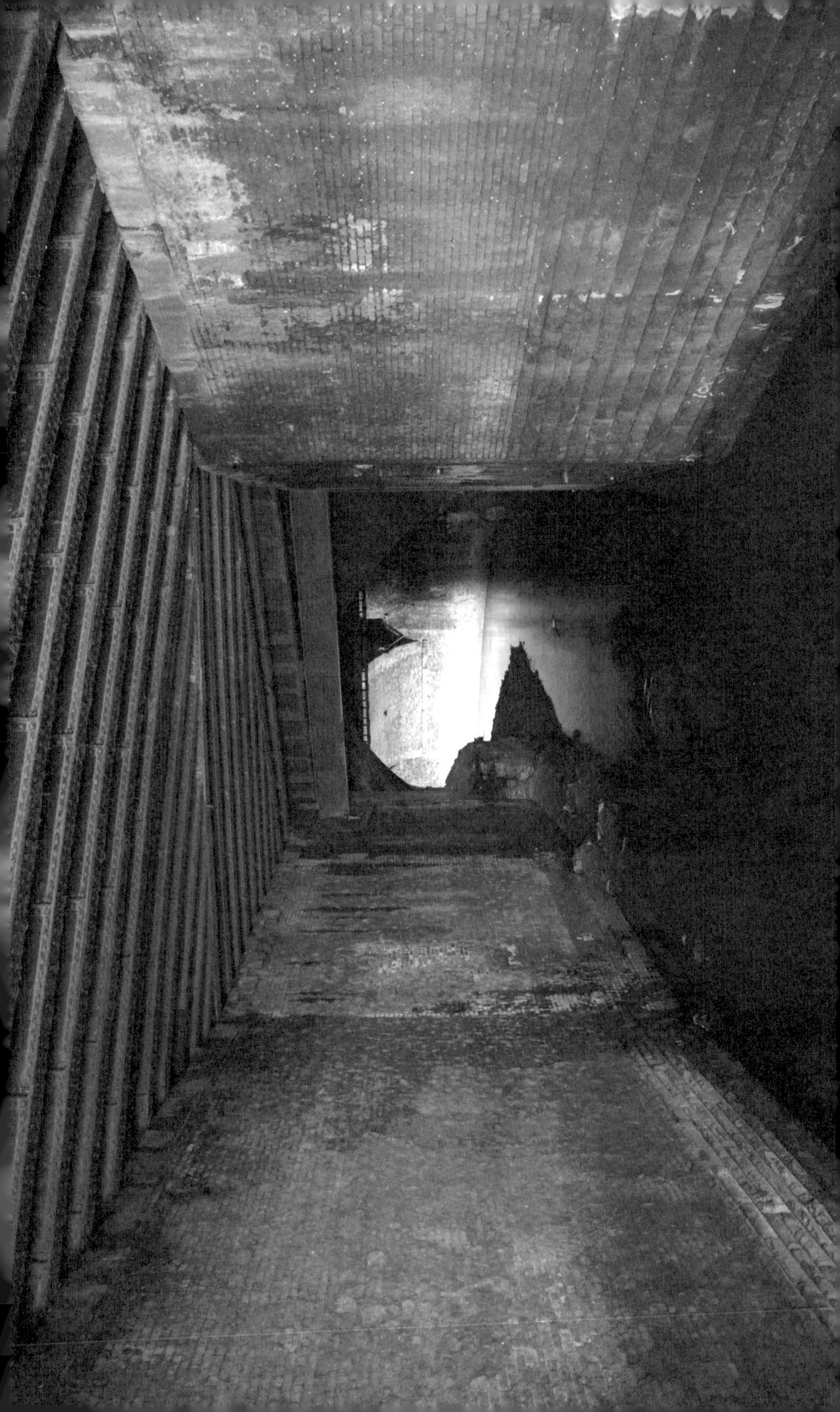

# Underworlds

> I was introduced to exhibitions of the most disgusting and loathsome forms of destitution, and utter vice and profligacy. We went into thirty or more different houses, from the most squalid to those which would not be inaptly termed elegant; and marched directly into parlours, chambers, garrets and cellars, crowded, in many cases like the cells of a beehive, but only in fullness, and beyond this I must adjure the comparison, and say rather like a putrid carcass filled with vermin.
>
> Henry Colman, Unitarian minister, visiting Manchester from America in 1843

Much of what makes cities function well lies under their streets. The subsurface infrastructure of sewers, gas and water pipes, and telecommunication and electricity cables, is almost always taken for granted, but these hidden networks keep the city working like a healthy body. We're only really alerted to their presence when something goes wrong – a blockage, rupture or cut that shows us how vulnerable we are to the sudden malfunctioning of infrastructure. But in contrast to almost every other European city of a similar size, Mancunians have never been able to travel underground: tube tunnels were planned once upon a time but never implemented, the city's expanding tram network effectively

**44** (Previous page) A culverted section of the River Irk, Red Bank, Victoria

providing its own version of the London Underground, replete with its new 'zones' of coverage.

Underground spaces are also imagined as underworlds: dark recesses of the city replete with danger, subversion and clandestine activities. But as Peter Kalu's 'Sewer' evocatively demonstrates, even the most utilitarian of underworlds can exert a powerful imaginative hold on us – in the case of sewers, of the monstrous concentration of our own wastes that we'd rather not think about once we've flushed the toilet. Death, also, is consigned underground: literally in the case of Cassie Britland's 'Grave', where a cemetery provides a way into a disturbing family history. Underworlds, of course, come to the surface all the time: brief glimpses of lives we would prefer not to know about, such as one recounted by Andrew McMillan, but which nevertheless share the same spaces we inhabit in the city. The same applies to a more visible, but no less alien, underworld – namely, Strangeways Prison, a landmark seen from miles around, and which Cassie Britland returns to in her story. And there are the spaces in between – not quite above ground, not quite below – the omnipresent railway arches of Victorian Manchester that have their own intriguing histories, opened up by Brian Rosa.

What's consigned to the underworld – both literally and symbolically – are all the elements of the city that make us uncomfortable, but which have to be put somewhere. If the unpleasant realities are underground, we imagine, they'll be contained and we'll be safe from them. But, just like the darknesses that lurk within each of us, it's not so easy to keep underworlds contained; indeed, to try and do so is inherently counterproductive because they always have to come to the surface at some point. Like giant whales breaching the ocean to breathe, underworlds erupt to the surface with a violence that makes us shudder – witness the 2011 city-centre riots – revealing that the darkness we're afraid of is really just a part of who we, and the city, are.

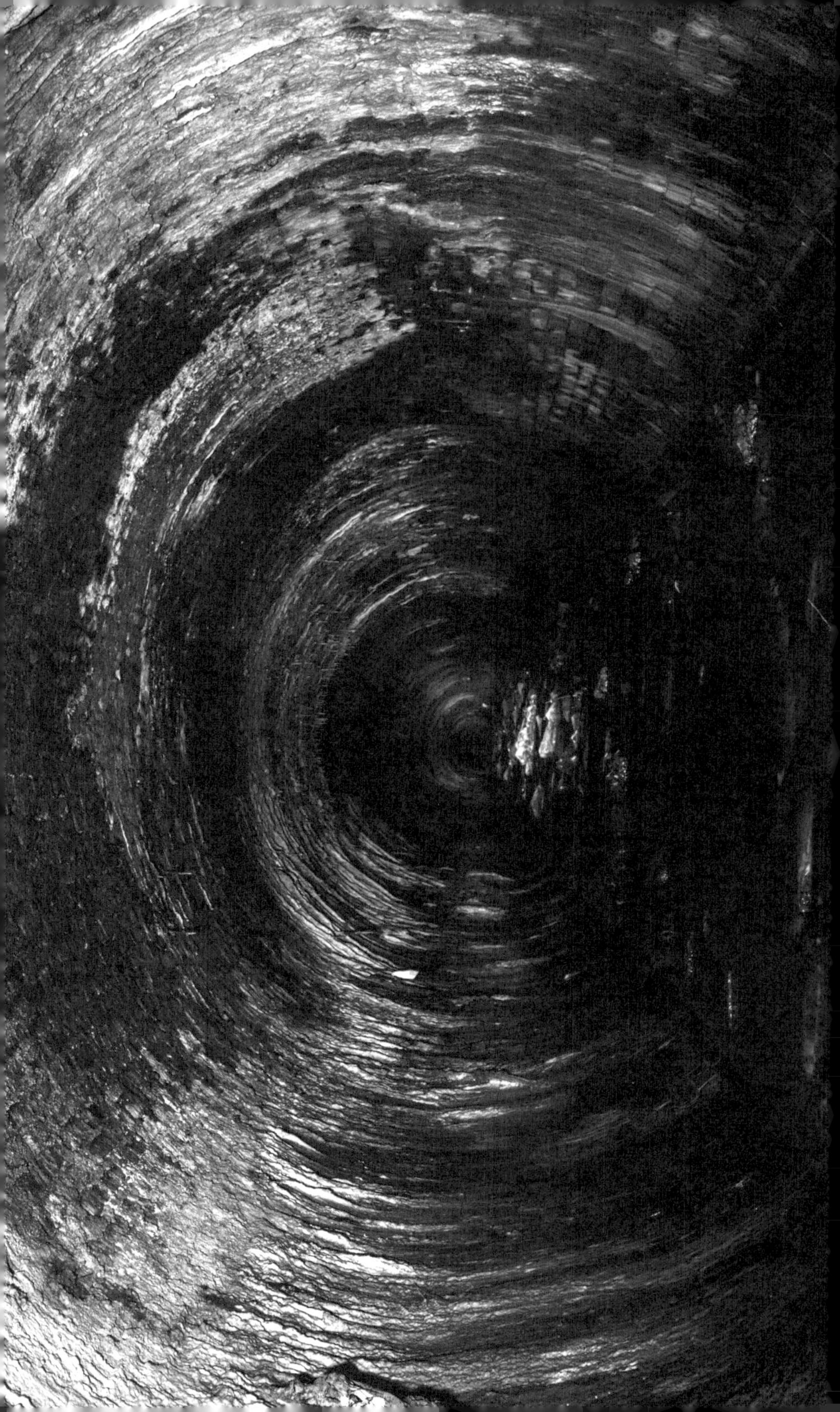

## Underworlds

### *Sewer* – Peter Kalu

We city dwellers are united by our shit streams. Down there among the feeding fatbergs and the guzzling rats, the sewers – sunken Victorian churches to ordure – are channelling all types of shit and shit's friends: wet wipes, needles, flushed drugs, stormwater runoff, chucked wedding rings, pregnancy tests, piss, spittle, hawkings, slobber, abscess gunk, wills, diet sheets, diagnoses, resolutions; they've all been shoved or thrown or ejected or flung or flushed to float softly in the foul untreated shit shat out by millionaire and pauper, cop and robber, toddler and septuagenarian. We city dwellers are united by our shit streams.

Unlike its strutting cousin, the fresh water system – that handsome, finely fluted construction that carries its glittering load in magnificently sculpted aqueducts arching grandly above green valleys, like a shining silver service, ferrying the purest fresh water from the Lake District to granite-sided reservoirs within open-air public parks such as Heaton Park – the sewers of Manchester are buried deep, the shame of their slop sunk low under the city, like an unloved child, abandoned and buried alive, underground. Occasionally the kid cries out for attention, kicks up a fuss, reminds us of its existence.

Subsidence, collapses, sink holes, blockages: the unloved kid wails. Then the Mancunian Way is throttled for nine months while repairs are performed requiring excavations the size of salt mines, the kid patched up and buried again, hushed. But not for long. Another cry, and the Oxford Street folded-napkin-and silver-service eateries around the city centre Palace Theatre reek for weeks of latrines because some guzzling fatberg has settled under there, clogging the city's colon. It's another tantrum that is put down with huge suction lorries and slithering rubber bypass

**45** (Opposite) Inside a combined sewer which flows into the River Irk

pipes running the length of Oxford Street's tarmac, leaking faeces, stepped over adroitly by theatregoers hoping to catch *Les Misérables*. More digging of tunnels. Then the kid is slapped quiet once more. And yet the sight of sewage unbound stays in the mind longer than the last big number of *Les Mis*. It clings to a sub-ego existence in the dark recesses of the mind, stirring to life in nightmares and winter stories of night creatures living there, the place from which stalkers emerge, bogeymen, cholera, plagues; the place where ghouls reside in between hauntings, shadows disappearing down sewers with hidden loot; the chopped-up bodies of lovers, journalists, diplomats, all shoved down there, gone the same way as unwanted kittens, old dogs and irksome guests who overstayed their welcome.

The tunnelling of the sewers does not criss-cross this city Hades alone. But it is the raddled, grande dame of all the other boreholes: the tunnels linking Manchester's civil servants' nuclear bunkers, the abandoned digs for never-built cross-city underground, cross-city rail networks, the lithesome, pretty blue, coiling water pipes, the snaking phone and internet trunk ways, the yellow-piped gas ways, the concrete culverts channelling marauding storm waters.

The sewers were an engineering solution that triumphed over slopping out – that wonderful tradition of flinging pails of faeces and piss out of an upper window onto the heads of those passing in rags in the street below. There is no better way for a costume drama film to establish its Elizabethan-era credentials than to show slops being thrown from bedroom casement windows.

The Victorian sewer is part of England's claim to glory, along with the two World Wars and the one World Cup. Sir Joseph William Bazalgette (1819–91) has his own statue in London by the River Thames for building London's main sewers in the 1860s. Manchester has yet to honour its sewer builders, yet they too did a fine job of keeping shit moving – as great a job as the canal builders who are so acclaimed, so memorialised, so plinthed.

## Underworlds

It all flows to the sewage treatment centres to be made into cake. The centres are fenced off, sometimes separated too by a rising, high bank of grass finishing in a plateau, tucked into some place away from housing, like the banks of the M60 Denton southbound exit, or by commercial zones like those of Davyhulme treatment works, close to the M60 that passes the Trafford Centre and Chill Factore. Somewhere there will be a wriggly, disguised approach road leading to an aluminium picket-fence gate onto which is bolted a sign: 'No Entry: United Utilities Water Treatment Works'.

Methane is a biologically active molecule with antioxidant, anti-inflammatory and antiapoptotic properties that can protect human livers and lungs. The farmyard smell in Trafford that hangs in the air for days in summer is due to a build-up of sludge which has not yet been converted to cake and removed to farms. United Utilities do good information. Whoever decided to call dried-out shit 'cake' should take a bow. Cake. Steaming cake is what causes that smell. The received product – raw sewage – is screened, pumped, filtered, sedimented and channelled into giant feeders where, by biological processes involving activated sludge, a bacterial digestion takes place. The end product is converted into high-grade fertiliser for farmers.

Cake. It sounds like a happy result – but spare a thought for the starlings. Studies have established that male starlings sing less than females if they feed on the grubs that eat sewage. Because the grub's dinner is chock-full of antidepressants. It seems we perturbed humans piss out a sea of antidepressants and our piss wrecks the love lives of grub-gobbling starlings.

The treated water of the Davyhulme works is released into the Manchester Ship Canal, United Utilities inform us. Again, the beautiful language. 'Released': like a freed tiger, or pet shop bird. There are other places it is released into besides the canal. Overflows runoff into rivers. I often walk by the River Mersey along the sweeping green golf fields and flood plains near Merseybank to catch the beauty of the riverbank reeds, the immortal sweep of the wriggling weight of water, the picturesque bob of its ducks, the soaring joy of its swallows. But when you slither down lower, get right down to the river's edge and look along, you may find concrete slabs, framing Bastille-like iron-gate guards that are the city alimentary system's colonic end – the arsehole through which effluent trickles out along a gently sloping concrete lip into the river. That sight ends any dream of loafing on the Mersey's banks, dipping toes in there before spreading out topless in summer in imitation of Seurat's painting, *Bathers at Asnières*. Nobody yet bathes in the Mersey.

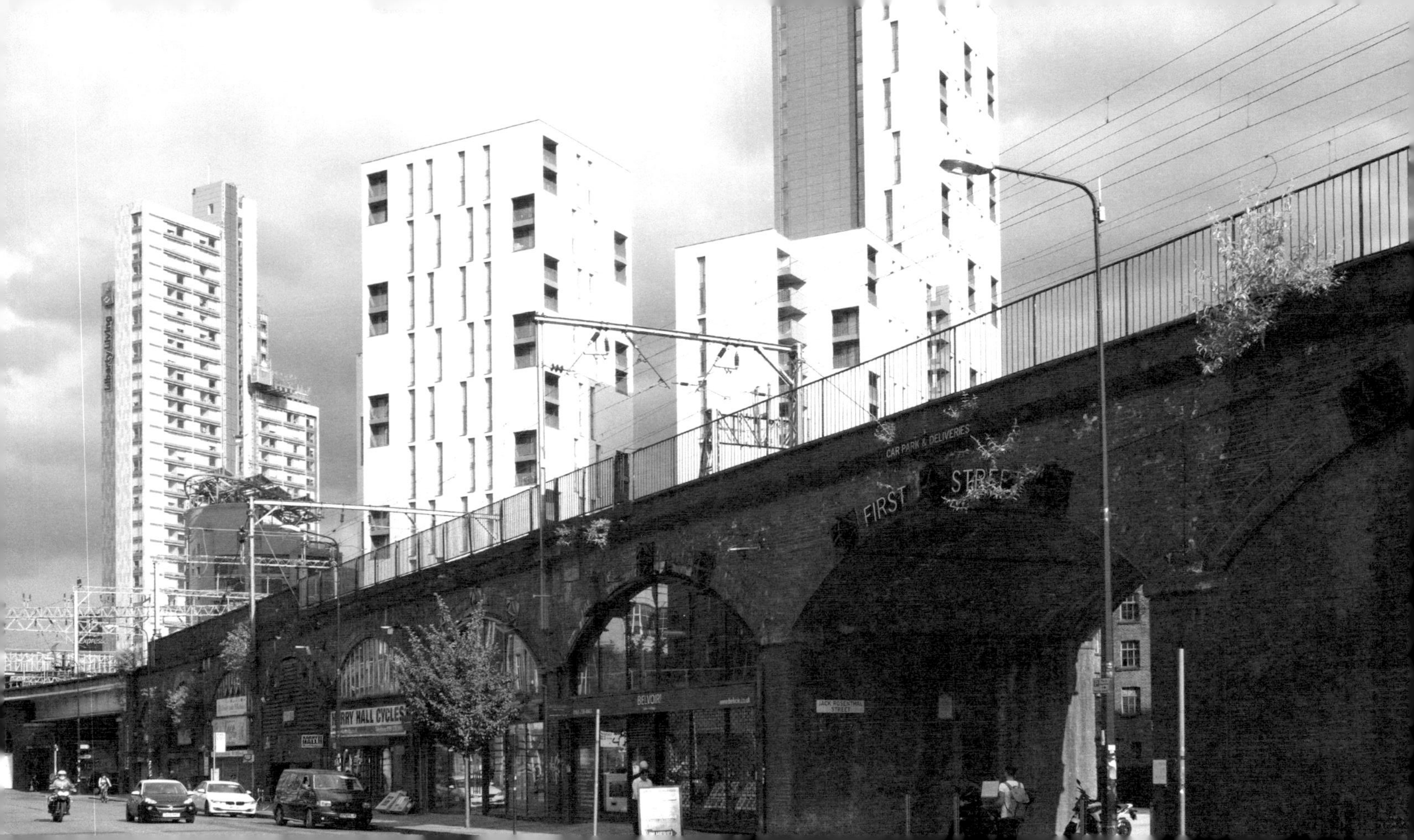

Manchester: Something rich and strange

## *Arches* – Brian Rosa

Railway arches are nothing specific to Manchester: they define the fringes of city centres throughout Britain and are such a commonplace element of the built environment that they often elude notice. However, there is a good argument to be made that Manchester, more than any other city, has been shaped definitively by the railway. With brick railway viaducts some of the largest and most dominating built structures of the city centre, the arched spaces beneath them have been inhabited since the railways' construction in the Victorian era. In the popular imagination, these arches are associated with shelter for the homeless and destitute, and they still clearly serve this function on the periphery of Manchester's urban core. They have also long been associated with criminality and various forms of dubious commercial enterprise, such as automotive chop shops, and the dodgy element of arches have long been played up as a trope for police procedural dramas and countless other cinematic representations of the British urban landscape.

Another common image of railway viaducts and their arches has been as a backdrop to working-class urban neighbourhoods, most famously in the opening credits of *Coronation Street*. Indeed, with Granada Studios having had a long-standing presence in Castlefield – the place where railway viaducts dominate most spectacularly – one can argue that the perpetration of industrial and railway landscapes as sites of lurid, urban twilight zones has constantly been reinforced for the sake of convenience. Why not have Sherlock Holmes chasing a suspect along the shadowy canals beneath the railways in Castlefield? After all, they were conveniently located right next to the studios.

Aside from these more long-standing cultural representations of railway arches as the sites of destitution, crime, and working-class

**46** (Previous page) Railway viaduct, Whitworth Street West

## Underworlds

industrial labour, these spaces have also been emblematic in the growth of new urban lifestyles: of clubs and cultural venues, coffee roasters and restaurants, gyms and design-savvy office spaces. The repackaging of railway arches as spaces of leisure and consumption – today most commonly associated with south and east London – was pioneered in Manchester.

As early as the late 1980s, cultural and entertainment spaces were opening in Manchester's railway arches. In 1985, the Cornerhouse cinema built one of its screens in an arch beneath Oxford Road station; and in 1987, an avant-garde theatre, the Green Room, opened next door on Whitworth Street West. Both of these establishments had built upon the momentum of the Haçienda nightclub further down the road, itself facing onto the railway viaduct which had defined the ragged edge of the city centre for well over a century.

Perhaps the most important and emblematic transformation of the railway arches in Manchester was Atlas Bar, opening in 1993 within an arch space formerly occupied by Atlas Motors, a car mechanic at the corner of Whitworth Street West and Deansgate. The new bar, tellingly, was jointly owned by a group of property developers and architects who were working on the post-industrial transformation of Knott Mill, the area located directly behind it. All of this was related to the work in the 1980s and 1990s of the Central Manchester Development Corporation, a public–private partnership focused on property-led redevelopment of the southern fringe of the city centre. This massive transformation was largely predicated on industrial displacement, the conversion of mills and warehouses, and a combination of heritage and post-industrial aesthetics.

Atlas – still existing today, though with different owners, design and clientele – should be identified as a key space in which Manchester's aspirations as a post-industrial city were first dreamed up. On the one hand, it was one of the earliest cafe-bars in the city, catering to the pre-clubbing crowd during the evenings and serving the growing office-based workforce in that part of the city during lunch hours. In the early 1990s, Knott Mill was being taken over by architecture and design firms such as SimpsonHaugh, and Simpson was also a consultant on the Knott Mill redevelopment and co-owner of Atlas with design-savvy property developer Nick Johnson. This was a primary site from which new aspirations for Manchester's city centre emerged – the embodiment of entrepreneurial, adaptive reuse with an aesthetic nod to the industrial past.

Just as lofts were beginning to offer new city-centre housing options for the design-conscious, cafe-bars provided many of the people who lived and worked in nearby converted industrial buildings an easily accessible place to work and/or socialise over cappuccinos or cocktails. Atlas was also the physical location where planners, designers and surveyors struck deals, rubbing elbows with artists and DJs. By 2001, it was dubbed 'the city's hippest bar', even as the crowd was, by then, becoming decidedly mainstream. Since then, arch conversions in Manchester have kept growing in scale: the Deansgate Locks development, across the street from Atlas beneath the old Central Station, saw a row of ten arches converted into bars and nightclubs – a centrepiece development leading up to Manchester's hosting of the 2002 Commonwealth Games.

After a relative lull in the years following the economic crash of 2008, the skyline of Manchester is once again dominated by cranes, and new businesses are appearing in districts experiencing intensive redevelopment. In recent years, microbreweries and gin distilleries have proliferated in the backstreets behind Victoria and Piccadilly stations – areas that, even five years ago, had no businesses operating in the railway arches other than the traditional uses of car mechanics, warehousing, and light industry. In 2019, plans were approved for six of the arches beneath the former Central Station to be converted into a massive gin distillery and bar.

## Underworlds

The transformation of railway arches in Manchester has once again become central in debates around the future of the city centre. The few remaining industrial businesses located in the arches on Whitworth Street West have begun relocating in anticipation of further redevelopment, and new businesses are opening within the arches behind Victoria station next to the Greengate housing development. Building upon the gradual conversion of railway arches into higher-value commercial properties, and stimulated by public disinvestment in railway infrastructure in Britain, nearly all railway arch commercial properties in England and Wales have been sold by the publicly owned Network Rail to investment firms Blackstone and Telereal Trillium for £1.6 billion. The justification for the disposal of these properties is that they are 'non-core' to the functioning of the railways and that the windfall payment can be used for other uses. What this means in practice, though, is that the ownership of the largest landlord of small business commercial properties in Britain has passed from public to private hands. As tenants in railway arches in cities across Britain have already been experiencing exponential rent hikes and lease terminations, the future of these affordable workspaces will continue to be central in processes of property-led development and commercial gentrification.

**47** Searching for the grave of Elizabeth Hannah and Thomas Britland in Dukinfield Cemetery

## *Grave* – Cassie Britland

I am standing in the reception office at Dukinfield Cemetery. I need help finding a grave.

'What's the name?' asks the receptionist.

'Elizabeth Hannah and Thomas Britland', I say. 'It's a family plot.'

'Britland, Britland…' The receptionist frowns. 'Why do I know that name?'

'I emailed about them recently. I'm researching…'

'A murder!' The receptionist, who tells me his name is Danny, gets excited. People often do when I tell them my story.

My name is Cassie Britland and I'm a writer working on a book about Mary Ann Britland, the first woman hanged at Strangeways Prison. She was Elizabeth Hannah Britland's mother and Thomas Britland's wife. In 1886, Mary Ann was convicted of poisoning her best friend, Mary Dixon. An inquest a few days earlier found her responsible for the deaths of her daughter and husband as well. Mary Ann Britland also happens to be my distant ancestor.

Danny takes a photocopied map from a pile on his desk. He writes a plot number on it and circles a corner of land halfway down the Ashton side of the cemetery.

'This one's hard to find. There's a few unmarked plots down there and no real landmarks to help you figure it out. But there's a big tree in the middle of it all, so you can look for that.' He hands me the map. 'This will get you to the rough area, at least.'

Dukinfield Cemetery (formerly known as the Ashton and Dukinfield Cemeteries) opened in October 1866 to what might now seem a surprising amount of celebration. The forty-acre site (of which twenty-nine acres were dedicated to Ashton's residents, and the remaining eleven to Dukinfield, Stalybridge and Hurst) was the Manchester region's first public cemetery at a time when they were still a very new idea. Less than twenty-five years earlier, traditional inner-city church graveyards were 'filled to overflowing [and] presented, as a rule, a most repulsive aspect'. Public cemeteries were created to ease the burden, and their quick universal adoption was hailed as 'abundant proof of the wisdom of [their] enactment'.[1]

Locals were proud of the cemetery. One reporter wrote:

> Nearly every important town in the kingdom has now its cemetery, which, in most instances, is one of the chief attractions of the district, and, happily, Ashton is no longer the exception. Few sites can be compared with the land now appropriated to interments for Ashton-under-Lyne and Dukinfield. In situation it is unrivalled; in point of substratum and drainage it is everything to be desired; and the approaches are excellent.[2]

Another was moved to near-poetry:

> Here, for succeeding ages, when the incessant demands of an ever enlarging commerce shall have covered the fields with factories, workshops, and houses, there will be a green and flowery spot, the last refuge of nature, where in sight of hills that lie beyond, and the broad plains that stretch far away, the toilers and sufferers of each succeeding generation shall be gathered to the host of the silent. And even as the traveller is hurried through the busy towns or the dwellers lift their eyes across the valley, they will see glancing in the sunshine or quiet in the storm the tombs of the dead in the sight of the living.[3]

Dukinfield Cemetery was a beautiful place, and nineteenth-century Ashtonians were right to be proud of it. But in reading these old newspapers, you get a sense that their pride comes from more than just aesthetics. While the consecration of the grounds, orientation of the plots (facing east – one of many pagan practices adopted by Christians), and Gothic Revival design were all reassuringly traditional, the new Ashton and Dukinfield Cemeteries were also a picture of modernity. Each building was equipped with gas lighting and a Haden's heating stove (the gold standard for any upstanding church or country manor in this period). The three

## Underworlds

chapels – one for each of Ashton's primary denominations (Roman Catholic, Church of England, and Nonconformist) – made generous use of glass, not only for decoration, but also for the mortuary chambers that adjoined the chapels, where the deceased could be laid out in full view of mourners, and then easily carried to their final resting place. And all of it was connected to sewage – a luxury that, in 1866, many living Ashtonians still did not enjoy.

As our reporter friend from earlier wrote, every important British town had a cemetery. Now Ashton had one too. Ashton was important. Ashton was on the map.

Today, Dukinfield Cemetery is still beautiful. Walking down the hill to Elizabeth Hannah and Thomas Britland's plot, the view is much as it would have been when Mary Ann Britland buried them here in 1886. Weathered rows of headstones, crooked like snaggleteeth, seem to burst from (or sink into) the green and soggy ground. There are no visible fences, but dense oak trees enclose the space. Beyond them are old mills and chimneys, but they're easy to miss if you stand in the right places. Our second reporter friend was also right – Dukinfield Cemetery is still a sanctuary from the twin forces of commerce and industry. Just don't look uphill to the south – that's where IKEA is.

With our map and Danny's instructions, we find the corner where Elizabeth Hannah and Thomas Britland are buried. They are in plot 1413, and we find plot 1414 without much difficulty: it has a headstone and the remains of a stone border. Like similarly marked graves, its plot number is engraved in the border's footstone. Elizabeth Hannah and Thomas's grave should be next to it on the left, but the plot lines are crooked and the numbering system is not chronological. The only way to be sure is to confirm that the grave on the left of the unmarked plot is 1412, but its stone border has sunk deep into the boneyard mud.

There's only one thing for it. Taking turns, we get down on our knees and dig – with our fingers and dirty twigs, hoping no one sees us and gets the wrong idea. We apologise to the worms we accidentally murder. We are about to give up when my companion feels a curved groove. Could it be the edge of a number two? It's too dark to see, so I put my camera down on the ground and use the flash to snap a photo. And there it is: 12, as in 1412. The plot to the right is almost certainly 1413. Elizabeth Hannah and Thomas Britland's grave. In this place, where history and modernity meet, I have found my connection to the past.

BELLA ITALIA

beauty

pharmacy

15

Manchester: Something rich and strange

## *Violence* – Andrew McMillan

I met my friend in Piccadilly Gardens and we walked through the loitering crowds on our way to the Gay Village. Everyone seemed to be looking at something. Standing still, their shopping bags resting between their legs, all eyes staring in the same direction.

A young black girl was on the ground; two, maybe three police officers were on top of her. She was screaming. One officer was holding a long kitchen knife, its blade as long as his forearm. Some of the people were filming the girl. She was screaming at them to stop.

My friend and I said nothing as we walked by, and then, almost when we felt we might have been out of earshot of the drama, we talked briefly about other stabbings that had been in the news. Then the news more generally. Then other things. Then nothing for a while, until we arrived at the bar.

A couple of days before all this I'd been coming home from the gym – having taken to waking without an alarm, and being at the gym before 5.30 am. It meant the streets were still quiet when I left the flat, before the city-centre businesspeople were even waking up. On one of the side streets I passed a young man in a car, who I assumed was parking up for his own workout. I ignored him, walked on, kept my headphones on and my head down.

I've never got myself in trouble in a city, never been mugged or threatened, but I always feel on constant alert. I was almost past the young man when he suddenly drove forward, first into the bumper of the car in front, pushing it out of its own parking space, leaving it stranded in the middle of the road, and then into the bumper of another parked car, shunting it forward. For the longest time I couldn't be sure that I was really seeing this, that this

**48** (Previous page) Greater Manchester riot police during the 2008 UEFA cup final riots

was really something that was happening. I kept walking, stopping every few steps to turn around and watch; a man in a suit who looked tired was wheeling a suitcase a few paces behind me. I kept trying to catch his eye, to have him as an accomplice to what I was seeing, but he kept his head down, started walking faster. The young man jumped out of his car, if it was his car, and ran down the side of the park over the road.

I didn't know what to do; should I call the police, not only to report what had happened but also the car that was now marooned across both sides of the road? An abandoned car in this current climate of suspicion could shut the whole city centre down for hours. Yet, as I walked back to the flat later, after a bleary-eyed workout, I couldn't fully accept that I hadn't been dreaming, and so opted to do nothing.

That afternoon, walking back from shopping, I detoured to the same road to see if there was any evidence of what I thought had happened; there wasn't anything. A row of cars parked neatly on either side, not even any debris in the gutter – but on Twitter, when the street name was searched for, one person's report of an abandoned car they'd spotted and reported.

It made me uncomfortable all evening, how such a thing could happen and only me and the man in the suit having seen it. My parents still live in the same small village in which I was born; if anything like that happened there it would be front-page news in their local paper. Mum would tell me about it on the phone; it would get spoken about for months. If something tears at the fabric of something small, the hole that's created seems bigger somehow.

Cities, on the other hand, can absorb acts of violence on a daily basis, without threatening to disturb the civility that keeps them functioning.

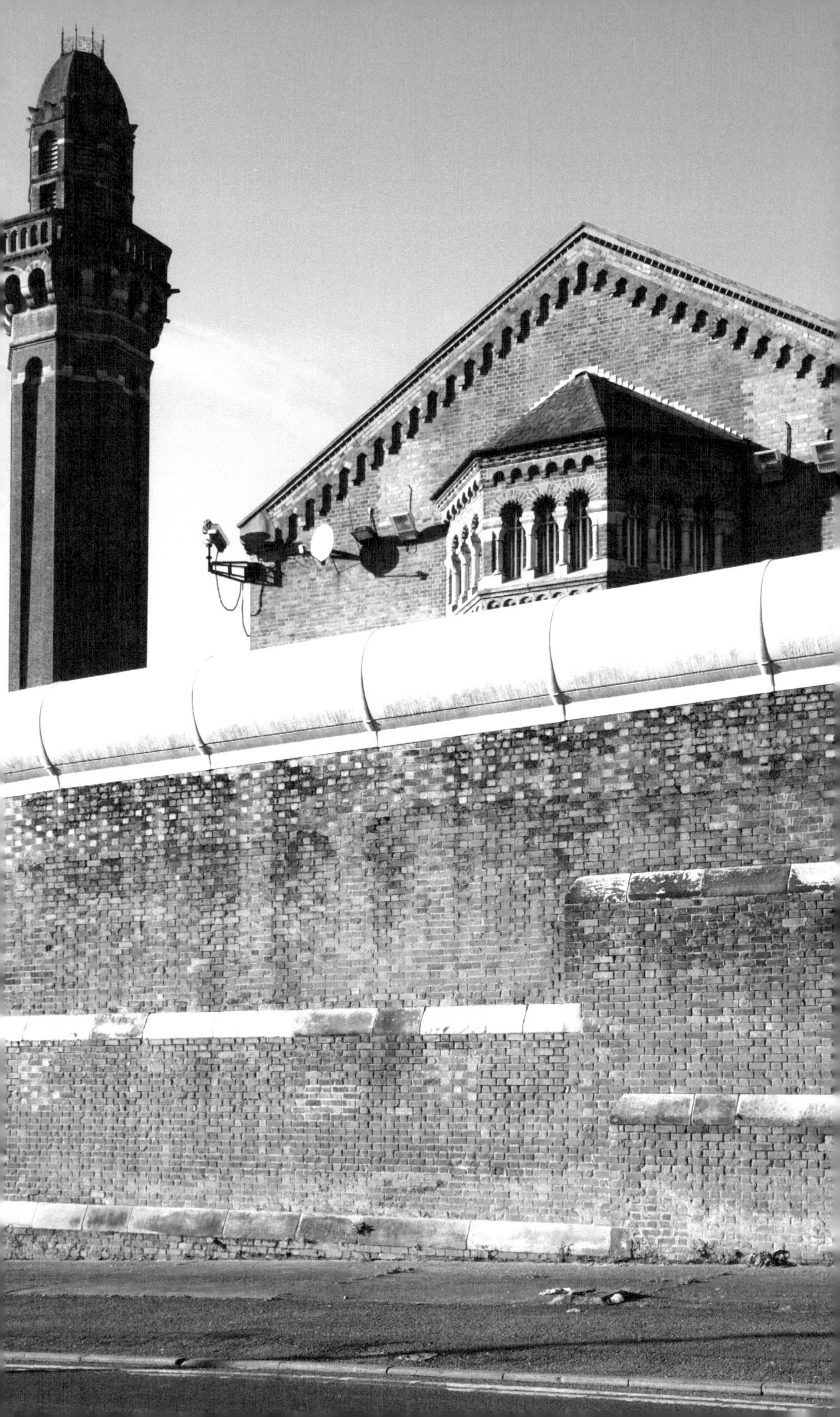

# Underworlds

## *Prison* – Cassie Britland

It's 8pm on a Wednesday summer night. The sun is still high in the sky, but hidden behind rain clouds and thick, black smoke. I am standing outside Strangeways Prison and an old mill next door is burning to the ground.

I was at work when a friend told me about the fire. It was a coincidence because I'd been to Strangeways the day before – had walked down Southall Street, where the doomed mill was located, and taken a photograph of it because I liked the way it looked. When I heard what had happened today, there was no question in my mind about whether or not I would come back for a look; only how close I could get without getting into trouble.

Strangeways Prison is where my ancestor and convicted murderer, Mary Ann Britland, spent the final months of her life. In 1886, it was still a relatively new institution – only eighteen years old. Designed by Alfred Waterhouse, the prison owes its distinctive radial design to the panopticon architectural concept and the 'separate' system of prison management. The separate system is all about solitary confinement – the idea that prisoners should do silent, solitary penance in their own cells. The panopticon is all about control – each wing radiates out from a single point, like a spoke on a wheel, allowing maximum visibility from the centre. Someone is always watching, so you'd better keep in line.

From its Gothic facade you'd think Strangeways' interior would be like a dungeon. But it's the opposite. When the prison was first opened, it was fitted with all the latest mid-Victorian mod cons. It was – and still is – tiled throughout, making it appear sterile, like a hospital. But the building's design and the severe overcrowding within it undermine that initial sense of hyper-cleanliness. In

**49** (Opposite) Strangeways Prison as seen behind the high brick wall on Southall Street

recent years, staff and inmates alike have condemned the conditions inside the prison. They have told how the small, barred windows allow for little natural light and even less fresh air to pass through. How, even with regular bathing, there is a constant sour smell of 'people' in the air – their breath, their sweat, their sickness. To a house-proud woman like Mary Ann Britland, it must have been unbearable.

I am fascinated by Strangeways – perhaps more than is appropriate. If I'm in Manchester with an hour or two to kill, I'll stroll over there and go for a walk around the prison's massive red-brick walls. It's the history that draws me: the people who have lived and died there. Suffragettes, serial killers, Britpop stars, supposed terrorists – all have done their time. But it's also the accessibility of the building. As an Australian, I am stunned that a prison like this is located in the centre of town – that I can walk right up to the walls and touch them. Back home, our prisons are away from the city centres, often on the side of a busy highway or surrounded by the harsh countryside of the bush. You can't just wander over to them after a day of shopping.

It's the walls that fascinate me, even more than the grand old gate or the iconic sky-piercing spire (which is actually a chimney, not a watchtower). The walls were there for all of it; every prisoner and every execution. They are more than a century older than me, and they will probably outlive me too. They've witnessed history, but also reflect it.

One event in particular has left its mark. In 1990, the inmates at Strangeways rioted, protesting the prison's increasing overcrowding (originally built to hold 1,059 inmates, Strangeways reached a peak population of 1,658 just days before the riot began), its deteriorating facilities, and a range of abuses committed by staff. They took over the prison for twenty-five days, almost destroying it in the process.

You can see all of it – the destruction and the violence – in those massive exterior walls. Whole sections have been rebuilt, and little of it is visually coherent. The new bricks – smooth and pinkish-brown – have been laid directly on top of the old ones, now greasy black and chalky white. The present and the future, built on top of the past. It would be poetic, except you know someone was just trying to save money.

Rumour has it that these walls are impenetrable: sixteen-feet thick. But every now and then you'll see a purple bloom of buddleia pushing through the bricks. It seems like escape is possible after all.

When I gaze upon those bricks, I often think of the records that were destroyed during the riot – prisoner registers, full of physical descriptions and biographical details that are invaluable to researchers like me. The few that remain were found dumped in a skip. I'm shocked that anyone could treat what I would consider to be such important documents with so little regard.

Then I'll notice a syringe next to my boot, the nitrous bulbs on the ground, and remember where I am. Strangeways is not a museum or a relic of history. It's not even called Strangeways anymore – it's now HMP Manchester, an active maximum-security prison. It's a place of broken lives and broken dreams; of trauma and heartbreak not only in some distant, almost abstract, past, but continuing today. While I take photographs of bricks, families sit in the visitors centre, waiting to spend just a little time with the men they love – men they may never see in the outside world again. They have more pressing concerns than the fate of some old books.

No one ever asks me to leave Strangeways like they would if I was hanging around a prison back home. Not even when there's a fire raging next door – in fact, a smiling young police officer actually helps me find the best view for a photo. To me, this is so quintessentially and wonderfully Mancunian. I feel welcome to go – and am welcomed when I arrive – anywhere, even in the back lanes surrounding a maximum-security prison. As a writer, researcher and visitor, I consider this an incredible privilege. But

## Manchester: Something rich and strange

it is one I must be careful not to abuse. While my research is historical and my subjects are long dead, the people and places I encounter through my work are all very much part of the present. A place like Strangeways is more than just its history, and history is more than just old stories.

### Notes

1 Anon., 'The cemetery', *Ashton & Stalybridge Reporter*, 13 October 1866, p. 4.
2 Anon., 'The opening of the Ashton and Dukinfield Cemeteries. Description of the chapels, &c.', *Ashton & Stalybridge Reporter*, 27 October 1866, p. 6.
3 Anon., 'The cemetery', p. 4.

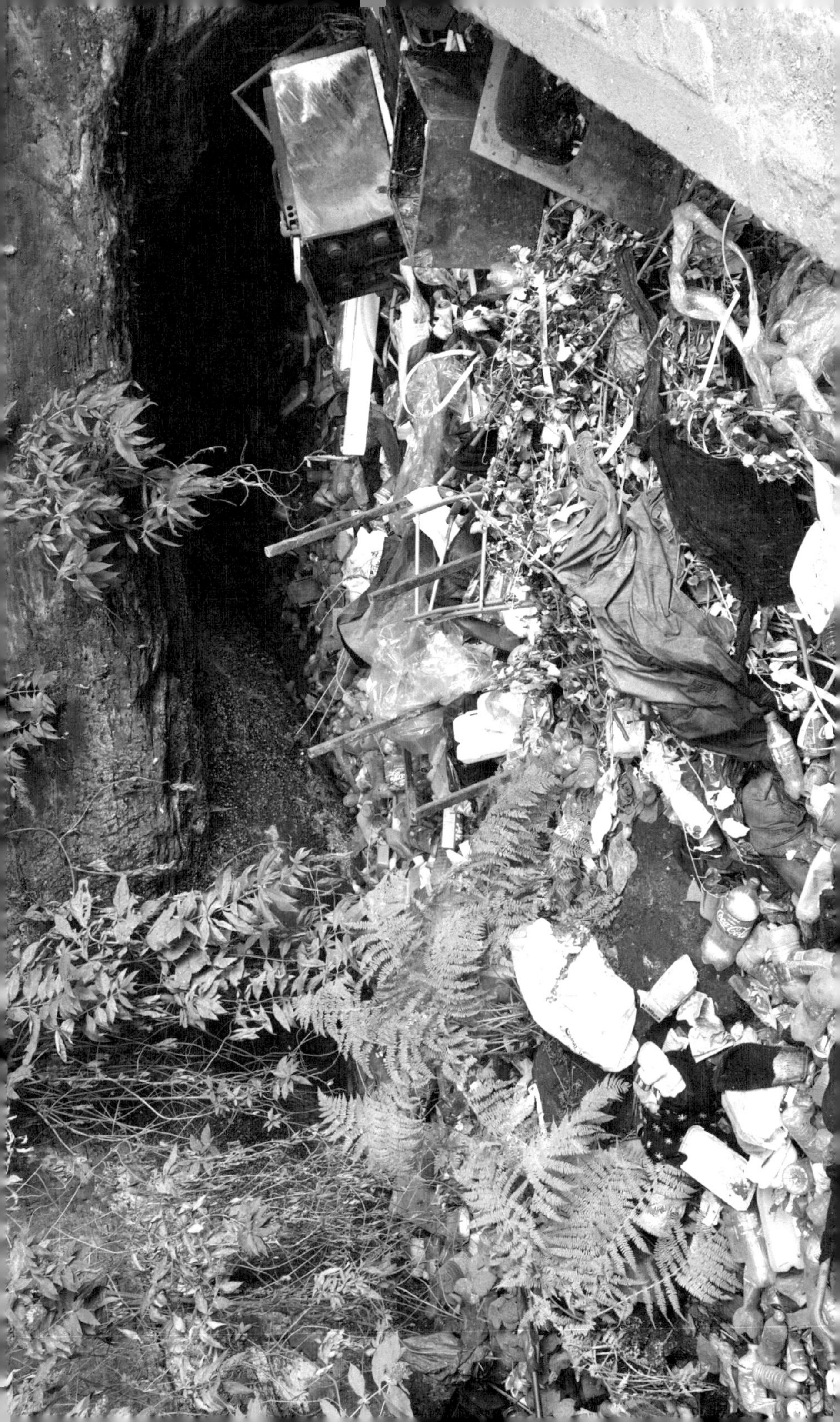

# Dregs

> It is in the middle of this vile cesspool that the greatest stream of human industry flows out to fertilise the entire universe. From the filthy cesspit flows pure gold. It is here that the human spirit attains complete development, and at the same time utter brutishness. Here civilisation produces its miracles and civilised man is turned back almost into a savage.
>
> Alexis de Tocqueville, French historian and diplomat,<br>on visiting Manchester in 1835

It's almost impossible to imagine Manchester in the 1830s – this astonishing description by Alexis de Tocqueville is perhaps the most powerful, but by no means unusual, picture of the city as an industrial hell. In calling Manchester a 'filthy cesspit', de Tocqueville well knew that he was tapping in on a repulsive image of the city as a very literal shithole. And this image lingers in contemporary perceptions of the city and its satellite towns, particularly those of outsiders – these places often gracing the top-ten list of 'crap towns' in Great Britain. It's a pervasive image that marketeers of Manchester, past and present, have done their utmost to dispel, the present makeover of the city centre and its immediate surroundings being perhaps the most obvious attempt to kick off these negative stereotypes.

**50** (Previous page) Detritus filling a spur of the Rochdale Canal in Castlefield

## Dregs

However, there are more rounded ways of thinking about the city's dregs, allowing the inevitable mess of wastes to become visible without being completely repulsed by them. Some of the dregs have a strange and terrible kind of beauty. So, as James Thorp explores in 'Dye', there's something miraculous about a toxic residue of industry turning ducks blue in Miles Platting; while the deadly arsenic uncovered by Becky Alexis-Martin was once regarded as an essential component of domestic products like wallpaper and clothing. In 'Shadows', Nick Dunn explores a more pervasive residue – namely the soot that once covered every single building in the city. More obvious dregs are the abandoned buildings and patches of waste ground that still litter the city, even though many are now being overtaken by rapacious development. Joanne Hudson reminds us of the value of these seemingly unproductive spaces, while Tim Edensor takes us to Burnage and the ambiguous pleasures of exploring an abandoned industrial building, again now completely lost to a Tesco car park. Finally, Matthew Steele visits Bradford, an area of Manchester that has been transformed so comprehensively that its industrial past, and the wastes that industry produced, have been almost completely erased.

Bringing to light lost histories of the city's dregs is not meant to make us feel nostalgic, as so many accounts of Manchester of the past are apt to do. Rather, they work best when they create an uncomfortable sense of dislocation, when the past we imagine is brought up short by an unpleasant reality we'd conveniently forgotten about. But, if we're game, there's also great pleasure to be had in this sense of shock – the joy of discovering anew what we thought we'd known, of finding in the dregs a kind of wonder.

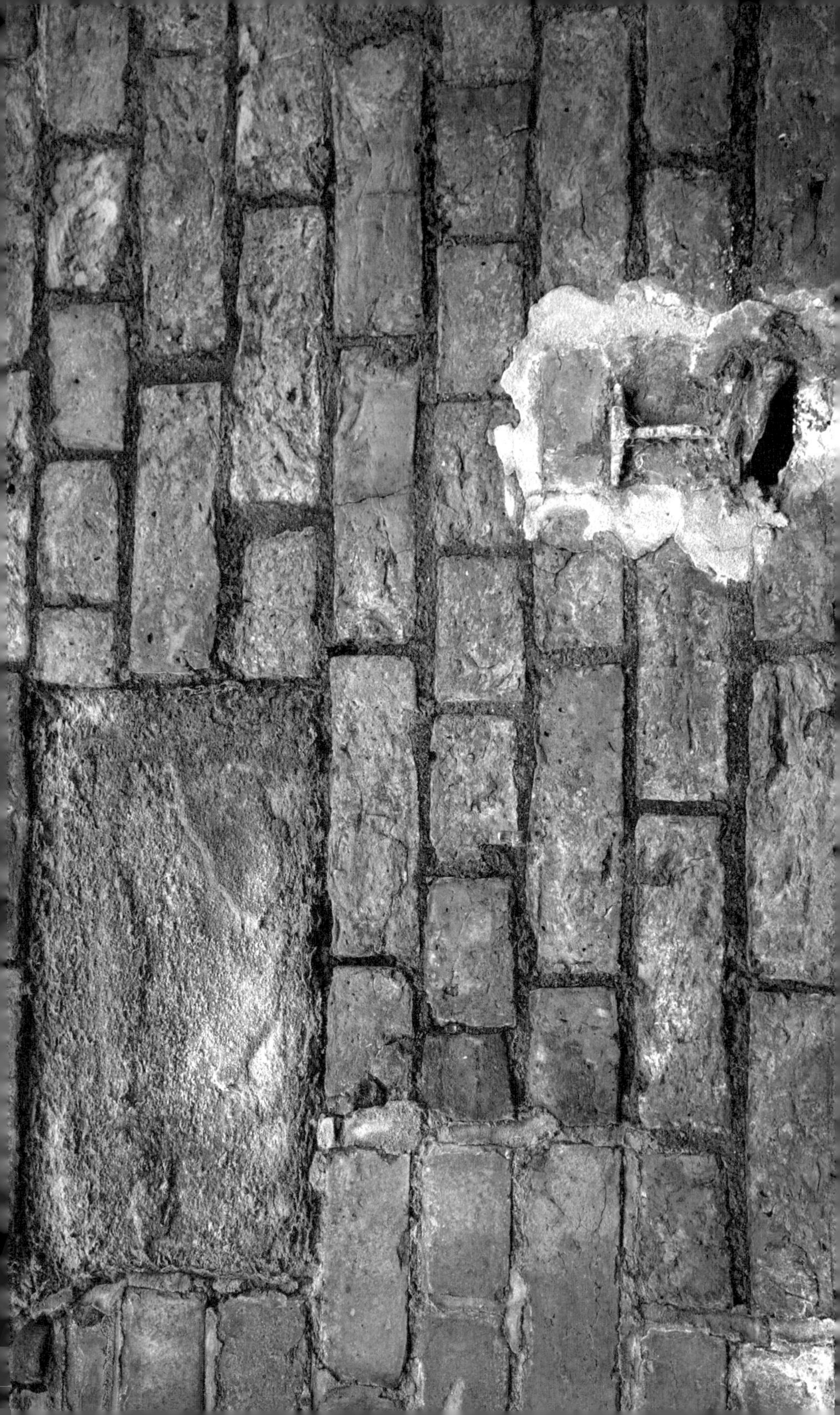

# Dregs

## *Dye* – James Thorp

My affinity for the site of the former Hardman & Holden dyeworks on Coleshill Street in Miles Platting started at a very young age. I just about remember the place as a functional manufacturing site. The name that the factory bore at that time – Degussa – sounded simultaneously exotic and industrial. Only recently did I discover that Degussa is actually an acronym of Deutsche Gold und Silber Scheide Anstalt (German Gold and Silver Separating Works) – now one of the world's largest chemical companies. Degussa closed their Manchester factory in 2005, and only the perimeter wall remains.

The production of synthetic dyes in Manchester owes its existence to pioneering chemists in Germany and the demands of the city's textile industry. Cyanol was the first synthetic blue dye, produced by Friedlieb Ferdinand Runge in 1833 as a by-product of the distillation of coal tar. The same substance was produced by a different method in 1841 and called aniline – the Clayton Aniline Company was another dye factory that served Manchester's textile industry until being regenerated by a different kind of blue: Manchester City Football Club. Neighbouring the aniline works in Clayton was Hardman & Holden's Clayton site, producing chemicals from coal tar liquor.

Josiah Hardman and John James Holden acquired the chemical works of Nicholas Varley in Miles Platting in 1870, and ten years later started a contract with the Manchester Corporation to process the by-products from the gasworks nearby in Bradford – namely, the iron thiocyanate left over after toxic hydrogen sulphide was removed from coal gas. This waste product was then used to make Prussian blue pigment at the chemical works. The

**51** (Opposite) Blue-dyed bricks and timber in the remains of Hardman & Holden dyeworks on Coleshill Street in Miles Platting

company became known as the Manchester Oxide Company, with Manox becoming a trademark following the formal acquisition by Hardman & Holden in 1897. Production of Prussian blue ceased around 1920 due to changes in the way gas was handled. Other dyes continued to be manufactured at the site until its eventual closure in 2005. Yet, even today, the production of those blue dyes many years ago has left indelible physical traces: blue-tinged bricks, timber and paving stones continue to act as visible reminders of the past.

Alongside the corporate machinations and decades of chemical production, many other lives were impacted by the presence of the Manox/Degussa factory. Newspaper records reveal a fascinating history of accidents and industrial malpractice, often at the expense of the workers, local residents or the environment. In 1899, following three explosions and the deaths of two men in a sewer attributed to effluvia from the works, a District Sanitary Association was formed by residents and their complaints heard at the City Police Court. The chemical works were having an impact on the environment, turning wood and stone blue. They also took their toll on public health. John James Cooper, honorary secretary of the District Sanitary Association, remarked that two of his children 'suffered in health',[1] often falling sick after eating. At the same time, the rector of the local St Mark's church complained that he 'had to suffer unbearable smells which causes headache and nausea and prevented him doing any thinking work'.[2]

Initially, Hardman & Holden claimed that it was impossible that the gases responsible for these incidents could have escaped from their works and were anyway 'too valuable a commodity'[3] to be disposed of. Upon investigation it transpired that carbon bisulphide and hydrocyanic acid had been discharged from the factory into the public sewers, but the company were not issued with a heavy penalty by the court. In 1905, they were directly responsible for a fatality when driver Joseph Lilley was overcome by gas in the factory. A doctor gave evidence at the inquest, explaining

## Dregs

that, as a result of a post-mortem, 'the man's brain presented a most striking appearance, being olive green in colour'.[4] The jury returned a verdict of death by poisoning and said that gas taps in the factory's yard should be enclosed. Even as late as 1971, the *Manchester Evening News* reported an 'evil smelling sludge'[5] found dumped on a recreation area next to Nelson Street Junior School, and children were warned not to play there.

In 2005, two startling reports once again made the *Manchester Evening News*. The first involved the sighting of blue ducks following a leak of dye into the adjacent Rochdale Canal in May. The entire canal was reported to have turned blue for several days. Representatives of Degussa and the Environment Agency sought to reassure the public that the dye was non-toxic and caused no harm to either water or wildlife. Yet, months later there were reports of blue-coloured pigeons gathering in Miles Platting. It transpired that the pigeons had been nesting in the factory and had became coated in the blue powder that gave them their new plumage.

Closure in 2005 and surrounding regeneration schemes have left a landscape with far less activity and interest than that seen in the preceding century. It is hard, if not impossible, to imagine the level of activity and industry that used to happen cheek by jowl with a dense residential community. All that remains of the factory are stubs of walls stained blue that unobtrusively border a wasteland visited by fly-tippers. Along the Rochdale Canal, crumbling walls of various ages are inset with deep-blue timbers and rusting steelwork. The company that currently owns the site specialise in the management of toxic industrial sites and plan to redevelop it. But for now, this part of Miles Platting is still waiting for that promised future to happen.

# THE CAKE OF DEATH

THE CONDEMNED WOMAN WAS ALLOWED TO SEE HER SON.

WALKED FIRMLY TO HER DEATH.

EXECUTION OF A WOMAN AT MANCHESTER.

## *Arsenic* – Becky Alexis-Martin

Victorian Manchester was blighted by a spectrum of industrial contaminants, and arsenic was one of the more insidious and abundant. Copper arsenite was used to create a verdant pigment known as Scheele's Green, first made in 1775. This vivid shade epitomised Victorian stylistic sensibilities, colouring everything from wallpaper to clothing and blancmange. However, these cheerful emerald walls concealed a major public health threat. Over time, vapours and inhalable fragments of this toxic tincture found their way inside the bodies of inhabitants, causing a nebulous collection of symptoms that are now described as *arsenicosis*. We now know that in 1857 each sumptuous sample of Manchester's Heywood, Higginbottom, Smith & Co wallpaper contained arsenic.[6] This beautiful dye also snuck into the food chain, with several children poisoned in Manchester by eating sweets coloured with copper arsenite during the 1840s.[7] This banal yet lethal element imprinted itself on Manchester, not just by the famed penny dreadful poisonings of disgruntled partners, but also through the lackadaisical attitudes of the city's manufacturers.

In addition, domestic rat traps were laced with arsenic, revealing its toxicity in plain sight, as poisoned rodents staggered to their deaths. Both mice and men were vulnerable, and it became a popular homicide choice, nicknamed 'inheritance powder' by the early nineteenth century. Francis Bradley was one of several Mancunians who poisoned their wives with arsenic, and was hanged on 3 September 1842. Mary Ann Britland gained the dubious honour of being the first woman to be hanged at Strangeways Prison on 9 August 1886, after murdering her daughter and husband with Harrison's Vermin Killer (see 'Grave', p. 179). In Ancoats in 1828, a mysterious cake was delivered by a young

**52** (Opposite) The cake of death: arsenic in Manchester's history boy on behalf of an old lady to a Mr Drummond. However, Mr Drummond's wife refused this cake, so the boy took it home to share with his neighbours. As his friends and family chewed, they didn't realise that this delicious treat was a 'cake of death', laced as it was with arsenic. One child died, and despite a reward being offered by the police, the old woman was never found.[8]

Arsenic's murderous popularity waned during the late nineteenth century, thanks to improved detection and new legislation. The 1851 Arsenic Act made it challenging to buy, and this reduced cases of poisoning, while local Acts of Parliament were introduced in Manchester and Stockport to prevent anyone younger than twenty-one from buying arsenic, requiring two witnesses for each purchase to deter any homicidal intentions. However, people still continued to suffer from arsenic exposure due to misguided medicine and a burgeoning English passion for unregulated capitalism. Manchester infirmaries provided arsenic treatments for conditions including rheumatoid arthritis, 'neuralgia', epilepsy, psoriasis and syphilis. An arsenic cure-all named Fowler's Solution became popular in the nineteenth century, having been developed in 1796. These treatments occasionally supported recovery from parasitic and sexually transmitted diseases, but usually just slowly poisoned patients.

Beyond the infirmary, those who chose to self-medicate with beer were also in danger. On 23 November 1900, two women died in mysterious circumstances at Crumpsall Workhouse.[9] Their deaths were blamed on alcoholism, but were instead the first signs of a baffling new epidemic. Thousands of patients were subsequently misdiagnosed as alcoholics while suffering from arsenical neuritis. Sociomedical prejudices were not addressed, and working-class people's description of their drinking habits were not trusted by doctors. By November 1900, 'alcoholic neuritis' was described for a quarter of acute admissions to Manchester Western Infirmary. Arsenical neuritis differs from alcoholic neuritis, as it also includes muscle cramping and skin discolouration. Dr Ernest

Reynolds of Manchester Royal and Workhouse infirmaries was the first medic to recognise the significance of this symptom set, and he diagnosed an arsenic poisoning outbreak across Greater Manchester. A Royal Commission into this epidemic had been ordered by February 1901.

Eventually beer was identified as the cause, and while local brewers destroyed their toxic barrels the puzzle remained unsolved. Brewers were criticised for not protecting their customers, yet the contamination originated from arsenious acid in brewing sugar produced by Bostock & Co in Liverpool. Only cheap 'four penny' beers brewed with sugar were affected. More expensive beers brewed with malt and hops were less contaminated, disproportionately affecting Manchester's working-class community. However, there was also a universal source, as malts processed over coal fires absorbed arsenic, which was then manufactured into all types of beer. The cultural memory of arsenic toxicity is still evident in Manchester. Rather than toxic beer, research at the University of Manchester now investigates the complexities of arsenic contamination through rice-based diets, in the city and worldwide.

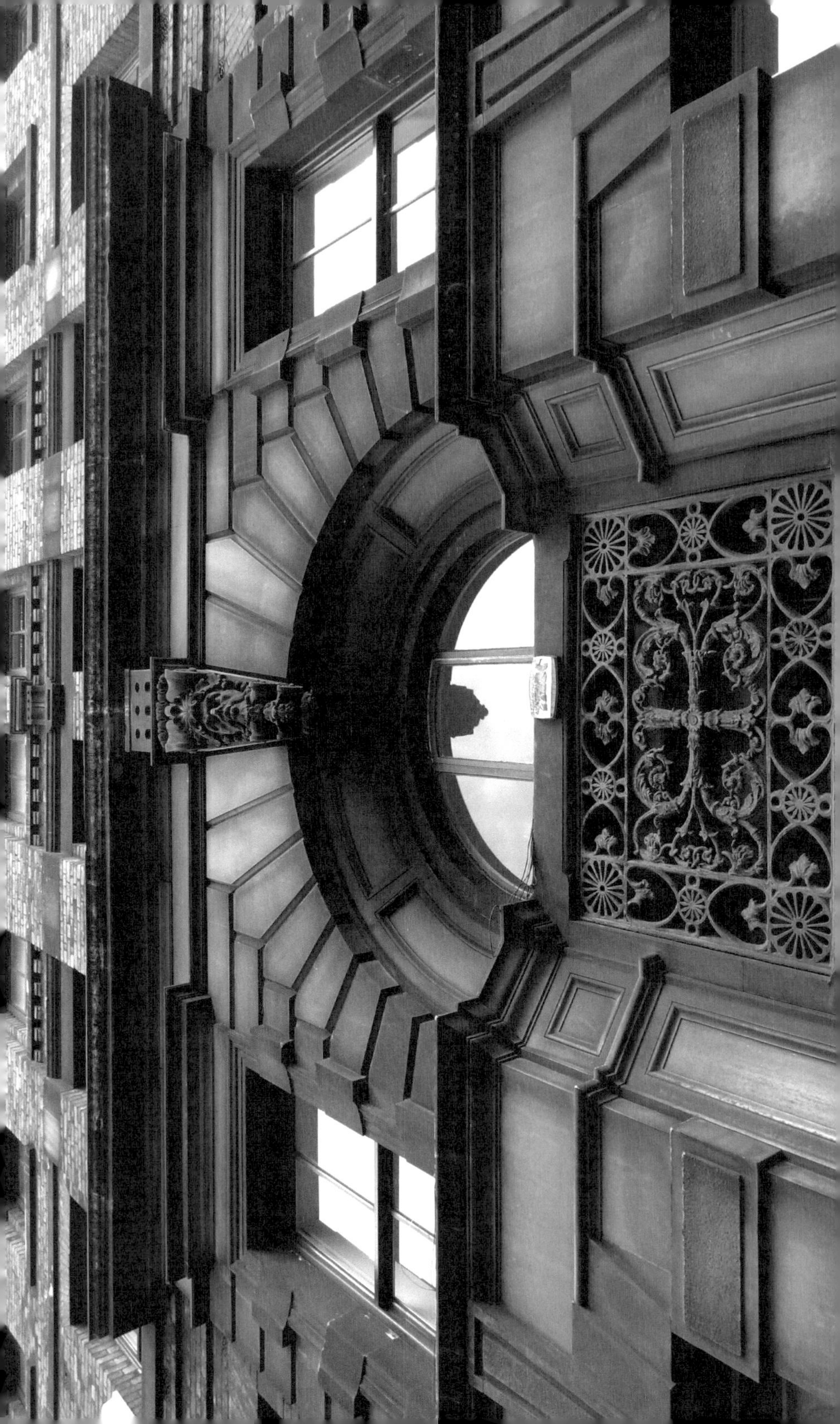

## *Shadows* – Nick Dunn

When we think of shadows we naturally think of light. The relationship between light and darkness is interdependent, the presence of one usually highlighting the absence of the other. But what of shadows? Do they really need the sun or artificial light to be formed? As with many things, Manchester has a special tale regarding such matters. The city has a considerable history of various types of light and darkness, especially in relation to its pioneering role in the industrialisation of cities. This has resulted in shadows, both metaphorical and physical, that continue to be cast in the present day. The physical shadows are dark remnants of a bygone era. They are notable for their scarcity in the contemporary city, but it's useful to understand how they were created.

The energy production needed to fuel the industrial transformation that changed a market town into a burgeoning city had a profound impact on the aesthetics of Manchester's increasingly urban landscape. In addition to the rapid growth of the city's population, which resulted in extremely poor and overcrowded living conditions for many who followed the new opportunities for work there, was the matter of soot. The soot created by the coal-burning furnaces that powered the machinery around them was airborne and quickly built up on the surfaces of the buildings across the city, leaving permanent 'shadows' behind. This dark and, admittedly dismal, landscape moved various writers, including Benjamin Disraeli, Elizabeth Gaskell and Charles Dickens, to evoke this new shadowy, urban atmosphere, the latter basing 'Coketown' in *Hard Times* (1854) on the city's bleak and blackened context. The living and working conditions in Manchester during

**53** (Opposite) Smoke-blackened stone on a former warehouse on Lever Street, Northern Quarter

this period were unquestionably grim for many. Echoes of the dirty, squalid and dangerous nature of some of its inner-city areas live on through place names such as Dark Lane in Ardwick.

The nascent industrialisation of Manchester soon accelerated both the need for energy production and the growth of an artificially lit urban landscape that came to be much copied around the world. The experience of being in Manchester at this time would have immediately disclosed the paradox that lay at the centre of the city's success. The processes of industrialisation, especially the development of artificial illumination, transformed people's perception of the world in terms of labour, culture and society. These lighting technologies, however, also gave rise to direct and fundamental changes in the natural light of the city in two principal ways. Firstly, the artificial illumination showed just how poor the quality of natural light was, due to the high levels of black smoke and soot that covered the city. Secondly, it created a city of greater contrasts in terms of light and shadow, making parts of the city appear even darker by their adjacency to artificially lit areas. This transition moved Friedrich Engels, upon rereading his own haunting description of Manchester penned in the 1840s, to admit his depiction was not dark enough in its attempt to convey the character of the place.

The city's role as a blueprint for the modern city is well documented. Less discussed is the shadowy, blackened architecture of Manchester and the legacy of this material deposit that would recall the city's dark history as its grandest buildings were covered with soot. The coal fires and smoke from the nearby industry effectively embalmed the city's landmarks with a black coat prior to the Clean Air Act of 1956, which reduced airborne pollution. Having laid claim to be the first industrial city in the world, during the first half of the twentieth century Manchester could arguably also have been the dirtiest. This blanket of soot formed a city that was dramatic, unified and uncanny; an urban landscape seemingly built from huge shadows.

## Dregs

Darkness is usually associated with night-time. But the sooty textures of industrial Manchester were capable of absorbing light during the day, and would have emphasised the sense of gloom in the twilight hours so that some elements of the city appeared almost to be in eternal shadow. This process spanned the late eighteenth century to the middle of the twentieth century, producing a specific type of sublime landscape that was wholly urban in character and distinct from its rural counterparts, the latter so enamoured of the Romantic poets. The application of the 1956 Act promptly removed the smog in the city and its architecture was generally returned to its former state, either as a result of cleaning or the soot being washed off by the rain. There are, however, a few examples of Manchester's shadowy 'architecture of darkness' that remain to the present day.

I use the term 'architecture of darkness' to refer to a two-fold aspect of the city's architectural landscape. In the first instance, two blackened buildings from the industrial era stand as testaments to Manchester's atmospherically darkened past in which the city's architecture would appear as three-dimensional shadows. These are the interior courtyards of the Town Hall by Alfred Waterhouse (1867–77) and 22 Lever Street by Smith, Woodhouse & Willoughby (1875). The gloomy status of the former is now in question as the building undergoes a major repair and refurbishment programme. The latter remains untouched to date and in public view. In the second instance, the gloomy environment offered a very particular context for Manchester's subsequent architecture. A striking example is the District Bank Headquarters on King Street by Casson & Condor (1969), which Casson likened to a 'lump of coal' since the building's cladding was deliberately specified to be dark to fit in with its soot-covered neighbours.

With 22 Lever Street, the once noisy warehouse now broods quietly amid a veritable smorgasbord of regeneration, with all the successes and failures that come with such investment and processes. This Grade II listed building is an architectural sponge, its shadowy appearance imbued with the dark matter of the industrial era in the crevices and surfaces of its facade, a silent witness to the enormous energy that transformed Manchester and reshaped countless cities around the world. The large two-storey sandstone arched entranceway on Lever Street itself is especially prominent in its filthiness. As a growing number of exposed brick walls appear in the city centre, along with the revival of names from Manchester's past, harking back to its industrial era, the physical shadows of the city's architecture of darkness are still currently visible at all hours – for now.

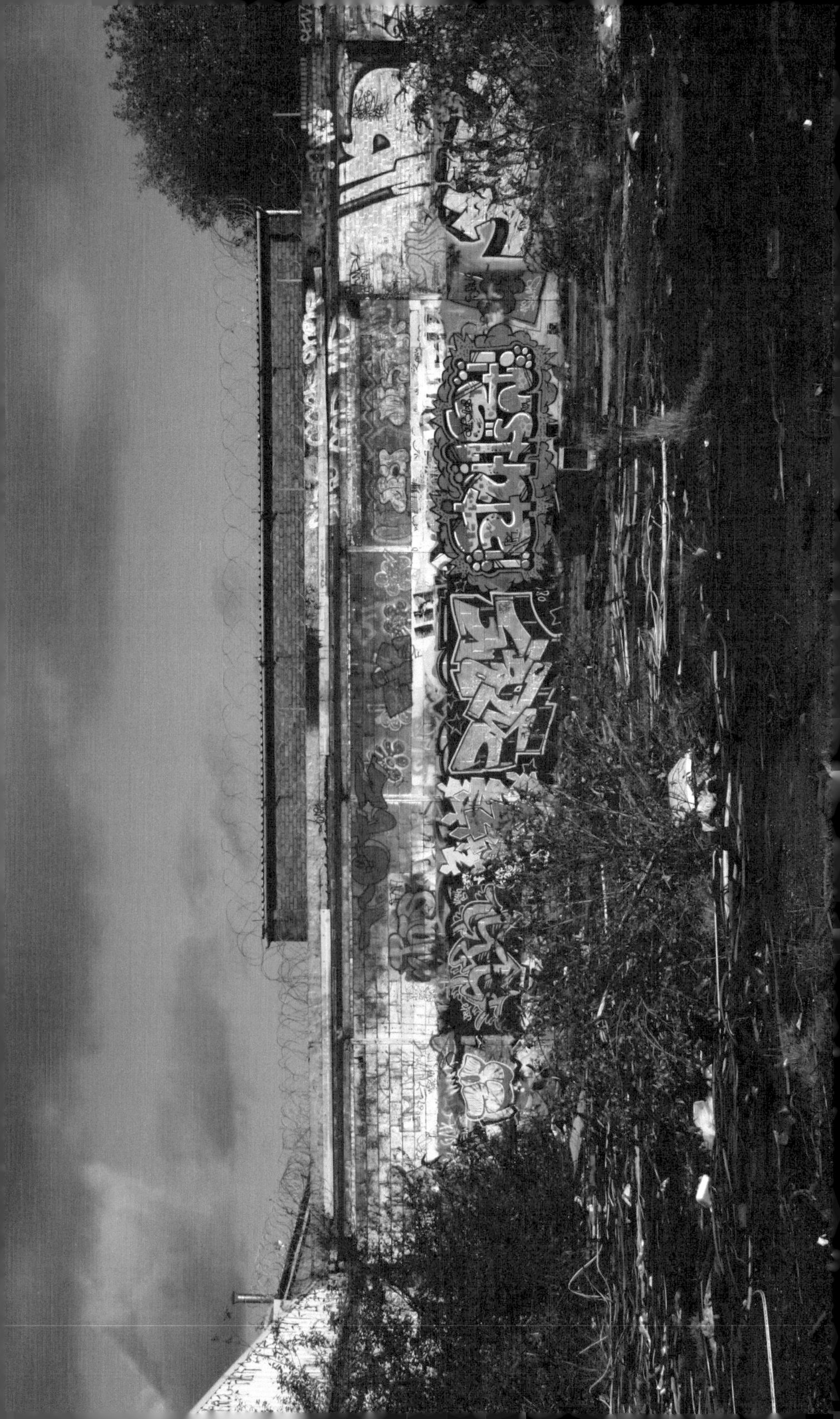

Manchester: Something rich and strange

## *Rhythm* – Joanne Hudson

Manchester is a city in perpetual change: a city of endless making and unmaking. It is influenced both by the ceaseless rhythms of global financial and property markets, and small-scale, everyday cadences that are often underappreciated and overlooked. At times, these rhythms complement; at others, they contradict. By looking at two sites close to Manchester city centre, the following insights highlight the rhythms of interwoven stories that shape the modern city. They also provide evidence that, despite attempts by urban elites to fix space and project particular images of the city, it is, in fact, a site of constant flux.

Following the much-lauded success of Salford Quays, guidance was sought to redevelop an extensive swathe of land on the banks of the former Manchester Ship Canal and River Irwell. Seen as an 'underused and unsightly fragment', redevelopment was intended to create a 'cohesive and distinctive' link between the Quays and Manchester city centre. Conceived during the property boom of the early to mid 2000s, this vision for 'Ordsall Riverside' – the name given to this reimagined site – was radically undermined as the 2008 economic crash unfolded.

As the subprime mortgage market collapsed and financial turmoil ensued, visions for a regenerated Ordsall Riverside ebbed away. The earlier planning guidance soon became at odds with what developers were prepared, or financially able, to deliver. The area, riven by volatile, conflicting time frames of contemporary capitalism, entered a period of widespread developmental stasis.

However, as landowners, developers and city bureaucrats were left waiting for change, other opportunists with more modest timescales appeared. These were concerned less with the future, and more with the 'present present'.

**54** (Previous page) Street art along the Manchester Ship Canal

## Dregs

Within the wider Ordsall Riverside master plan, a partially derelict site continued to be appropriated by graffiti writers. Over previous decades, they had turned it into an unofficial 'hall of fame', evidenced by an assemblage of everchanging artworks. For some writers, their relations were fleeting. Others, however, had formed longer-standing engagements with the site spanning many years. The site's surfaces became woven into writers' everyday rhythms and routines acting as a form of autobiography for specific individuals and crews, and the work as a whole constituted a collective site biography.

Today, even as the buoyancy of the property market has returned and the multiple cranes dotting the skyline evidence an upsurge in investment, this section of the wider developmental jigsaw remains incomplete. Hence, writers still paint the vast walls facing the once industrious Manchester Ship Canal. Huge artworks, visible from nearby train and tram lines, announce the site to commuters, emphasising the modest and everyday temporal routines that help shape the city – routines that exist both underneath and alongside those that influence the city in more prescriptive, less malleable ways.

Another site in Salford – Middlewood Locks – adjacent to the River Irwell and Trinity Way, tells a similar and equally pertinent story. From the mid 1990s to the late 2000s, this site was subject to a number of policy revisions as visions for the future of Salford changed. During this time, a range of future plans were envisaged for Middlewood Locks. One of these – SnoWorld, described by the *Manchester Evening News* in 2001 as a 'winter wonderland for skiers and shoppers', offered the public some persuasive imagery, as did the initial Middlewood Locks scheme which prompted boastful headlines such as 'The world has designs on Salford'. However, following the turbulent times of the late 2000s, as deep capital destabilisation caused accelerated financial and property markets to grind to a halt, effusive statements were replaced in 2010 by headlines like 'For Sale: The remains of a £600m dashed dream'.

**55** Homeless shelter within a railway viaduct at Middlewood Locks

Indeed, as large-scale market forces retreated, a number of opportunistic practices were shaping the site at a micro level. Exploiting the literal cavities of the city, individuals and groups were able to reclaim time as well as space. Numerous people occupied it for a range of purposes. One such purpose was that of shelter and homemaking by Manchester's ever-present homeless population. Their occupation, like that of the graffiti writers, was underpinned by uncertain temporal horizons. However, their itinerant practices matched this uncertainty.

Individuals and groups occupied two railway arches that bounded the site. These brick edifices were seen as problematic in planning and development terms, as they formed a physical barrier to the surrounding city, but for the homeless they provided much-needed privacy and shelter. Commonly, groups tended to occupy the larger arches to the north of the site, whereas individuals would fleetingly appropriate various smaller niches that fronted Trinity Way. In some cases, residency was clearly evidenced by the demarcation of territories. In others, however, it was more difficult to gauge the number of inhabitants, or indeed if they intended to return to claim their scattered belongings. One group who thought beyond the present, and who eventually remained in excess of six months, imbued the repurposed archways with a personal sense of time. They began to domesticate their environment, acquiring furniture and repurposing architectural features. Making use of the opportune times created by the accelerated global economy, these everyday interventions actively transformed the architecture of place, turning this underused cavernous space into a home and subtly changing the physical and social environment. Displacing the original and intended functions of space, residents became the architects of their own environment and produced a counter-narrative to meet their own needs.

These micro-habitations are however at odds with corporate developmental visions. As the buoyancy of the property market returned, and in recent years a cohesive scheme for Middlewood Locks became a reality, land was cleared, fenced off and policed. Accordingly, these opportunistic, personal, everyday rhythms have been replaced with a variety of other cadences.

These spatio-temporal stories of competing rhythms describe the contemporary city and highlight how it moves at different speeds, in different directions and on multiple levels. Despite attempts to fix space and provide particular narratives, there is always the potential for these to be undermined, challenged and rethought. Indeed, Manchester in its gloriously ambiguous state remains open to be made and remade as multiple time frames and rhythms continue to define the city – the one constant being that Manchester is constantly changing.

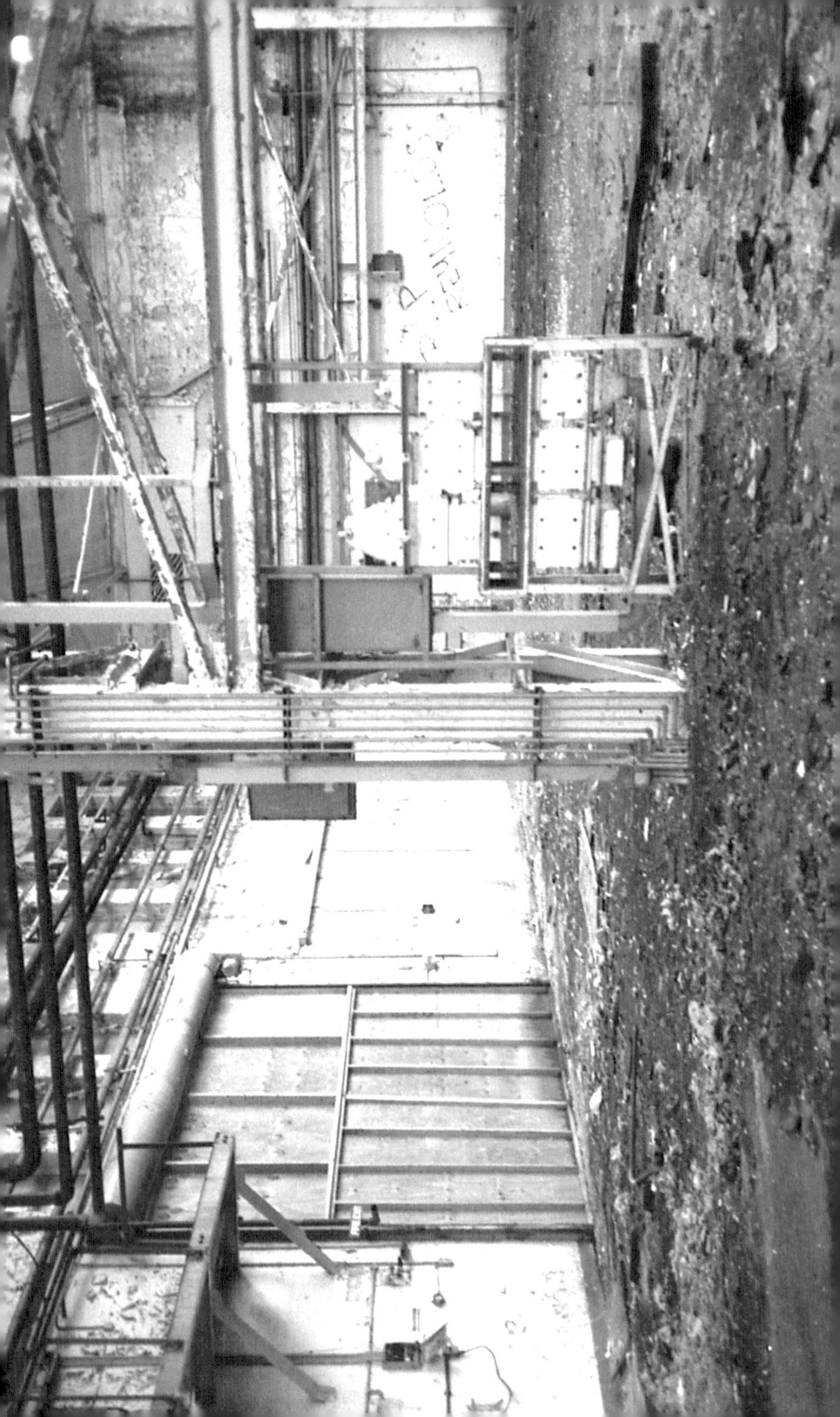

Dregs

## *Ruins* – Tim Edensor

Swiss entrepreneur Hans Renold, an inventor of some ingenuity, arrived in Manchester in 1873. He invented the bush roller chain, widely used in the textile and bicycle industries, and initiated a series of innovations in the production process that improved chain production and made manufacture more efficient. After opening chain-making factories in Salford and central Manchester, in 1906, Renold opened a large operation in Burnage to expand his growing business. After a brief hiatus during the First World War, when production focused on munitions, the factory increased the manufacture of chains to satisfy overseas demand. A patrician, socially conscious employer, Renold instituted a profit-sharing scheme for workers and subsidised a Wakes Week outing to Blackpool as well as funding a works Christmas party. He also presided over the Hans Renold Social Union that accommodated a range of leisure activities.

The factory closed down in the late 1980s due to the archetypal pursuit of 'modernisation', though the head offices of Renold remain in Manchester. The buildings were gradually stripped of most of the machines, though some remained to the end, and the site lay derelict until 2005. To the relief of local residents, who were concerned about the potential for wayward youths to get up to nefarious activities in the ruins, as well as the threat to the value of their properties, Tesco bought the large derelict site, demolished the buildings and subsequently opened up a huge store, despite owning a smaller supermarket less than half a mile away.

I visited the sprawling ruin in late 2004. Climbing over the pale green railings that surrounded the site, I made my way across mossy tarmac and then what was once a carefully manicured

**56** (Opposite) Interior of Hans Renold's chain-making factory in Burnage in 2004 before it was demolished to make way for a Tesco supermarket

lawn, now bordered by dead perennials. I entered the vast complex through a broken window. As with most industrial ruins, graffiti covered areas of wall and toilets; windows were smashed; and empty beer bottles and syringes littered parts of the floor. But the first impression that greeted me was the enormity of the shop floors, almost empty save for the crunchy debris that had fallen from above, pools of water that reflected the large glazed areas of the roof, and scrawny weeds that sought out cracks in the floor and reached towards the luminous skylights. Renold's son, Charles, succeeded Hans as chairman in 1928, and along with his father was an enthusiastic proponent of Taylorist scientific management, the time-and-motion process through which workers' labour was measured and timed to increase productivity. It was intriguing to imagine the more than 2,000 employees who toiled at this now empty site being put through their paces across these vast shop floors, their manoeuvres regulated and their bodies disciplined. Their absence in this large, empty place conjured them up in my imagination. Now only the creaks of the swinging light fixtures and the flurries of pigeons punctuated the thick silence. It was strange being in such a quiet realm in the heart of the city, with only the occasional muffled car engine audible from the world outside.

After wandering through several equally large interconnected shop floors, I entered an elongated, rectangular room with a remnant piece of industrial equipment, a long conveyor belt that rose and then descended into a vat full of oil, presumably to lubricate the chains. Having already visited numerous industrial ruins, I had encountered nothing that frightened or disturbed me. Other adventurers and security guards were usually pleased to see another person, and heroin addicts and homeless people were unperturbed as long as they were given a wide berth. Yet in Renold's factory I was truly horrified, if only briefly. I carefully advanced up the rising conveyor belt to the container and saw something that pierced my reverie, shocking me into immobility. There, submerged in the oily bath, was what seemed to be a dead body: a boy curled up and motionless. Spinning panic reigned, and was then followed by an urgent calm: a focus on what to do. Yes, that was it. I had to swiftly leave, run to the nearest phone box and call the police. But then I looked again. It was no human but an inflatable alien, emptied of some of its air, its green hue bleached out. Wide, black, almond eyes mockingly stared at me. I felt slightly foolish. But the most overwhelming emotion was a sense of relief.

Having recuperated from my fright, I left the conveyor belt and arrived at a series of machine shops, with some rusting steel relics nestling amid the rubble. As with many industrial ruins, the floor was strewn with all kinds of matter: fragments of broken ceramics, electrical wiring, shards of plaster, parts of tools, chain links, bolts, and indefinable substances spewed out by production processes. In this part of the factory were several elegiac reminders of those who had once routinely inhabited this place, revenants of those who had laboured and bantered with each other, and had customised their workplace to make it more homely. On one end wall of a large chamber was daubed the misspelt lament, R.I.P. REYNOLDS. In a small adjacent closet were several metal lockers installed to store workers' personal effects. A particularly potent display of vernacular surrealism featured a juxtaposition of canine and equine creatures and a sticker advertising the Isle of Man TT motorcycle races, with the owner's name, S. Wilson, inscribed on the steel surface. More bafflingly, somehow remaining affixed to an area of painted brick wall next to the skeletal remains of a telephone, was a label bearing the words 'THIS WALL IS NOW AVAILABLE IN PAPERBACK!' The scrawlings that once likely adorned this peeling surface had vanished.

And now the factory itself is long gone. Like the other abundant ruins that were scattered across old industrial Manchester, in Salford Docks, Oldham, Stockport, and large areas of the north of the city, these derelict factories, workshops, mills and foundries, large and small, have disappeared. In most cases they have been replaced by retail parks, housing and industrial units; in some cases by erasure, with empty land yet to be developed. No doubt ruins will be spawned by the next economic depression, but this time they will be different. No longer will large brick and stone-built buildings be expensively demolished; instead, most of the much lighter structures that have replaced them will be simply disassembled, leaving little trace of their existence.

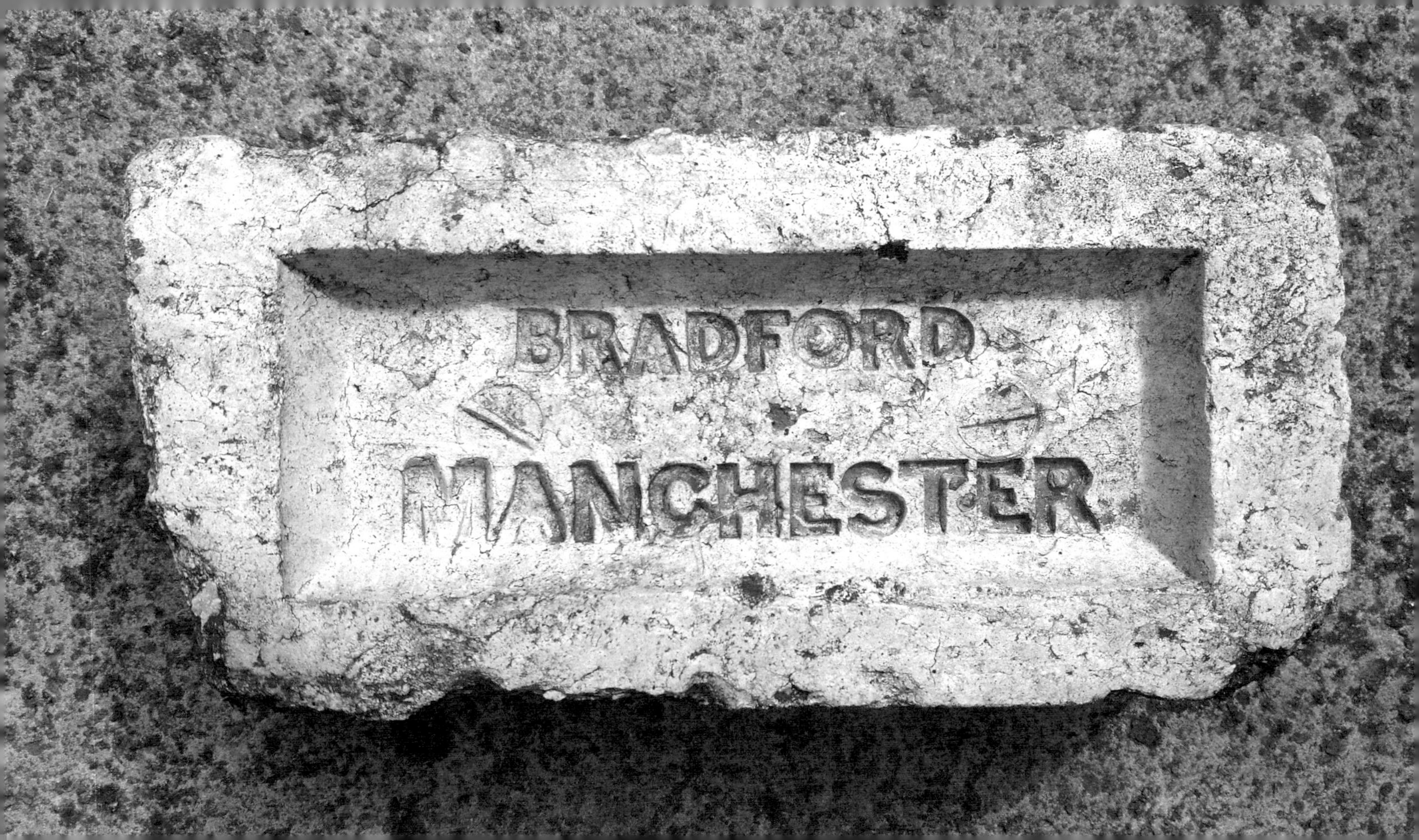
BRADFORD
MANCHESTER

## Redundant – Matthew Steele

On 11 May 2003, Manchester City played their final competitive football match at Maine Road, Moss Side. Having negotiated a long-term lease on the City of Manchester Stadium, the sports stadium built to host the 2002 Commonwealth Games, the following season would see the Blues relocate to Bradford, an area two miles east of the city centre, with Maine Road, once hailed as the Wembley of the North, becoming redundant. Not being overly familiar with Bradford, or 'Eastlands' as the council had attempted to rebrand it, I did wonder whether 'going to the match' would ever feel the same again (see 'Stadium', p. 151).[10] Navigating my way through Eastlands, or 'Wastelands' as waggish fans of that other Manchester team have dubbed it, has revealed Bradford to be an intriguing area – one that has undergone, and continues to undergo, significant change.

Once nothing more than 'meadow and pasture land and heath', Bradford came to prominence with the onset of the Industrial Revolution in the mid eighteenth century.[11] Whereas neighbouring Ancoats evolved to become the world's first industrial suburb, with workers' housing built in close proximity to the cotton mills of McConnel & Kennedy and the Murray Brothers, it was coal from Bradford Colliery, established in the early seventeenth century, which powered the machinery in those mills. The Ashton Canal, completed in 1797, and the Beswick and Ardwick branch railway lines which followed, ensured further industrialisation of the area: Beswick Goods Station, for example, meant that an ironworks established in the mid nineteenth century by Richard Johnson & Brother (later Richard Johnson & Nephew) had rail access to both east Lancashire and the south of England. Meanwhile, deep-shaft mining at Bradford Colliery led to the discovery of rich seams of

57 (Previous page) Fireclay brick from the Bradford Colliery

## Dregs

fireclay and the construction, in the 1870s, of the Bradford Colliery Brickworks on the north-east corner of the colliery site. Bricks made from fireclay could withstand constant heating and cooling without cracking and, therefore, were useful for lining furnaces.

As had happened in Ancoats, widespread industrialisation brought about the construction of workers' housing and other associated amenities, blurring the boundaries between Ancoats, Bradford and Beswick in the process. Public houses, such as the Bank of England on Pollard Street and the Mitchell Arms on Every Street, were among the earliest in the area (licensed around 1830 and 1840 respectively), while in 1860 Cronshaw's Alexandra Brewery was granted a licence to open a brewhouse on Palmerston Street. Church building abounded too. Examples included All Souls, Every Street (1840) by William Haley; Christ Church, Church Street (1862) by Hayley & Son; and St Mary, Hillkirk Street (1878) by Paley and Austin – the latter depicted by the artist L. S. Lowry in 1929. Other recreational needs were met by Ardwick Lads' Club, Palmerston Street (1898) by W. & G. Higginbottom.

Bradford continued to prosper into the twentieth century but, as with many inner-city and suburban areas of Manchester, post-1945 planning brought about radical change. Slum clearance programmes saw back-to-back housing in Bradford and Beswick demolished in the late 1960s, and the resident populations relocated to new developments such as Coverdale Crescent and the Wellington Street Estate (both completed in 1972 and derisively nicknamed Fort Ardwick and Fort Beswick by residents). For many of Bradford's churches, the loss of their congregations forced mergers and, in some cases, redundancy: both Christ Church and St Mary were merged with All Souls, and subsequently demolished.

Industry suffered too, with Bradford Colliery closing in 1968 owing, not to a lack of coal, but the threat of subsidence ongoing mining might cause to the wider area. Closure of the ironworks followed in 1986, leaving Bradford an industrial wasteland,

## Manchester: Something rich and strange

contaminated and criss-crossed with mine shafts and tunnels: not the most promising location to host the 2002 Commonwealth Games, one might think. Nonetheless, with deep-shaft mines capped with concrete and surrounding land decontaminated, Manchester City's future home began to rise in Bradford.

So what is the present-day experience of 'going to the match'? Despite the huge changes that have occurred in recent years – new apartment blocks and an extension of the Metrolink tram system – one can still observe vestiges of the area's past. Walking down Palmerston Street, one will encounter The River public house: derelict and deteriorating with each passing season, this was the brewhouse opened by Cronshaw's in 1860. Presently, it is difficult to imagine the bell for last orders ringing once more at The River, the Bank of England, or the Mitchell Arms, all of which are extant but closed. This is peculiar, given the increased footfall on match days. Further along Palmerston Street, standing outside where Ardwick Lads' Club once stood (it was demolished in 2013), one can still see the church of All Souls on Every Street – its square, soot-blackened brick pilasters topped with pyramidal stone caps rising above the treetops. Closed for worship since 1984, and poorly maintained ever since, only its Grade II listed status has staved off demolition.

But perhaps it's not too late for any of these buildings. Recent years have seen other redundant churches, such as St George in Hulme (1828) by Francis Goodwin, repurposed for residential use, while St Peter's, Ancoats (1860) by Isaac Holden is now home to the Hallé orchestra. Similarly, the social, as well as historical, significance of the city-centre Sir Ralph Abercrombie public house was belatedly recognised amid recent plans to demolish it and redevelop the site. As the population of Bradford increases with the construction of each new apartment block, hope remains that at least some of old Bradford will survive into the future.

## Dregs

## Notes

1 Anon., 'Chemical nuisances at Miles Platting: manufacturers summoned', *Manchester Guardian*, 1 July 1899, p. 6.
2 Ibid.
3 Anon., 'The Manchester sewer fatality: resumed inquest', *Manchester Guardian*, 13 January 1899, p. 10.
4 Anon., 'The death at a chemical works', *Manchester Guardian*, 11 November 1905, p. 6.
5 Anon., 'Clay cleared from site near school', *Guardian*, 20 May 1971, p. 6.
6 Lucinda Hawksley, *Bitten by Witch Fever: Wallpaper & Arsenic in the Nineteenth-Century Home* (London: Thames & Hudson, 2016).
7 Jerome O. Nriagu, 'Arsenic poisoning through the ages', in William T. Frankenberger, Jr, ed., *Environmental Chemistry of Arsenic* (New York: Marcel Dekker, 2002), pp. 1–26.
8 *Annual Register* (1828), pp. 79–80.
9 Matthew Copping, 'Death in the beer-glass: the Manchester arsenic-in-beer epidemic of 1900–1 and the long-term poisoning of beer', *Brewery History* 132 (2009), pp. 31–57.
10 *Going to the Match* (1928) is a painting by the artist L. S. Lowry depicting football supporters arriving at an unspecified stadium set in an industrial landscape.
11 William Farrer and John Brownbill, 'Townships: *Bradford*', in *A History of the County of Lancaster: Volume 4* (London: Victoria County History, 1911), pp. 274–5.

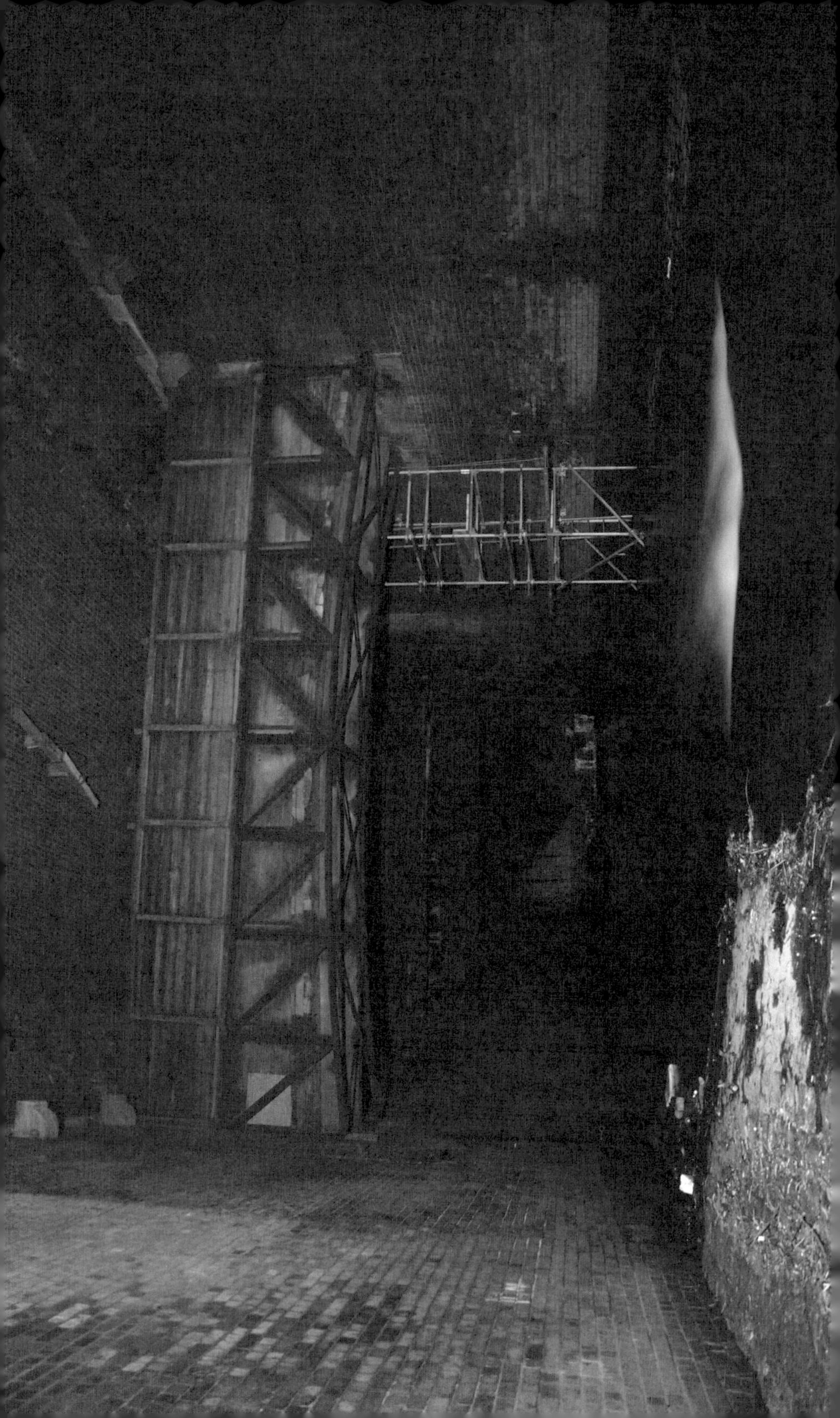

# Secrets

> The grey daylight shines on the map of this city which is still so unfamiliar, which conceals itself as the folds of a cloak conceal other folds, which shuns scrutiny as though the light scorched it, like a woman whose face one cannot see except by forcibly tearing away her veil: the map which is, so to speak, the city's ironic response to my efforts to see it whole and to take its census, forcing me at each fresh glance to admit other times are superimposed, with other points of interest, other references, other networks, other systems of distribution – in short, other maps which, though vague and fragmentary at first, are gradually growing fuller and more precise.
>
> Michel Butor, *Passing Time*, 1963; original in French, 1957

Maps of cities are supposed to tell us all we want to know about them – to plainly show us the things we desire and need and how to get to them. But, as Michel Butor's strange novel *Passing Time* demonstrates, a city like Manchester can never be known in its maps. There are just too many things that can't be shown on them – the city's secrets, both large and small; its lost or suppressed histories; the things it has forgotten, or would prefer not to remember.

Manchester's secrets are something different from either its dregs or underworlds – they're a mixture of invisible processes going on all the time – for example, the many different kinds

**58** (Opposite) Victorian railway footbridge preserved in the culverted section of the River Irk under Victoria Station

of 'Facade' explored by Steve Hanson; and specific things that happen in the city's spaces, like a convent hidden in inner-city Collyhurst, as described in Clare Archibald's 'Cloister'. They are lost stories from the past – of migrants and women throughout Manchester's history, as documented by Jenna Ashton in 'Thread'.

Secrets are also sometimes hidden in plain sight. We can easily guess the reason why Radium Street in Ancoats is so named, but as Becky Alexis-Martin argues, this name covers over a complex web of evolving research centred on Manchester's scientific and medical institutions. Places that hold secrets can also connect us – the everyday backyards of Manchester's terraces and the passages that connect them providing respite for generations of city dwellers from the brutal rhythms of industrial work, as Paul Dobraszczyk brings to light in 'Passage'. And, as Tim Edensor shows, the cobbles that line the ground of these passages can point us to the city's connection with its broader region and to the labour and skill of those who hewed and laid the stones. Here, glimpses of everyday secrets of the past serve to strengthen our sense of belonging.

So, when we look at a map of Manchester – whether the old-fashioned way on a sheet of paper or on our smartphone screens – it pays to think about what we're not being shown, the things that evade the all-seeing eyes of the Ordnance Survey or Google. There's always so much that we're not seeing, so many points of reference that escape us at any given time. That may make us feel uncomfortable, but it's also what keeps the city perpetually interesting – the knowledge that we can never really know it fully.

**59** Demolition of part of the Manchester School of Art building taken from Oxford Road, 2018

## *Facade* – Steve Hanson

Manchester is a city of facade. All Saints, where the Fifth Pan-African Congress was held in 1945, is at present nothing but a facade.

At the time of writing, the Manchester Metropolitan University All Saints campus is being reconfigured. On the walls the words 'leave' or 'go' have been spray-canned by builders to designate which walls are to be left standing and which are to be demolished.

At the same time, the incompetent government Brexit negotiations continue. To 'leave' and to 'go' here mean different things – that wall is to be left standing, this one must go – but the words, taken out of their context, mean the same: in Manchester, always attend to the facades, and to what they are telling you.

The Free Trade Hall, we are always told, is where the Sex Pistols ignited a whole generation of Manchester musicians. For years, people thought the famous 'Judas' Bob Dylan gig had been recorded at the Royal Albert Hall in London. Not so, it was recorded at the Free Trade Hall in Manchester. Yet the Free Trade Hall is now a Radisson Blu hotel. All that remains is the frontage, as a facade. The Radisson Blu hotel uses the consumable, middle-class friendly term 'Edwardian' to sell this facade, with some token, idealised art in the foyer referring to the Peterloo massacre. This place, where private individuals made themselves radically public, is now where public bodies make themselves expensively private.

Looking even further back, it is tempting to claim that history repeats itself, because a series of terraces designated slums were flattened to create the Crescents during the post-war consensus around housing and modern urbanism. These cleared terraces are often still referred to as 'back-to-backs', though this isn't quite correct. The Crescents themselves were again designated as places of deviance and criminality in their turn, and flattened. This does

## Secrets

have a long and sadly rich history, most obviously to be found in Engels' 1844 book, *The Condition of the Working Class in England*. The places the working classes are designated in Manchester only have a presence in the city as a series of 'facades', because Engels described how the middle-class dwellings served to cover over the basement spaces where whole families and sometimes livestock lived together. These were the people who actually produced the city's wealth and standing as a radical, industrialist place.

Yet, for most people, the facade is all that is seen, the decent shopfront which literally stood in front of, or even over, the slum dwellings.

The term 'facade' seemed to be acknowledged in the Haçienda nightclub and Factory Records with its post-Warhol obsession with facile surfaces. It was always winking at us, long before it passed into the condition of full facade itself.

The former yacht showroom that became the Haçienda was eventually demolished and flats built on the site. Peter Hook bought the name. Many people bought bricks from the demolished building for £5.

An anthropologist might not be surprised by the buying of bricks, for here are totems, belief trinkets. They are objects and signifiers that circulate to perpetuate a past spirit that is no longer here in concrete form, and never was here except in the myths that endlessly circle the city. History, as Hegel pointed out, passes into system. This process does not end with the Haçienda; it is a key quality of the city of Manchester. It is worth repeating: in Manchester, always attend to the facades, and to what they are telling you.

The stories themselves, then, are the biggest facades in the city. For instance, the blurred afterimage of Romanticism completely obliterates the figure of Thomas de Quincey, a biological racist, at the same time as the place where the Fifth Pan-African Congress was held becomes nothing but a thin, preserved frontage. These are just some of the contradictions that can be found.

## Manchester: Something rich and strange

The story of Manchester as a city of radicalism completely obliterates the underlying reality of a city that hosted the first fully neoliberal Labour council, well before New Labour existed, and continues to do so. Yet very different stories of radicalism serve as comforting bubbles for Manchester citizens to inhabit, to partially shield them from the cold, pull-yourself-up-by-your-bootstraps reality they actually live in.

E. P. Thompson explained how the cult of Joanna Southcott clung on in this region as the industry, rooted in Enlightenment science and mechanism, swept such ancient belief away.

When you strip everything except the aesthetic frontage away, the history can be conveniently reconstructed too. The facades mean that a mythical version of the city can be created, and we can all conveniently sidestep living in the reality of Manchester.

**60** Stained-glass windows of the Presentation Sisters convent in Collyhurst

## Manchester: Something rich and strange

## *Cloister* – Clare Archibald

Your approach to a city is often connected with your first memory of it, the way in usually controlled by road or rail lines. Markings on your mind delineated by stopping and starting again. The Manchester of my mind is built of stereotypical red bricks, bricks that do not move. Except as with all buildings made of any material, there is movement within and around. The red bricks of my first Manchester memory build up in hidden patterns of motion, of women who have been cloistered yet who still grooved paths in the outside. My city gateway is the red-brick Presentation Convent on Livesey Street in Collyhurst.

Walls of solid red are held together and softened, even by the sometimes harsh silk of many women's stories. The convent, one of a half dozen that still remain in Greater Manchester, came into being when an Irish silk merchant made recompense for using the labour of girls in his silk factory by providing £2,000 for the education of young females. Collyhurst, an area of high levels of Irish immigration and working poverty, was where the money was eventually used, when three nuns of the teaching order, the Presentation Sisters, were persuaded to travel to Manchester from Ireland in 1832 to assist in removing some of the barriers to education for working-class girls. The Sisters lived wholly within the confines of the convent building, engaging with the wider world only in clearly delineated lines of movement, brick wall to brick wall, door to garden. In the very early days of the convent the Sisters relied on food parcels brought by the parish priest, and were at times almost completely starved out by him. Their graves are still contained within the boundary walls that they did not go beyond after first entering.

If you were to walk down Oldham Road now, past the Chinese supermarket, the Post Office depot and the funny little is-it-a-mini-garden-centre-yard before turning left into Livesey Street, you

## Secrets

might wonder what microcosm lies beyond the walls. You might imagine the lives wrought in iron, brick and stained glass. You might even wonder if it is indeed a convent.

The walls there are many. High ones surround the gardens; internal ones connect the seen and unseen compartments of the contained lives; invisible ones were erected by watchers, separating the women who do not move through spaces in the same way because of different cultural or religious beliefs – and levels of confidence, accessibility or opportunity – from the ones who do. Imagining what is behind the wall of other. Whatever you or I think about the beliefs of the Sisters, the movement and textures contained within that space in Livesey Street have been felt as a part of the city, of the community that it has emotionally or spiritually tunnelled out in time towards.

I first visited my auntie there as a toddler, with no idea until recently that she chose to be part of an order that, until the mid 1970s, did not allow her to move outside the convent walls, other than through the cover of an internal corridor to the school where she taught next door. I have seen the blandly glossed door that connects the unseen, and find it hard to reconcile this with the feistiness of the mainly octogenarian nuns of now who reject ideas of patriarchy in their own internal thinking, despite my failure to understand how this can be.

For years, red brick was my idea of Manchester. Brick with no connection to other parts of city knowledge, standing in isolation, speaking loudly in its echoes of imagined life. Buildings are libraries that we borrow mental blocks of history from; we all have our own preferred or given editions of them. Sometimes we conjure the worst, or have false faith in what happens within; perhaps all buildings carry elements of both mindsets. My idea of Manchester will always be a strange layering of the private and the public mixed with my own family history.

The main convent building has a later addition that houses the private chapel and the wood-panelled dining room where different permutations of the same Sisters have met all or most of their adult lives. In it stands an almost wall-length set of aluminium lockers, all now vacant bar those of the six remaining nuns – metal relics of the time when the only external communications were letters from family, and this was a thriving hub of female spirits. Held within those empty lockers are the lives of both the changing city and the nature of religious faith, as well as the unwritten movements of the nuns who have died. Whatever their seen and unseen connections to the wider city, they are an embedded community within a community, a palimpsest of layers of belief and reality cemented in red brick.

Adjacent to the convent is a Catholic primary school, still linked by the corridor which no longer flows with nuns passing through invisibly on their way to work. In the very early days there was also an orphanage, later removed as part of a compulsory purchase order by a city council that needed to extend the iron train lines to bring food to a growing industrial metropolis. The railway arches now lie abandoned, the ground in between growing an as yet unnamed new history as Collyhurst reimagines itself. The plaque commemorating children who died in the orphanage is dated 1836, and reassures a public mind that has grown to expect hidden tragedy within the walls of institutions.

We can borrow from buildings, but never fully know the lives underwritten by them. Manchester for me will always be red brick and wondering what will happen to the space when the last nun is gone and all that has been cloistered within is no longer. Will the bricks of outside still glow red with imagined lives?

**61** Embroidery sampler made by Alice Pitfield in the Alice Pitfield archive at the Royal Northern College of Music

Manchester: Something rich and strange

## *Thread* – Jenna C. Ashton

The needle is used to repair the damage.
It's a claim to forgiveness. It is never aggressive, it's not a pin.

Louise Bourgeois[1]

I am in the Alice Pitfield archive at the Royal Northern College of Music (see also 'Hair', p. 156). The archivist brings out two wrapped artefacts, one soft, the other with a hard edge. Two textile pieces produced by Alice – a smaller embroidery sampler in a thin wooden frame and a larger linen piece, the latter likely created to be hung on a wall, the former a hobbyist creation. Both so different, and no information attached to either. These are like orphaned objects, and I must speculate to make sense of their presence and relevance here in the archive.

Cottonopolis makes itself known once again: Alice's family owned cotton mills in Russia; Alice's husband, Thomas, grew up in the shadow of the cotton-spinning mills of Bolton; Thomas's own mother was a dressmaker. Cotton – thread – is an ever-present material for Alice and Thomas.

The needle requires its 'eternal thread'. Connecting us back and forth across time and place, it holds us together. Stitches, darns, closes the wound, seals our fate; tighter, tighter, don't let it unravel. Repair the damage. Industry, revolution, movement, displacement; we find hints in Alice's writings, but perhaps best visualised in these two pieces. Her thread replaces words. The two textile pieces encapsulate the complexities of a Manchester that it is both domestic and public, international and local, traditional and modern.

The linen of the embroidery sampler is stained with ageing, despite being pressed and held behind a glass frame. The threads are still gaudy and punchy: royal blue, lilac, buttercup yellow, burnt orange, a lime green and pastel shades of pink and cream.

## Secrets

Alice revels in her access to the variety of newly created chemical colour combinations. Writhing on the natural-coloured linen, the threads burst through the surface to produce floral patterns in the style of traditional folk cross-stitch and free-form curvilinear motifs. Flowers and fruits, once popular imagery for traditional costume on the outskirts of Moscow (Alice and her family lived in Balashikha before the 1917 Revolution), gently cluster together in the centre of the linen. The work seems too fresh and the frame too modern to be a Russian-based creation. Is this Alice's moment of nostalgia, her Russian childhood? A tenderness and fragility pressed behind glass, a memory in thread.

The second piece, in stark contrast, is her modern triumph. A large abstract work, the flower motifs have lost their delicacy and fastidiousness; in their place are chunky triangular applique tulips and geometrical shapes. More akin to Russian Constructivism or Bauhaus design than traditional embroidery, it is an abstract painting in linen. Royal blue, yellow, black and natural beige are the only colours used. It is bold and confident.

It is tempting to offer an interpretation here of female empowerment and emancipation, the second work resonating with a shift from traditional domestic expectations of daughter-wife-mother (as represented by the first embroidery) to one of modern internationalism and freedom of self and expression. Of course, I have no evidence at all of the dates of creation, nor motivation behind the works, and I am only presuming Alice is the creator as they reside in her archive. But we must be wary of the tricks played on us by the archive. We can be seduced by artefacts and read into them what we will (I frequently am and probably do so too often).

Symbolically, these two pieces perhaps signify something of greater importance – the lack of evidence around refugee, exile and émigré communities and individuals in Manchester. Alice's story – her voice as a British-Russian, is frustratingly absent. Hers is a lived experience of movement and adaptation between two international contexts connected by the insatiable global need for cotton to be spun into usable threads. Her situation evidences a moment of historical flux, of a world on the edge of a war, a changing class and economic infrastructure, in which her own family were a small cog in a much larger and exploitative machine. Her family escaped the bloody Revolution; many others didn't. I wonder for a moment how the workers in her father's factory suffered.

Manchester is its refugees, exiles, immigrants and émigrés; up to 200 languages are spoken in the city. Where are these people, these lived experiences in the archives?

In 2018–19, I curated the Travelling Heritage Bureau, a co-research project and supportive network with and for international women artists based in North West England. The project worked with around twenty-five women artists and included refugees, those seeking asylum, and first- and second-generation immigrants. Through arts and curatorial practice, the Bureau explored methods for identifying, documenting, performing and sharing the cultural heritage and lived experiences of international women artists. Textile and thread can offer a form of evidencing, in place of other missing documentation around trauma and journeying.

Alice's textile pieces materialise the magic of needle and thread to simultaneously repair and create anew. This creativity as a form of archive reveals the gaps. Stitching all the orphaned textile pieces from across Manchester's archives would create a new kind of document, harking back to the etymology of the word 'textile' – meaning to weave, or woven – which is the origin of 'text'. Textiles are woven texts. In place of missing words, thread can weave together different histories of people and places.

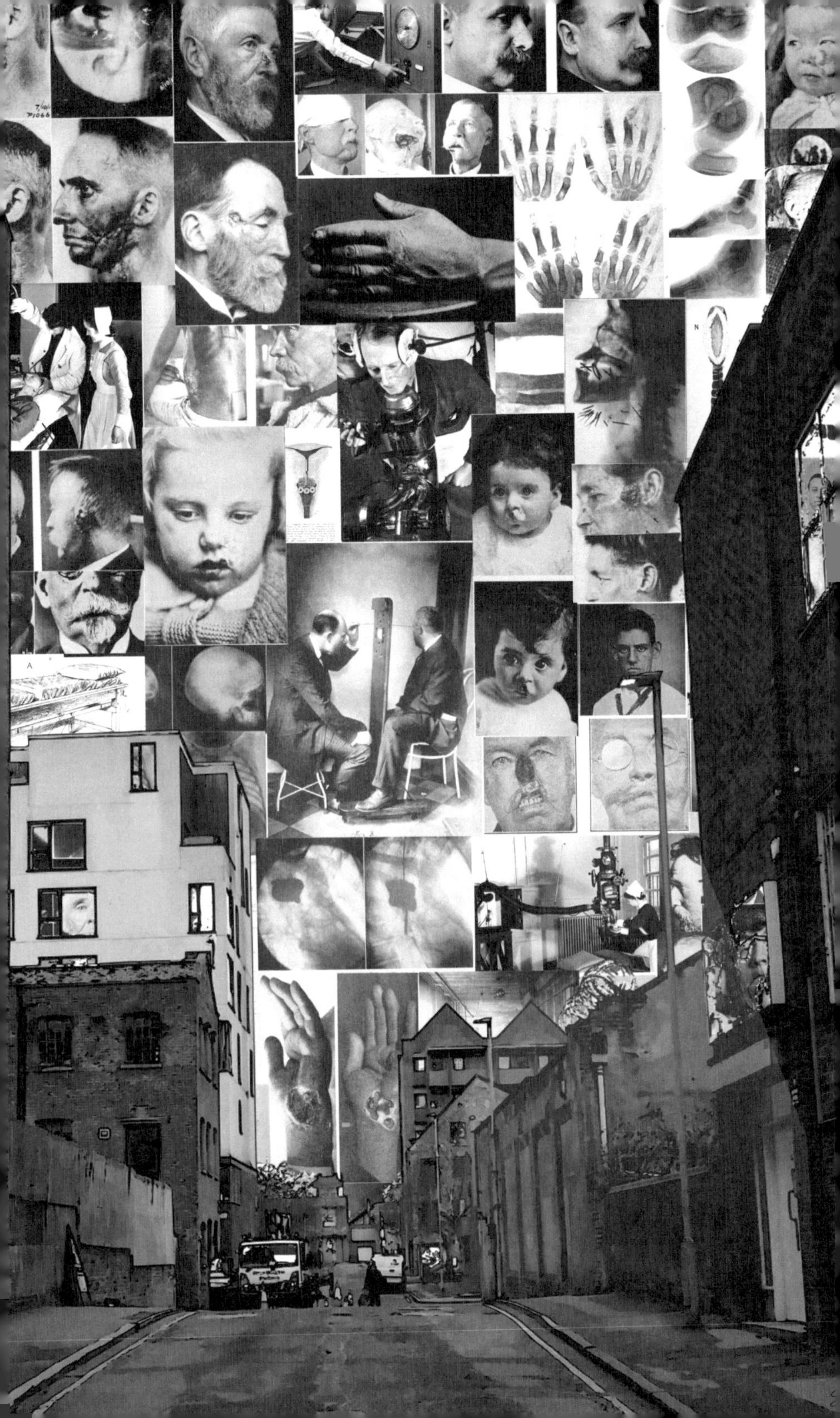

# Manchester: Something rich and strange

## *Radium* – Becky Alexis-Martin

Nestled between carefully conserved cotton mills and glimmering new developments in Ancoats is a little road named Radium Street. It is unusual for any place to be named after a radioactive element, beyond the confines of military 'closed cities' where nuclear weapons are manufactured. Radium Street was originally called German Street, after a German toy importer's warehouse that was located in the area. The street was renamed after the First World War to conceal its Teutonic heritage, and to commemorate Manchester's achievements in nuclear medicine.

In the nineteenth century, cancer was a stigmatised and poorly understood condition. It was considered untreatable, contagious, and was usually associated with sexually transmitted diseases. However, increased pollution from Manchester's factories and cotton mills meant that carcinogens, and therefore occupational cancers, such as mule-spinners' cancer of the scrotum, had become more abundant. Unfortunately, the only Victorian treatment for cancer was surgical, and this was often unsuccessful. 'Cancer asylums' were established to provide palliative and psychiatric care for terminal patients. They had exceptionally high mortality rates, but nonetheless provided a place to trial treatments.

In Manchester, the Cancer Pavilion and Home for Incurables was founded in 1892 by a legacy from Sir Joseph Whitworth. A first site was established for eleven inpatients at Stanley House, Oxford Road. As attitudes towards cancer changed, the word 'Incurables' was dropped from its title. By 1901, the Cancer Pavilion had a thirty-bed capacity and had been renamed again: the Christie Hospital. At the Christie, a form of electromagnetic radiation known as Roentgen waves had come into use as an

**62** (Previous page) The bodily effects of radium superimposed over a view of Radium Street in Ancoats

## Secrets

'X-ray treatment' for cancerous growths. Professor Robert Briggs Wild, a pioneer of X-ray treatment in Manchester, became interested in the benefits of a newly discovered element called radium-226. This element had been identified by the Curies in 1898, and then isolated for use by 1902. Three years later, in 1905, Professor Wild trialled radium treatments for cancer at the Christie. His experiments were a surprising success.

The discovery of radium's specific medicinal benefits also inspired manufacturers to include this toxic and expensive element in everything from cold remedies to face cream and soap. These products offered no special benefits to their users, but invoked a glowing aura of luxury and health. Beyond the craze for quack radium cosmetics, nuclear medicine was becoming a burgeoning specialty. In 1914, a £25,000 fundraising appeal had been launched to create the first Manchester and District Radium Institute (MDRI). 'Radium Days' and donations from workplaces and social clubs provided some funding, and Sir Edward Holt of Holt Breweries created a Manchester and District Radium Fund. Professor Ernest Rutherford, who had split the atom at the University of Manchester, was a member of the Technical and Scientific subcommittee of this fund. By August 1914, £31,000 had been raised for the new 'Holt Institute'. Therapeutic radium was purchased, and a small department was established in the basement of Manchester Royal Infirmary, directed by Dr James Ralston Kennedy Paterson.[2] This was the first centralised, standardised medical service accessible to all local hospitals.

MDRI swiftly became renowned for radium treatment, maintaining the second-largest supply of radium in the UK by 1920. This was accompanied by a move to its own facilities at Lister House on Nelson Street, and advertising of clinical assistantships for 'candidates desirous in obtaining experience in radium and x-ray therapy'.[3] Radium was still expensive until the UK government set up a National Radium Commission in 1930 to supply it to national centres, including a new Northern Radium Centre at the

## Manchester: Something rich and strange

Radium Institute. In 1932, all facilities were merged and placed on one site, as the Christie Hospital and Holt Radium Institute in Withington.

Pooling of facilities and increased patient numbers meant that Dr Paterson and physicist H. M. Parker had the resources to develop a new biophysical method for the clinical application of radium to cancerous tissue, that became known as the 'Manchester Method' and provided accurate guidelines for dosages in milligrams and duration of treatment in hours. It became an internationally accepted standard, and Manchester's Holt Brewery created a 'Paterson Ale' to celebrate Dr Paterson's achievements and honour the Holt–Paterson legacy of nuclear medicine in Manchester. Although other centres temporarily closed, radium treatments continued in Manchester throughout the Second World War as staff were able to securely store radium in the depths of the Blue John Cavern in Castleton during Luftwaffe air raids on the city.

Innovations in machine-generated X-rays meant that radium-226 therapy became redundant by the 1950s. And in 1962, the Holt Radium Institute was renamed the Paterson Institute for Cancer Research. However, it continued to develop new cancer treatments – from breast cancer drug Tamoxifen, to photodynamic therapy for skin cancer. As part of the Christie Hospital, it has subsequently grown into the largest centre for cancer treatment in Europe. The story of Manchester radium is still not over. A different isotope, radium-223, was EU-approved for the treatment of prostate cancer bone metastases in 2013. Unlike radium-226, this isotope has a half-life that expires in a matter of days rather than centuries. The legacy of radium therapy and Manchester's Radium Street have both been revived.

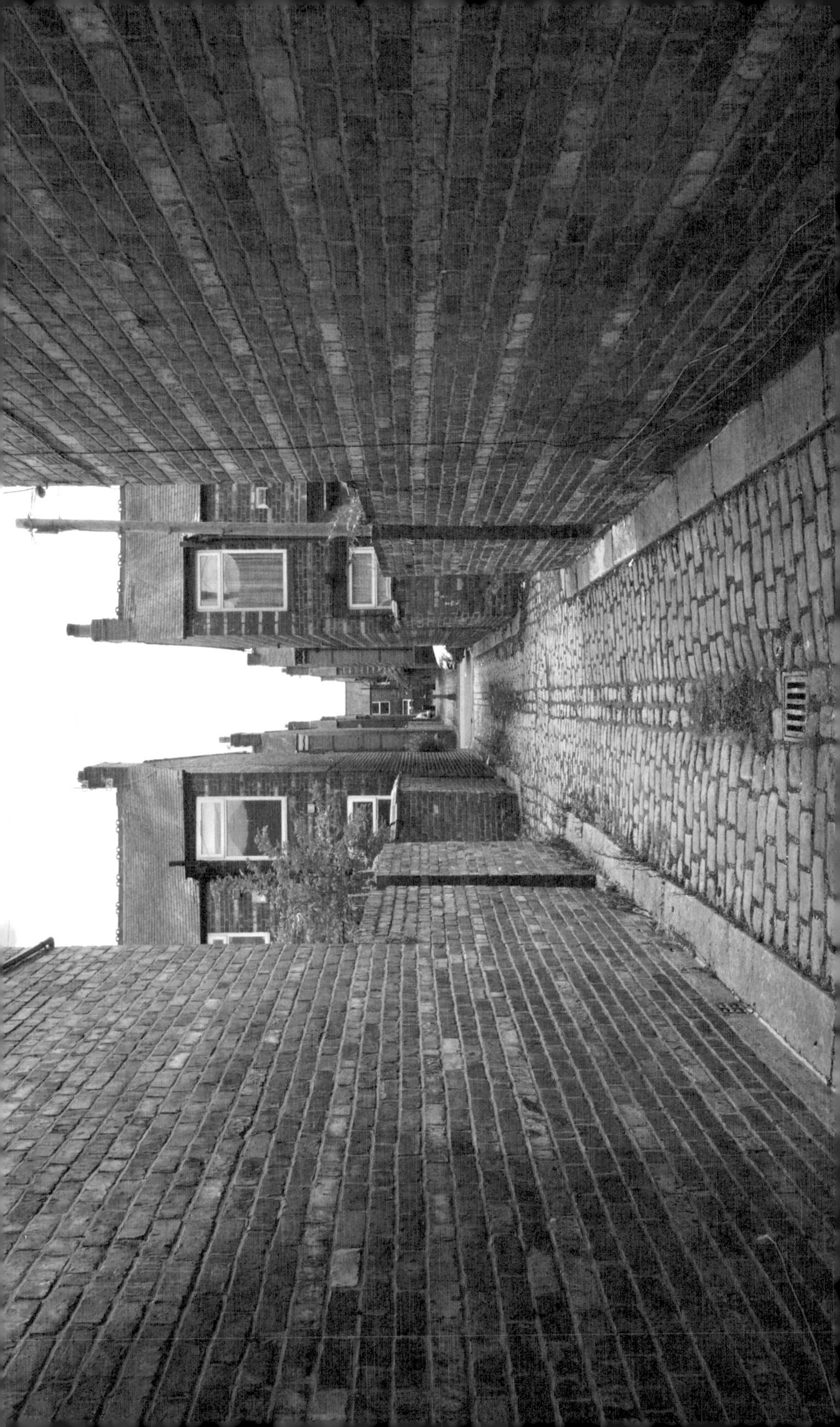

Manchester: Something rich and strange

## *Passage* – Paul Dobraszczyk

They go by a variety of names: in common English parlance they are alleyways, passages, lanes or paths; in regional variations, they are, to name but a few, jitties (West Midlands), jiggers (Liverpool), pends (Dundee), ten-foots (Hull), and closes (Edinburgh). In Manchester, they are most often called ginnels or genells or, more rarely, snickets. All of these words describe either a narrow passage between houses or a longer and wider walkway situated at the backs of terraces and between two streets.

In the early decades of the nineteenth century, when back-to-back terraces were the norm in industrial towns, these passages were known as courts: narrow paved yards between terraces and other houses that were cut off from street traffic and often accessible only via dark covered entrances. Widely condemned as unsanitary breeding grounds of disease, back-to-backs and their courts were mostly replaced in the second half of the nineteenth century by the more ordered rows of terraces that still characterise most British towns and cities today, and particularly industrial ones like Manchester. These cobbled passages and alleyways were laid out to provide easy access to the backs of terraces for the delivery of basic goods such as coal, and the easy removal of rainwater and household wastes. They predominated in working-class areas of industrial cities where building speculators maximised the available space for housing, while also abiding by the sanitary regulations laid down by the municipal authorities.

In the 1960s, it seemed, for a time, that the Manchester alleyway would become a thing of the past. In this decade, Victorian terraces were generally viewed by those in power as outdated and troublesome remnants of the nineteenth-century city that impeded the application of modernist principles of urban planning. In

**63** (Previous page) Cobbled passageway in Moss Side

## Secrets

each year, from 1963 to 1967, 4,000 Victorian terraced houses in Manchester were demolished by the council, with little attempt – at least in this period – to replace them. As testified by architectural critic Ian Nairn's BBC programme, *Nairn Across Britain*, by the early 1970s whole swathes of the terraced city were transformed into vast fields of rubble, their connecting alleyways remaining only as spectral outlines on the ground. The eventual rebuilding of these areas would see the disappearance of alleyways – the backs of the new houses opened up to adjoining car-parking spaces and public lawns.

In the early to mid 1960s, when the decrepit Victorian terraces of Hulme were scheduled for demolition (to eventually make way for the brutalist high-rise concrete housing of the Hulme Crescents), the council's official photographer obsessively documented the back alleys of this area. In these images, the narrow cobbled lanes are found to be places of unhealthy congestion – dark, waterlogged and, in the case of one set of images picturing a fallen wall that killed an unfortunate resident, a literal danger to life. As with much official photographic documentation of slum housing in this period, the case for demolition is made by casting a negative light on the existing built environment. In these photographs of Hulme, alleyways recur because they are viewed as both redundant, unhealthy and ungovernable – spaces that are clearly unfit for habitation (and there are never any people in these images).

And yet, at exactly the same time as these official images of Hulme were being gathered, the amateur photographer Shirley Baker was capturing another aspect of the alleyway, namely as a place of human connection. In some of her poignant images of the backyards and alleyways of Hulme, children and adults gather in shared moments of freedom. The alleyways of Hulme in Baker's images are as rubbish-strewn, waterlogged and structurally unsound as they are in the official photographs; yet their human occupants speak of them as places of value, where demolition will not only result in the erasure of spaces but also of valued memories.[4] Despite the loss of Hulme's and other areas' alleyways in Manchester, some still survive today, mostly in small pockets of densely built Victorian terraces in areas like Moss Side and Whalley Range, where their names – 'Passage No. 1', 'Passage No. 2', and so on – ring out like a common refrain that links together otherwise scattered districts of the city.

They may be taken for granted, grounded as they are in everyday life; but alleyways have always been ambivalent spaces. They are neither public nor private; rather a mix of the two – liminal places that are both valued and feared. As Baker's photographs show so clearly, householders connected with each other in alleyways, whether in chance meetings or in shared activities like putting the rubbish out. But the wider public are often seen as a threat, taking advantage of the public yet hidden nature of alleyways to engage in all manner of nefarious activities: drug dealing, sexual assault, burglary (the most common stories you'll find if you search for 'Manchester alleyways' online).

This ambivalence has resulted in two opposing approaches to alleyways in the contemporary city. On the one hand, the widespread gating of back passages in areas like Oldham has effectively severed the alleyway's link to the outside world, turning the public into the private; on the other, the 'greening' of alleyways, such as a few in Moss Side in the late 1990s, has reclaimed them as valuable communal spaces, where potted plants jostle with wheelie bins and discarded objects for ascendancy. Even when tidied up, it seems, the disorderly nature of the alleyway can't be fully tamed. The fundamental ambivalence towards these spaces derives from the fact that they are spatially unstable and dependent on the existence of other places and boundaries to define them. In this sense, alleyways are not only physical boundaries in the city but also metaphorical ones too – boundaries between the present and past, where a host of secret stories, both good and bad, linger on in these cracks in the city.

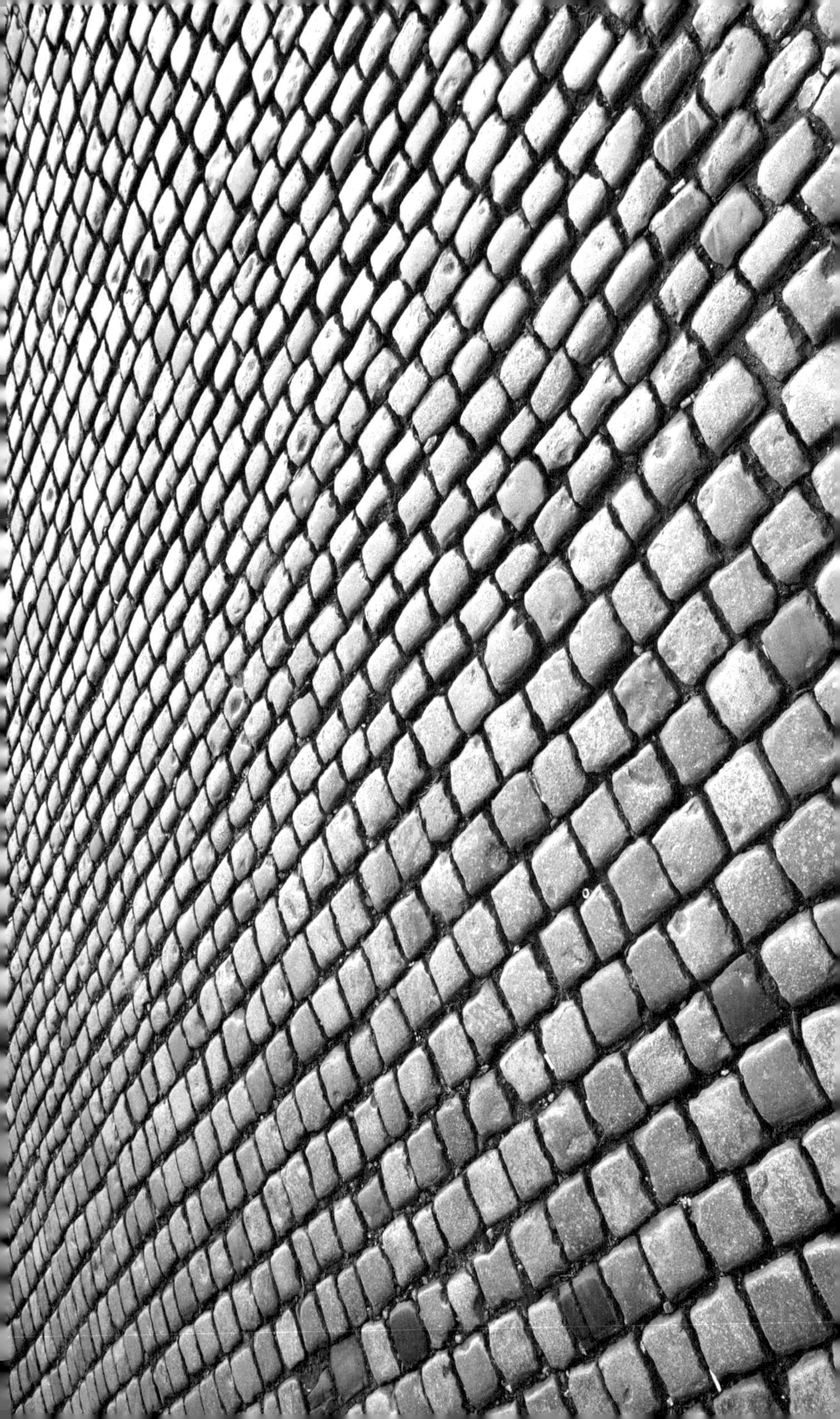

## Manchester: Something rich and strange

### *Cobble* – Tim Edensor

Outside my house in Didsbury, lying in a small gap between the asphalt road and the stone kerb, stretch a line of cobbles, or setts – three parallel rows that extend along the length of the street. Cobbles like these persist in the gutters of numerous streets across Manchester and, in those places where they burst through the surfaces of neglected roads, reveal their enduring presence under the covering asphalt.

Though the Romans first deployed these road technologies, in the UK cobbled streets are medieval in origin, formed from smooth, round stones typically obtained from river beds to fabricate more durable roads. In Victorian times, these were superseded by the rectangular, harder setts that were laid down across the streets of Britain's growing industrial towns and cities, shaped so they could be fitted together with greater exactitude. These setts afforded a more comfortable journey for passengers and horse riders, besides adding extra traction for horses' hooves. Typically around 300 mm in length and 50 mm thick, setts constitute a tightly bonded, compact assembly, bedded into a flexible base of gravel or lime mortar, and with joints filled with fine sand or mortar. These dense, solid road surfaces have proved extremely durable and continue to retain their functional qualities. Though they may have been worn down by heavy traffic over the years, conservationists recommend that rather than relaying old groups of setts, it is preferable for them to remain in place because they have been worn down together to form an evenly smoothed, if depleted surface – a pleasing patina that signifies their age.

Manchester's cobbles or setts derive from multiple locations.[5] They exemplify how the city is continuously assembled out of materials from elsewhere, and testify to numerous historical

**64** (Previous page) Cobbles, Jutland Street, near Piccadilly

connections with sites of supply. Unlike cities with extensive, high-quality supplies found within the city boundaries, most of the setts that line Manchester's streets are made of Pennine gritstones and coarse-grained sandstones. These stones possess a high proportion of quartz, making them resistant to weathering and less susceptible to the impact of the iron-shod hooves and iron wheel rims that once plied these roads. Popular stones used for setts include Upper and Lower Kinderscout Grits, Huddersfield White Rock, Holcombe Brook Grit, the white-grey Ousel Nest Grit from the western part of the Lancashire Coalfield, and Helpet Edge Rock from around Rochdale and Oldham. From further afield, stone setts from Upper Haslingden near Rossendale and hard Shap granite were brought to the city.

In Manchester, most eighteenth- and nineteenth-century streets are laid according to a *coursed* pattern in which rectangular setts were positioned at right angles to the direction of traffic, but as with those in my street, embedded setts were situated longitudinally. Elsewhere, in a few civic spaces, as in Albert Square in the city centre, cobbles were organised into more elaborate, decorative *European fan* arrangements. Rather differently, in the centre of nearby Rochdale's town centre, the removal of the tarmac that covered the narrow King Street has revealed that the road remains entirely lined with wooden cobbles that were laid in the early nineteenth century so that the racket of horses and carts would not unduly disturb the patients of the hospital that was once situated there.

As Chris Otter contends, 'a street is a site where nature, society and matter meet and mingle, a permeable membrane on, through and under which bodies, pipes, dust and liquids ambulate, circulate, dribble, sink and collect'.[6] For road surfaces to endure, to ensure that what lies beneath does not messily erupt to the surface and that water drains away into the ground below, technical know-how is essential. Particular layers of matter need to be laid horizontally to create a stable and solid surface, and building material that will not quickly corrode under wet or freezing conditions is required. But even this is not enough, for systematic maintenance procedures to repair holes, remove vegetation that colonise cracks and sweep away superfluous matter, is also essential to the longevity of a road's surface.

The many remaining cobbled streets of Greater Manchester can be conceived as embodying one aspect of the vast expenditure of labour that has gone into producing the complex material composition of the city region. It is thus important to honour the energy expended and the skills deployed by the set dressers who repeatedly forged cobbles by splitting them into comparable shapes, not to mention the hauliers, cart drivers, bargemen and railway workers who transported them, and the road builders who laid them down.

All cities are palimpsests, composed out of heterogeneous material elements from many historical periods that are assembled together. Coming across cobbles that continue to serve as the surface for the city's streets or remain visible where tarmac has been worn away can suddenly, unexpectedly, conjure up a sharp impression of the past and deepen a feeling of belonging to place. At once we may sense the affordances of the streets of one or two hundred years ago, feeling the pleasing grip of the road and unevenness that massages the soles of the feet. And we may abruptly realise that, not so very long ago, these streets served as routeways for the passage of horse-drawn carts, in which the rich aroma of plentiful horse manure pervaded everyday experience. The rhythmic clattering of the unyielding iron of cartwheels and horses' hooves coming into contact with stone has been replaced by the softer sounds of rubber on asphalt. These stony remnants of an otherwise vanished world in which horses were ubiquitous also invokes the prevalence of stables in most parts of the city to house them. In Didsbury, some stables lingered on until the extinction of the horse-drawn bus that plied a route from the city centre until 1913, put out of business by the advent of electric trams. Some of

## Secrets

these stables have been converted into houses, while others have disappeared.

Cobbled streets have, of course, become part of the iconographic signature of northern England, a cliche that continues to resonate in black-and-white photographs of terraced streets and in realist cinematic representations of the soot-blackened alleyways that the protagonists of kitchen-sink dramas traverse. Most archetypal, the plaintive brass theme tune to *Coronation Street*, Britain's longest-running soap opera, has long been accompanied by images of slate roofs, brick facades, ceramic chimney pots and the cobbled street in which the action unfolds. Representations of these setts are integral to the power of a northern English aesthetic in which deep-grey streets absorb a weak sunlight or are varnished with rainwater and reflect the dark, drizzly grey skies above.

### Notes

1 Louise Bourgeois, cited in Robert Storr, *Intimate Geometries: The Art and Life of Louise Bourgeois* (London: Moncaelli Press, 2016), p. 526.
2 Brian W. Fox, *Christie Hospital and Holt Radium Institute: A Brief History of a World Famous Cancer Hospital* (Manchester: Christie Hospital NHS Trust, 1996).
3 The reports of the Radium Institute, from which much of this article draws, are held in the Manchester Medical Collection: Sections 3–16. University of Manchester Library. GB 133 MMC/9/23/3.
4 See Shirley Baker, *Without a Trace: Manchester and Salford in the 1960s* (London: The History Press, 2018).
5 See C. Johnson and M. Fletcher, *Strategic Stone Study: A Building Stone Atlas of Greater Manchester* (Swindon: English Heritage, 2011).
6 Chris Otter, 'Streets', in Stephan Harrison, Steve Pile and Nigel Thrift, eds, *Patterned Ground: Entanglements of Nature and Culture* (London: Reaktion, 2004), p. 212.

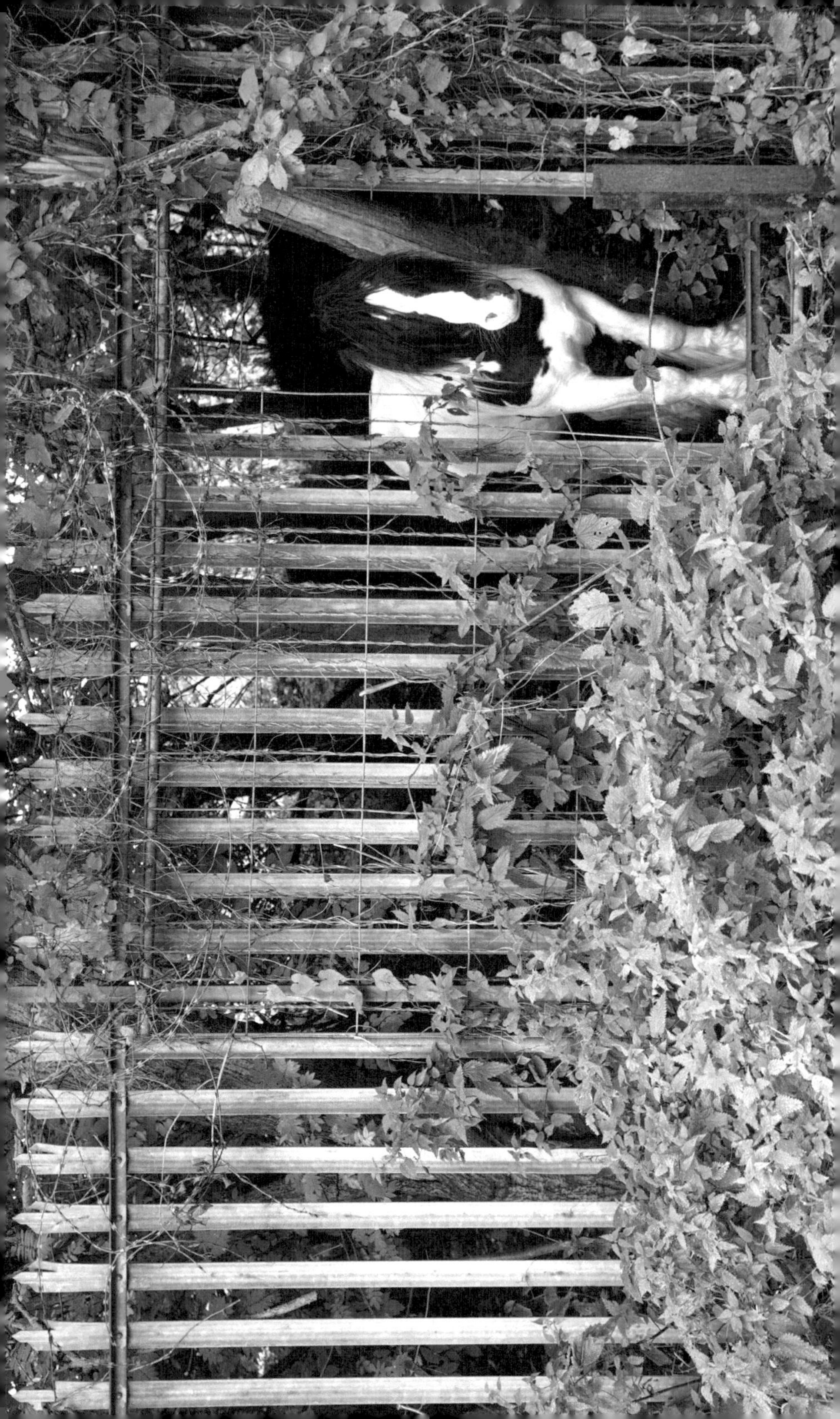

# Nature

> There were so many pleasant footpaths, that a pedestrian might walk completely round the town in a circle, which would seldom exceed a radius of two miles from the Exchange, and in which he would scarcely have occasion to encounter the noise, bustle, and dust of a public cart road or paved street. The beautiful undulating country between the valley of the Irk and Cheetham Hill; and the fine valley of the Irwell, with its verdant meadows … all this delightful scenery lies open to the pedestrian.
>
> The edges of Manchester in 1826, according to The Manchester Association for the Preservation of Ancient Public Footpaths

Often set up in opposition to each other, nature and the city in fact coexist and intertwine. They complement each other: cities providing spaces and conditions for nature to thrive; nature offering spaces of reflection and escape to city dwellers. They also challenge each other – nature overtaking development sites, as explored by Joanne Hudson in 'Wildscape'; the city's concrete impacting water reabsorption, and pollution from traffic and industry damaging flora and fauna.

Nature in Manchester encompasses the hills on the city's edges; the city's water – from its famous rain to its canals and rivers; individual gardens; overgrown wastelands; street planting and

**65** (Opposite) Waste ground near the Ashton canal, Openshaw

parks. A mix of the naturally occurring and the artificially created, nature both asserts itself in the city and is invited in to enhance the cityscape and indeed help reduce pollution, climate change and human stress. Central Manchester might not have the 'green lungs' of a city like London, but there are still pockets of nature in Whitworth Park, Ardwick and Miles Platting and, as we reach towards the edges of Greater Manchester, there are larger parks, nature reserves, gardens, and even a small slice of the Peak District National Park.

Many of the pieces in this section consider the idea of edgelands, the 'scuffed and unloved fringes' of the city as Nick Dunn writes in 'Edges'. Such spaces offer both respite and potential danger, as Morag Rose notes in 'Canal'; they are wild spaces where the city has lost a degree of control, where we might go to escape for a moment, but where we might also feel unsafe. Permeable, flexible, ever-changing, they also question the boundary between the countryside and the city, and between what is artificial and what is natural.

Nature offers its different timescales to the city. Alongside the daily and yearly rhythms of the city sit nature's seasonal cycles of birth, growth and death; and nature operates on much longer timescales too – with trees outliving buildings and city initiatives by centuries. Manchester's nature holds and reflects the essence and history of the city. As Becky Alexis-Martin discusses, trees can record changes in climate, war and human behaviour, and Manchester's adoption of hibakujumoku ginkgo trees (which share their DNA with the six ginkgo trees that survived the atomic attack on Hiroshima) stand in memory of the city's association with both the development of, and resistance to, nuclear warfare.

Nature in the city also engenders myth and story, creating spaces for us to exercise our fears and imaginations of these wild places. Morag Rose examines the ghost stories, folklore and urban myths that 'haunt' Manchester's canals, stories of murders and monsters, which manifest the city's 'fascination, and fear, of the

## Nature

waterways'. We return to the more mundane edges of the city in Matthew Steele's 'Gardens', which charts how private gardens have shaped the evolution of Wythenshawe. Even if we don't have a garden of our own, there's still pride to be taken in the green spaces that are almost everywhere in the city between the concrete, brick and asphalt.

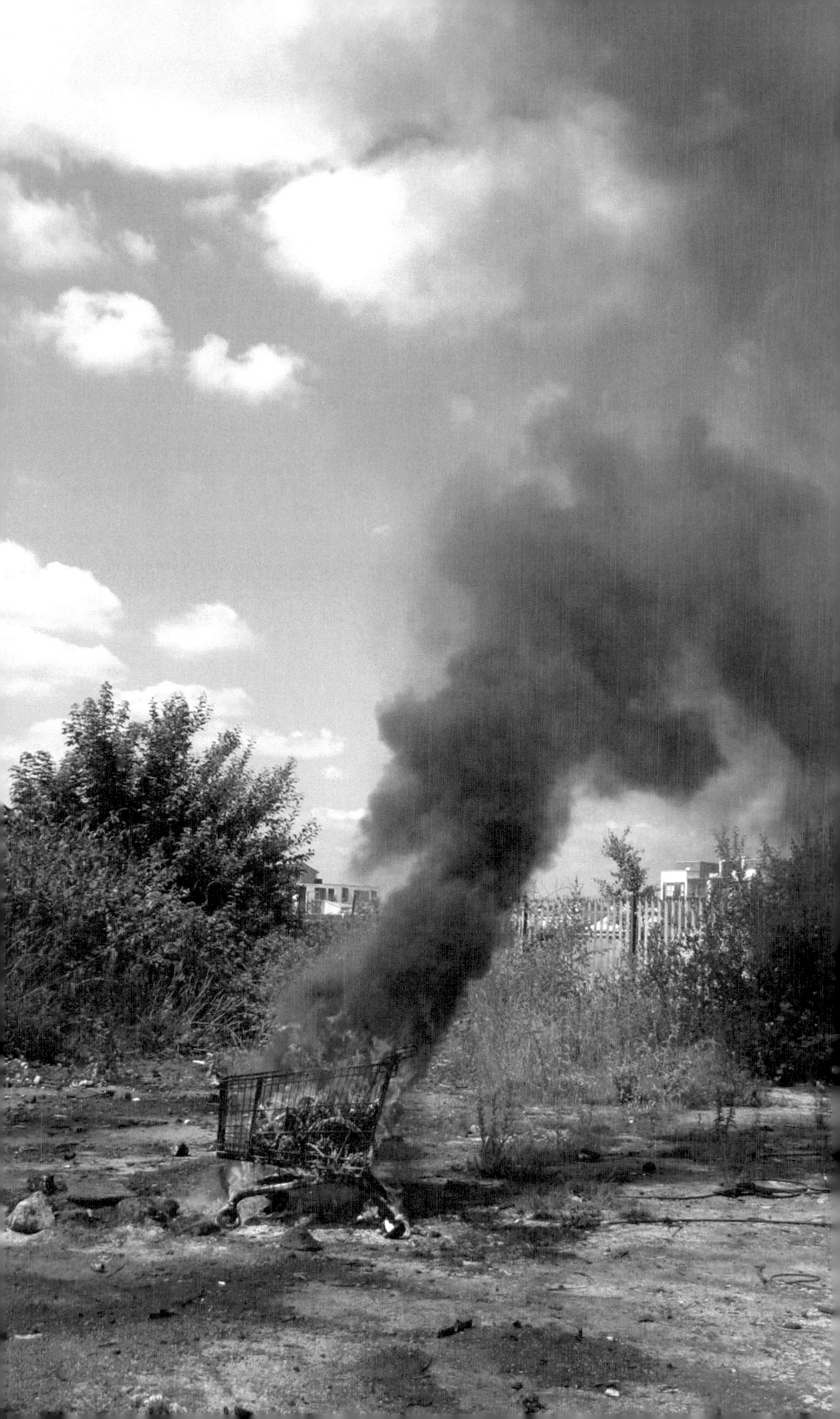

### Nature

## *Wildscape* – Joanne Hudson

An area of West Gorton, five kilometres to the east of the city centre, previously part of the Openshaw ward, today strikingly reveals the instability of the city and its constitutive processes. A verdant urban *wildscape*, its appearance offers a visual reminder of the multiple timescales that shape urban space.

West Gorton was once a focal point for industry, with population figures rising eightfold from 1851 to 1901, as the area housed companies such as Ashbury Railway Carriage and Iron Company, Gorton Locomotive Works, and the Beyer and Peacock foundry. But in the second half of the twentieth century, the social, economic and cultural wealth that this industrial belt created slowly ebbed away following deindustrialisation and large-scale economic restructuring. Today, although new developments are appearing apace, as Manchester emerges from the financial turmoil of 2008, pockets of post-industrial wastelands persist. One such site, still caught in a developmental time gap caused by multiple fractures in capitalist rhythms, located adjacent to Gorton Road, and in close proximity to Ashburys railway station has, as a consequence of natural succession, become an urban wildscape.

After centuries of urban development, this area is now shaped by natural as opposed to human agencies, and it supports an ecologically diverse and enchanting community. Few traces of a landscape formerly structured by a vast network of clocking-on times, repetitive tasks and timetabling remain, as nature's rhythms have been allowed to proliferate, concealing many vestiges of the former industrially productive site. Nature no longer provides a neutral aesthetic background to a site once defined by industrial output; now the eye is overwhelmed by grasses, shrubs and trees as successive growing seasons coalesce

**66** (Opposite) Scrappers at work on waste ground in West Gorton

to produce a varied natural habitat unfettered by human maintenance procedures.

Following abandonment, a variety of plants and animals have been able to gain a foothold. The soil, contaminated by acid, alkalis and heavy-metal deposits from former industrial practices, has afforded ideal growing conditions. The plethora of species it contains has thrived on neglect; being ignored has stimulated diversity. Plant species including buddleia, rosebay willowherb, common ragwort, soapwort, mugwort, red valerian, common stork's-bill, white campion, young silver birch, common alder, and various willows, are in abundance. Species normally separated or absent, due to their labelling as weeds, co-mingle here in a 'chaotic' assemblage.

A series of Second World War air-raid shelters, constructed to protect workers from German bombs, are today hidden beneath long grasses and plants, such as red valerian. With tough leaves and long flowering seasons, plants provide bursts of shocking pink, their flowers complementing the ageing brickwork of the shelters and the rusting remnants of the once prolific Ashbury Railway Carriage and Iron Company.

As a consequence of a lack of surveillance, the site has also regularly attracted fly-tippers and asset strippers – colonies of unofficial entrepreneurial 'scrappers' who see value in society's waste. Entering nearby abandoned buildings soon after they were closed and sitting empty, the scrappers would remove valuable material. Copper piping, stainless steel, aluminium and, less frequently, lead and brass, their stash would be brought to the wildscape. The vast expanse of land afforded a relatively hidden space in which to sort through their plunder and engage in the processes of dismantling, stripping and removing unwanted outer casings by burning to access the prized metals inside, before selling on to scrapyards. These activities introduced a further disorder to the wildscape. Normally zoned according to species, colour and aesthetic, plants and grasses grew in and around discarded clothing, bags and suitcases, various remnants from the asset-stripping practices and discarded household items, including the occasional bathroom suite.

Urban wildscapes such as this site in West Gorton have not had any form of external identity imposed on them; they are unique and tell their own stories – their very existence the tangible result of a set of interactions over a sustained period of time. The plant species that have opportunistically occupied the wildscape provide an informative site biography. Colonisation is not a static process but one that changes over time, and which is related to the longevity of the site. Within one growing season initial colonisers prepare the ground for taller perennial plants, which then stake their claim to the wasteland. Within the first year of abandonment, perennials, shrubs and grasses such as common evening primrose, purple loosestrife, cow parsley, fennel, creeping jenny, and goat willow, appear. Approximately five years later, these earlier species give way to grasses – common bent and timothy grass being the most prevalent. Meanwhile, common willow, birch, hawthorn, elder and various brambles have dug in for the long haul, allowing even an untrained eye to conclude that the site had existed for some time. Just as specific architectural styles and nuances allow us to date the urban environment and provide evidence of time passing, wildscapes and the species they contain also provide us with an ecological history of dereliction.

Urban wildscapes provide us with the opportunity to interact with nature, as they usually lie in close proximity to inhabited spaces. They introduce a sense of wild nature into the city, not normally deemed a place for such things to exist, thereby challenging our notion of what constitutes the urban and our assumptions of where a wilderness is. If you judge wilderness differently – as places that are overlooked, unplanned and undervalued – then the Highlands of Scotland would score low, while this wildscape in inner-city Gorton would score highly. Although rarely valued as beautiful by conventional aesthetic standards, their beauty commonly lies in their 'out of placeness', which can surprise and stimulate.

The greatest threat to these diverse habitats is, of course, redevelopment. These natural niches and their inherent richness are rarely recognised as such in redevelopment plans. Consequently, they are denuded in preparation for permanent built forms. Thus, these diverse ecological temporalities are lost; spontaneous and contingent growth patterns are replaced, and plants labelled weeds – the botanical equivalent of waste. Plants out of place are exchanged for classified species, carefully selected and arranged to require minimal maintenance and project an aesthetic of order. Yet, as exemplified above, nature is always waiting, ready to transgress boundaries, transforming spaces of former order to introduce a plurality of temporalities and affordances that can create positive and enduring relations.

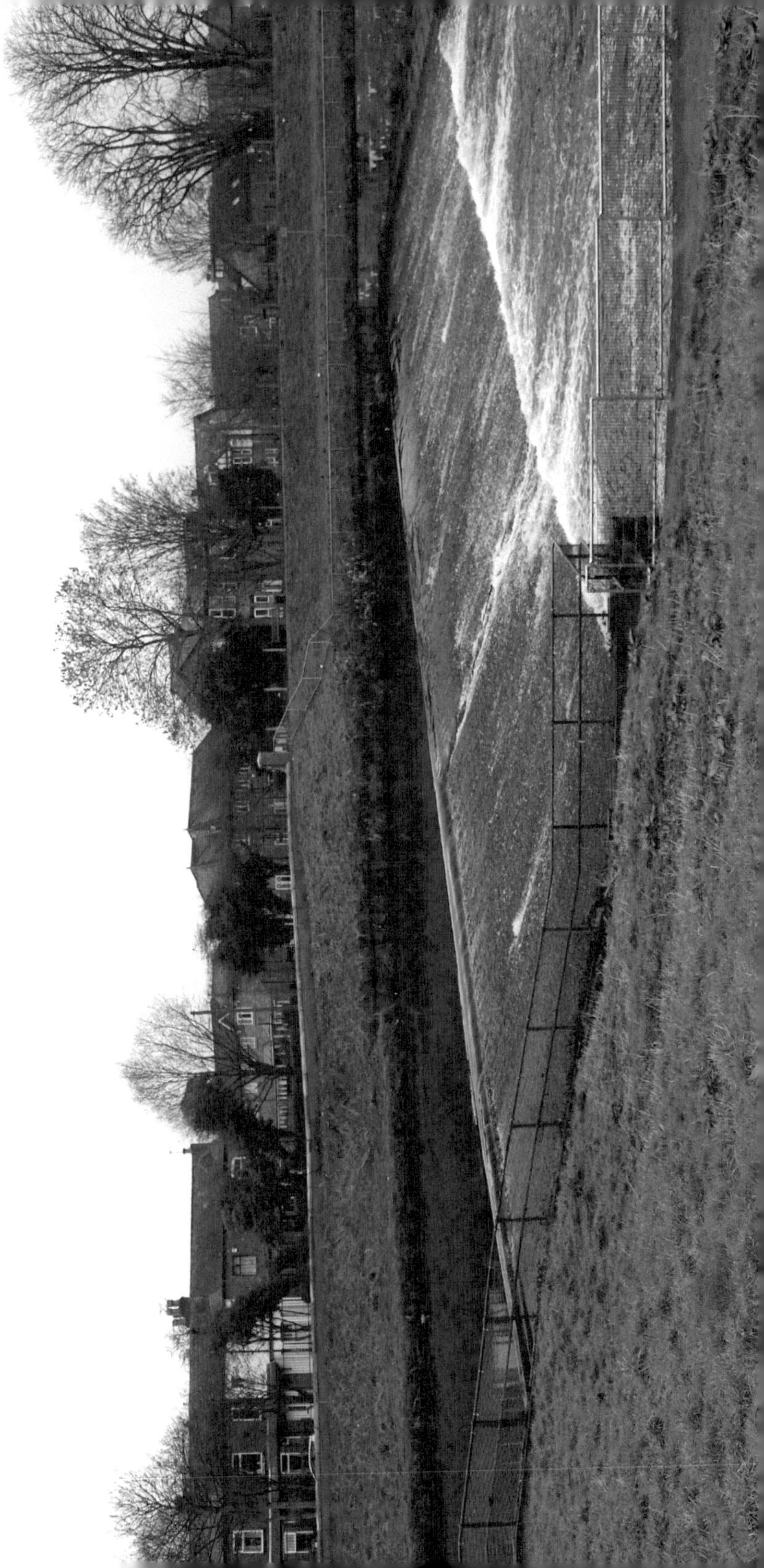

Manchester: Something rich and strange

## *Edges* – Nick Dunn

Manchester is often said to have an edge, its people embodying a strange mix of warmth, humour and no-nonsense attitude. But what happens when we encounter the physical limits of the city? Or perhaps more specifically, where does this happen? Greater Manchester itself is formed of ten metropolitan boroughs and has the counties of Cheshire, Derbyshire, Lancashire, Merseyside and West Yorkshire as its neighbours. The borders between these could reliably constitute an edge, but would they be so far removed from the city itself that it might be difficult to consider them related to Manchester anymore? Edges take all forms – from officially designated boundaries, to informally appropriated demarcations; from the sharp lines of man-made routes, to the fuzzy outlines of natural features and reclaimed landscapes.

For me, the edge of the city is behind where I now live, the outer suburbs held within the pinwheel of the M60 motorway. It is where the suburban is disrupted by the River Mersey, which flows along the southern rim of the city. Its waters are deceptively fast, its seemingly gentle nature brought into white-foamed cacophony as it passes over weirs. It is undeniably an edge, only to be crossed via bridges. It is also the connecting thread that weaves together the woodlands, meadows, artificial lakes, flooded gravel pits, and so much more, as it snakes along the perimeters of Priory Gardens, Sale Water Park, Chorlton Ees, Kenworthy Woods and Chorlton Water Park. Walking from my home to the river, I move along the edges of streets, allotments, a brook and two woodlands. These edges are so familiar to me now that I rarely stop to consider them.

Though some of these features appear resolutely fixed, such edges are not static but vibrant matter, subject to daily and seasonal changes that can dramatically alter their character or quietly

**67** (Previous page) Weir on the River Mersey in Chorlton-cum-Hardy

nuance it. There are two sets of dynamics at play along these edges; sometimes these work in tandem and sometimes they do not. First are the processes and changes, ecological and otherwise, happening within the place itself that evolve its identity. Second are the imprints, movements and legacy of those passing through that redefine the identity of a place through their encounter with it: ducks, anglers, dogs, cyclists, foxes, runners, kingfishers, walkers, herons, countless insects and other creatures, both above and below the surface of water features. This tract of the Mersey Valley is 'the unofficial countryside' that naturalist Richard Mabey mapped out during the early 1970s as he brought attention to the overlooked, scuffed and unloved fringes of cities. Not that this area isn't held dear by the many that use it – a wondrous green lung amid Manchester's suburbia.

Edges in places such as this alter the body. Feet are presented with a spectrum of crunchy, soft, wet, squelchy, powdery surfaces and textures not found in the cityscape's hard lines. The pace and posture of the body are engaged with the rhythms of these various materials and the movements they support or prevent. The land itself appears to blur with the body, leaving its imprint upon it and vice versa. It's as powerful an escape from the inner city as is imaginable, yet it lies less than five miles from Piccadilly Gardens. It is at the edges of urban life where things quieten down that it is also possible to reflect on ourselves, our relationships, and our lives, with the respite such places provide.

There are moments in these places where it is hard to imagine being near a city at all, let alone Manchester. Walking this section of the Mersey Valley with two lurchers has ensured that I have often been led off the beaten track and able to appreciate the richness and diversity of its nature reserves and flora, even if much of the fauna swiftly disappears as a result of my four-legged companions. This has led to the encounter of edges new to me, invisible to the eye, but described by the limits of an animal's scent trail. It has also taken us to awkward edges in pursuit of stirrings in the undergrowth and woodland unseen by myself, where due only to good luck and familiarity of reading the landscape have I not ended up in one of the hidden ponds as my agile and spring-footed friends bound onwards in a different direction.

On those occasions where we follow the edge of the river closely, we arrive at Northenden. Located at an old crossing place of the River Mersey on the salt road from Cheshire to Manchester, it fared well in medieval times. Edge along the river further and behold – Northenden Weir. This is particularly remarkable as it is the location of Manchester's only fish ladder. A flat and wide weir with a thin sheet of water running down it, the fish ladder enables migrating salmon and sea trout to get upstream. In 2005, salmon were spotted for the first time in two hundred years, reflecting vast improvements in the river's health. I cannot claim to have seen these fish for myself, defying the river's current by travelling back up over the weir's edge, but it must be quite a sight. That this edge of Manchester now teems with even more life, connecting the city to the vast seas beyond, is a useful reminder of just how permeable borders and edges are. No mere frozen lines on a map, they are dynamic forcefields for the identity of place and its people.

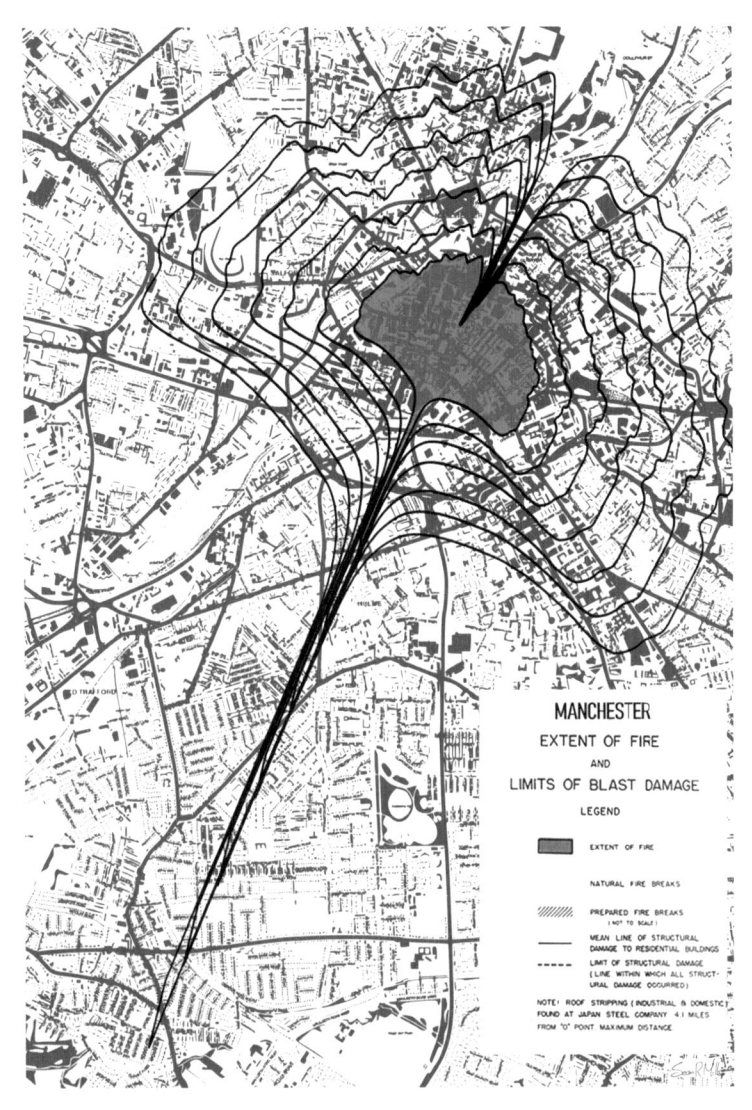

**68** Outline of a ginkgo leaf superimposed on a map of Manchester showing anticipated damage from a nuclear bomb attack

## *Ginkgo* – Becky Alexis-Martin

The green spaces of Manchester are the adopted home of a living fossil. The paired lobes of the leaves of *Ginkgo biloba* are marked by prehistoric striations, unchanged for 270 million years. Like *Homo sapiens*, the ginkgo is the sole survivor of a once ample family tree. Unlike us, a single tree can survive for over 2,000 years, outliving our regimes and empires. The ginkgo has somehow persisted, seemingly oblivious to the melodramas of both dinosaurs and humans. However, isotopic traces of our human age are sequestered away within the ginkgo's trunk during each growing season, to be accessed only by the dark art of dendrochronology. To unlock the secrets of the ginkgo and humankind, you need to perform surgery – to drill deep into its heart and extract a slice of history.

There are already ginkgoes dotted across Manchester, if you know where to look for them. Eleven specimens grow on Stevenson Square in the Northern Quarter, planted on 19 May 2017. However, the tale of the Manchester hibakujumoku ginkgoes traverses scientific discovery, warfare and, finally, peace. It began when Ernest Rutherford split the atom at the University of Manchester in 1917. Rutherford described his particle physics as 'moonshine', never envisaging that his work would provide the science to create weapons of mass destruction (see also 'Atom', p. 295).[1] He died on 19 October 1937. Eight years later, the first atom bomb was tested in Alamogordo; then, on 6 August 1945, 'Little Boy' was dropped on the city of Hiroshima. This nuclear attack killed approximately 100,000 people and changed the nature of warfare. It precipitated an international scramble for the bomb, and the world became a more dangerous place.

As the Cold War crept into being, nuclear weapon tests flung carbon-14 and other isotopes into the global atmosphere, and trees locked away some of these radiation residues with each growing season. The charred stumps within Hiroshima's blast zone began to thrust out fresh buds. Six ginkgoes recovered. While the blast had destroyed their foliage, their underground root networks endured. These trees became known as *hibakujumoku* – the A-bomb survivor tree – and Hiroshima regrew and recovered around them. In 1951, the new President of Hiroshima University, Tatsuo Morito, sent a letter to universities worldwide, asking for their support in further replanting the razed grounds. A global response to his request provided 261 trees of 103 varieties, and 934 sachets of seeds to Hiroshima.

Meanwhile, in the UK, the British government was responding to the burgeoning threat of Soviet nuclear warfare by instigating nuclear war preparedness measures. Reassuring but useless pamphlets were sent to the public, while subterranean bunkers were carved into the earth in an attempt to ensure the survival of the state. Clandestine excavations began thirty-five metres beneath Manchester city centre in 1954, to create an extensive dual-purpose network of reinforced concrete tunnels and facilities known as the Guardian Underground Telephone Exchange (GUTE).[2] The GUTE opened to telephone traffic at 8am on 7 December 1958. However, in the advent of thermonuclear warfare its protective subterranean specifications had already become redundant. By 1968, the GUTE had been declassified. When the GUTE's existence entered the public domain, it became clear to the people of Manchester that nuclear warfare was an unsurvivable threat. Their reaction was anti-nuclear pacifist action. By 5 November 1980, Manchester had declared itself the world's first Nuclear-Free City. By the end of 1982, 150 local authorities had joined it in opposing nuclear war.

Mayors for Peace supports the elimination of nuclear weapons, and was founded in Hiroshima by Mayor Takeshi Araki in 1982. Manchester is Vice President City, and works with Hiroshima to develop peace tours and exchange programmes, and contribute to the United Nations Institute for Training and Research

(UNITAR) disarmament policy. In 2011, Nassrine Azimi, Director of Hiroshima UNITAR, created a new initiative called Green Legacy Hiroshima. She organised for hibakujumoku ginkgo seeds to be collected, and shared with other places committed to social and ecological peace worldwide. Manchester received hibakujumoku ginkgo seeds in 2014, and the city's seedlings successfully sprouted at Hulme Community Garden Centre. Two Manchester hibakujumoku ginkgo seedlings will be planted in a peace garden on Lincoln Square.[3] Ginkgoes have been planted at 'Project G' peace education schools across the city, and also at Manchester Children's Hospital.

Each Manchester hibakujumoku descendant shares its DNA with trees that were destroyed, and then regenerated after the atomic bombing. These trees have a hidden radioactive heredity, despite looking similar to any other ginkgo in the city. The radioactive bombardment will have changed their genetic material, creating harmless mutants. While they are too young for their trunks to harbour traces of our nuclear history, they will record future changes to both climate and warfare. It remains to be seen if the hibakujumoku ginkgoes will outlive the city. In a burgeoning age of ethnonationalism and political extremism, they serve to remind us of the very real risks and possibilities of our human age.

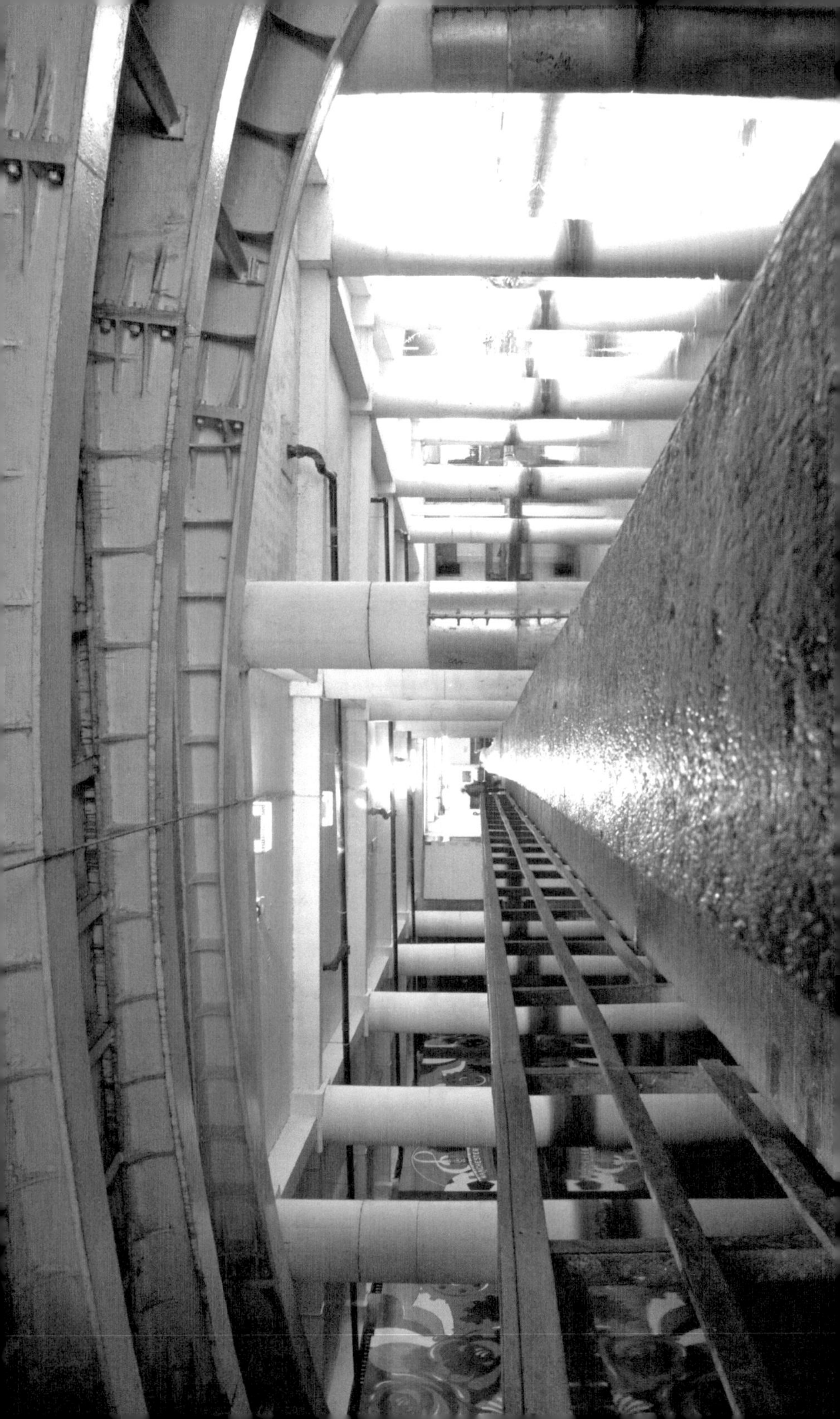

Manchester: Something rich and strange

## *Canal* – Morag Rose

Of all the fantastic tales this city tells itself, those focused on our canals are perhaps the most tangled and confused. For example, the Manchester Ship Canal is an engineering marvel, but from the very start it was mired in controversy. There were petitions, near bankruptcy, feuds with Liverpool and years of prevarication. The age of the train, and later containerisation, meant that, even when the canal opened, its glory days were limited. Unsurprisingly, the project took a fatal toll on the workers who made it, and beneath its surface lie the tales of those whose labour goes unrecognised: 130 men were killed, 165 permanently injured and 997 slightly injured. Those who still had some capacity for lighter toil were redeployed as watchmen or such like, joining the ranks of 'Walkers' fragments'.[4]

Today, like its brethren canals – the Manchester, Bolton & Bury, the Rochdale, the Ashton and the Bridgewater – the ally-ally-oh (the colloquial name for the Manchester Ship Canal) occupies a strange position in the psyche of Manchester. Canals flow 'betwixt and between, both absolutely central and integral to the topography of the city but also apart, separating and separate and frequently hard to traverse'.[5] I've asked people to imagine our city as a body, a living organism, and then to tell me where the canals would be, and there is no consensus. They are variously described as the city's heart, guts, veins, arteries and bowels. Full of love, nourishment, blood and shit.

Compared to many cities, Manchester has been slow and disjointed in its approach to waterside development. It's not always been celebrated and swathes of waterside have been relatively neglected. This means a walk on any of Manchester's canals can offer a brief respite from the frenetic energy of the city and a

**69** (Previous page) The Undercroft, Piccadilly Basin

chance to reconnect with nature. There are mercifully few billboards, but plenty of flowers. Deindustrialisation, and the dedication of environmentalists and volunteers, mean flora and fauna can thrive. Waterfowl are the custodians of much – perhaps the secret rulers of the city. Tourists and leisure seekers find much to enjoy, despite (perhaps because) the rest of the city has turned its back. It changes over time of course, and it feels like you can chase the line of regeneration – the flow of capital – as you head outwards from the city centre.

For a long time, my favourite canal walk was through Castlefield basin, past the apartments and bustle of St George's, and out into the sanctuary of Pomona island. Once there were pleasure gardens here dedicated to the goddess of abundance; then fire, fashion and the ship canal changed everything, and they were gone. The docks too have had their day, and this became a feral edgeland with traces of abandoned futures: a liminal zone to lose yourself in. Abandoned to the elements, Pomona became a breathing space and secret playground for games with no rules, some dark and shameless. A wanderer could find a ghost lamp post, a bird of prey, a patch of tarmac or a tree bursting with golden apples. It could never last, of course, and developers are currently building some of the most banal apartments on the island, despite spirited opposition. On my last few visits, the only people I saw there were photographers of course – fashion shoots in the apocalypse. Ruin porn. All the city is a giant photoshoot, no more, no less; nothing below the surface.

There's an edginess to many of the canals – not just the literal drop down with no barrier, but a sense of menace that stops many enjoying a stroll. One section of the Rochdale Canal, known as the Undercroft, is closed at night for reasons of 'public safety'. It lies adjacent to Minshull Street Crown Court and joins Canal Street – the bar-lined party place of the Gay Village – to Piccadilly Basin. The PSPO (Public Space Protection Order) was challenged, both on principled grounds as a right of way, but also because of suspicions it was stigmatising and victimising the LGBTQ+ community. Closing a towpath won't tackle homophobic and transphobic crime, of course, but it may protect the sensibilities and profits of nearby businesses. The Undercroft is just a small subterranean section of the canal network, and certainly not the only place folk don't feel like walking alone.

Whether justified or not, there are stories of monsters and ghouls that haunt Manchester's canals. The most notorious of these is the Pusher, currently implicated in hushed tones of up to eighty-six deaths (numbers vary depending on your tabloid or website of choice). Personally I am sceptical of his existence (and despite varying accounts his assumed gender is consistent). I think perhaps Jack the Dipper is the latest manifestation of the city's fascination, and fear, of the waterways. This manifests as folklore, ghost stories and urban myth. Enchantment wasn't killed off by the Industrial Revolution, a supposedly rational age hailed by a plethora of chimneys.[6] The tales that swirl in those murkier waters demonstrate its persistence. For example, old ladies still talk about Ginnie Greenteeth, the monster they were warned about as children. She lives in dirty, dangerous water and serves as a threat to keep wandering youths tamed. She has family worldwide, including the Australian Bunyip and Japanese Kappa. Several others have shared accounts with me of the elusive Messie, a creature glimpsed fleetingly at various locations. Theories abound about what Messie may be: a giant eel, a stowaway on a cargo ship, a manifestation of dark energies conjured by sinister figures with mutable motives, a drunken misunderstanding of shadows, a trick of the light, the flow of capital, the soul of the city.

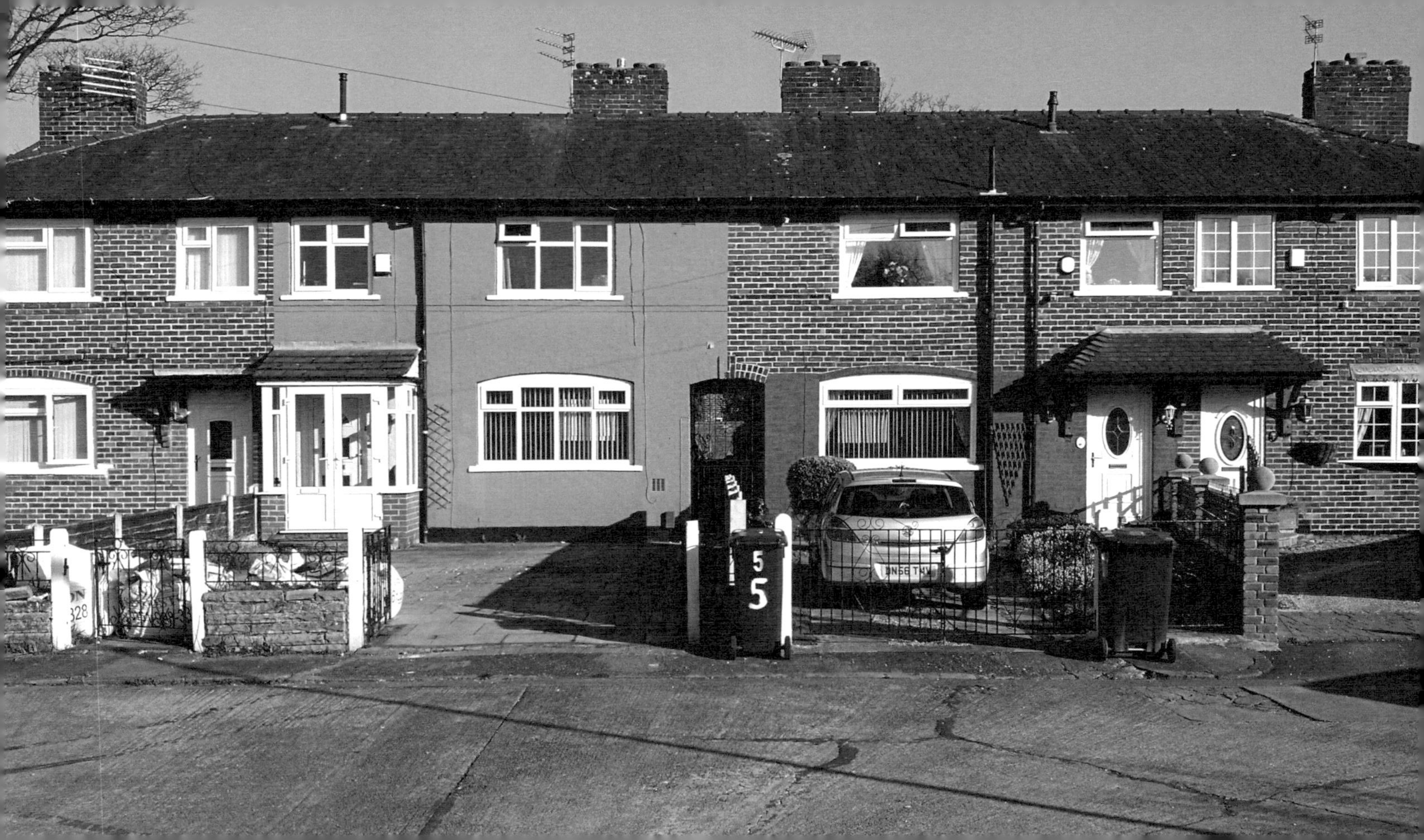
5
5

## *Gardens* – Matthew Steele

Accounts of Manchester often gloss over the wider conurbation in which it sits and pay little attention to the character afforded by its many and varied suburbs. As the journalist Paul Barker noted of the suburbs in *The Freedoms of Suburbia* (2009): 'Here weren't dragons, or elephants, but sunrise garden gates and privet, privet, privet.'[7] Yes – mile upon mile of privet demarcating the private gardens of suburbanites. Barker, in making his observation, no doubt had places such as Hampstead Garden Suburb in mind; founded in 1906, master-planned by Barry Parker and Raymond Unwin and, since 1968, a designated conservation area. What of Parker's later Wythenshawe Garden Suburb in Manchester, however? Unconstrained by such designations, it is an area whose character continues to evolve and, therefore, is more revealing of present-day attitudes to private gardens.

Manchester's first foray into planned garden suburbs came in 1906 with the creation, by Manchester Tenants Limited, of Burnage Garden Village: eleven acres of co-partnership housing, each with a private garden and set around open recreational space. Other private enterprises followed, including those at Fairfield (1906), Hollins Green (1908), Alkrington (1909) and Chorltonville (1911), before the passing of the 1919 Housing Act which, through the promise of government subsidies, encouraged municipal authorities, including Manchester Corporation, to follow suit. In keeping with the recommendations of the Tudor Walters Report (1918), the Act stated that new municipal housing was to be built at a density of no more than twelve to the acre and, preferably, on undeveloped land on the outskirts of cities. In Manchester, the death of Thomas Tatton in 1924 presented the corporation with an opportunity to purchase 2,538 acres of undeveloped land from

**70** (Previous page) A row of 1950s houses in Yew Tree Drive, Wythenshawe

his family estate, which it duly exercised in 1926. This land, along with a further 1,053 acres it subsequently acquired, was incorporated within the City of Manchester on 31 March 1931, allowing the building of Wythenshawe Garden Suburb to commence.

Initial development included the Royal Oak and Roundwood estates, south of Wythenshawe Park and Northenden village respectively. However, construction of the Lawton Moor estate, north of the park, and on land formerly used as Britain's first municipal airport, saw hundreds of couples, young and elderly alike, stumble 'over rough land' eager to see the new houses.[8] Each was replete with its own private garden, while wide grass verges separated roadways from footpaths. The importance placed upon landscaping by the corporation was evident in the General Powers Bill it had brought forward in February 1934, which allowed for a twenty-shilling fine to be levied against any pedestrian who 'wilfully' walked on the grass verges.[9] Although this seemed rather officious, the attitude of the corporation, nonetheless, instilled a sense of pride among early tenants in their new surroundings.

In August 1934, a competition organised by Wythenshawe Residents' Association attracted over 700 entries, as tenants competed for the honour of best kept garden – the overall winner being the resident of 8 Yew Tree Drive, Northenden. Presiding over the occasion, Robert Tatton, son of the late Thomas, commented: 'Where I used to see hundreds of fields, I now see hundreds of square yards of houses. But what impresses me more than anything is the neatness of the gardens.'[10] Privets, never allowed to grow higher than the little garden gates, meant that tenants could enjoy views of each other's gardens – proving, in the words of Lady Simon of Wythenshawe, 'that a private garden is a real public service'.[11] Indeed, a survey of the tenants revealed an overwhelming enthusiasm for 'the gardens, the fresh air, and the country surroundings'. It must be said, however, that those who failed contribute to this 'public service' did so under threat of eviction. One resident of Carloon Road, whose garden was 'covered with dandelions, dock, and rank grass', was subject to a possession order which was suspended only on condition of the situation being swiftly remedied.[12]

Unfortunately, if the proud aldermen of Manchester Corporation were to take a walk around their prized garden suburb today, one suspects many more such possession orders would be sought. The 'Right to Buy' afforded council tenants, consequent to the passing of the 1980 Housing Act, inevitably reduced the council's power of influence as more and more houses fell into private ownership. And without the controls afforded to designated conservation areas being put in place, the character of those early estates, such as Lawton Moor, is being slowly eroded. Brick walls and six-foot-high fence panels have, in many instances, replaced the low-rise privets – presumably for ease of maintenance, but at the same time engendering exclusivity. Elsewhere, a privileging of the motor car, a problem not unique to Wythenshawe it must be said, has seen many private gardens grubbed up – at best replaced with a paved driveway, at worst left as open ground 'with dandelions, dock, and rank grass' growing rampant among the recycling bins and discarded household goods. No twenty-shilling fine for those who would 'wilfully' park on the grass verges either. And what of the neighbourly competitions once so keenly contested? Sadly, these too are a thing of the past, the diminution of private gardens contributing not only to a lack of visual, but also social, cohesion.

Thus, while Barker is celebratory of the unfettered freedoms of suburbia – 'permissive, not prescriptive … forbid as little as you can' – it is an approach that has not served Wythenshawe well.[13] But perhaps there is still some hope for the future. The extension of the Metrolink tram system which, since 2014, has passed through Wythenshawe en route to Manchester Airport could, in time, help reduce private car ownership and the need for driveways. Moreover, with a growing awareness of environmental issues such as biodiversity, the importance of private gardens is

### Nature

being recognised once more. Could this bring about a return to the aesthetics, if not principles, of the original garden suburbs in Wythenshawe?

### Notes

1. John G. Jenkin, 'Atomic energy is "moonshine": what did Rutherford really mean?', *Physics in Perspective* 13:2 (2011), pp. 128–45.
2. See Richard Brook and Martin Dodge, 'The Guardian Underground Telephone Exchange', *Lancashire & Cheshire Antiquarian Society Transactions* 108 (2014), pp. 20–55.
3. Sean Morris, 'Manchester City Council seeks to create new contemplative peace garden', *Mayors for Peace* website, June 2018, available at www.mayorsforpeace.org/english/whatsnew/activity/180619_Manchester_peace_garden.html (accessed 17 June 2020).
4. Nick Robins, *The Ships That Came to Manchester: From the Mersey and Weaver Sailing Flat to the Mighty Container Ship* (Amberley: Shire, 2015). Thomas Walker was the civil engineer contracted to build the Manchester Ship Canal.
5. Morag Rose, '"There's something in the water!" A psychogeographical exploration of what lurks beneath the surface of Manchester', in Karl Bell, ed., *Supernatural Cities: Enchantment, Anxiety and Spectrality* (Martlesham: Boydell & Brewer, 2019), pp. 290–310.
6. Karl Bell, *The Magical Imagination: Magic and Modernity in Urban England, 1780–1914* (Cambridge: Cambridge University Press, 2012).
7. Paul Barker, *The Freedoms of Suburbia* (London: Frances Lincoln, 2009), p. 10.
8. Anon., 'Looking at houses', *Manchester Guardian*, 21 August 1933, p. 11.
9. Anon., 'Keep off the grass', *Manchester Guardian*, 16 February 1934, p. 13.
10. Anon., 'City flower shows: Wythenshawe starts well', *Manchester Guardian*, 20 August 1934, p. 6.
11. Ibid.
12. Anon., 'Badly tended garden: house possession case', *Manchester Guardian*, 22 October 1943, p. 3.
13. Barker, *The Freedoms of Suburbia*, p. 221.

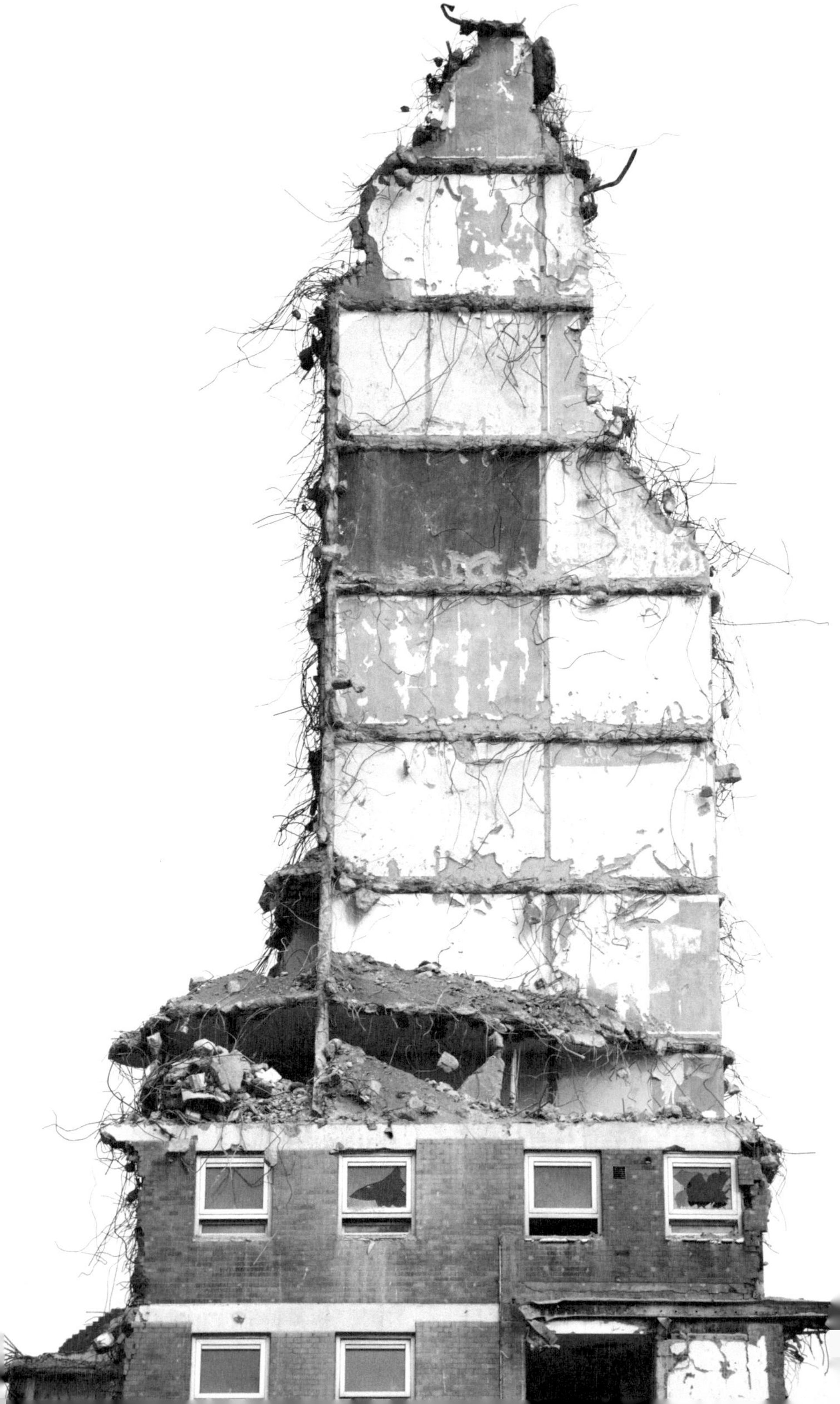

# Destruction

Only last week it had been a row of houses. Fairlawn Street [in Moss Side] next to St Bees Street next to another road James couldn't remember the name of. Each house had three floors and a million stairs to the top. Only last week the street was full of kids playing catch and cars driving past the women gossiping on the corner. But not any more, all that was gone and all that was left was a pool the size of a school yard and a reflection of a church spire. The church was the only building left, apart from the pub at the end of what used to be St Bees Street. The pub had a large poster of a man and a woman smiling at the skies like they'd seen a bird. If they'd been looking to the ground they wouldn't be smiling. Who would when all that was left was a big pool the size of a school yard? It was like the 'blitts' as Aunty Mary called it, like a bomb had exploded and all the houses disappeared in a puff of smoke and a loud bang.

Joe Pemberton, *Forever and Ever, Amen* (2000), p. 52

Destruction is everywhere in cities. Perhaps most obvious in Manchester today is the constant churn of demolition and rebuilding that sees buildings torn down to be replaced by new ones, invariably because the new promises a higher return than the old. There's also a sense in which cities are always on the edge of destruction: even if we can't see it, the built environment is always

**71** (Opposite) Demolition of Wenlock and Armitage Court, Gorton, March 2014

on the verge of ruin – only ceaseless maintenance prevents this. Witness the emergence of cobbles from underneath the tarmac of so many of Manchester's streets – the ruins of the past returning to remind us of the city's buried remains.

There are also more specific acts of destruction in the city's history, events that cast long shadows over the present, even as their impact gradually lessens over time. Until its recent 200-year anniversary, the 1819 Peterloo massacre was an underexamined tragedy in the city's distant past: now it's been resurrected as a powerful reminder of the dangers of unchecked social inequality, the subject of new books, a film, memorial, and, here, in Sarah Sayeed's 'Flower', which revisits the spaces of this violent event. At the same time, the impact of the city's most recent outrage – the suicide bomb attack at the Manchester Arena on 22 May 2017 that left twenty-two dead – remains a raw wound for many, a reminder that destruction may come seemingly out of the blue, changing so many lives in a shocking moment of violence.

That attack looms large here in Paul Dobraszczyk's 'Bee' – an account of how one of Manchester's historic symbols of industriousness changed overnight into one of strength and unity. Moving backwards in time, Sarah Butler uncovers the impact of the 2011 city-centre riots through a fictional retelling of one person's involvement, while Steven Hanson uses the history of nuclear science in Manchester as a way of framing a less visible form of destruction – that of social ties and solidarity. Telescoping us back to the very origins of modern Manchester, 'Tudor' takes a tour of some of the city's oldest dilapidated remnants, exploring how they can take on new life if they're reused, rather than left to rot.

Thinking through destruction in cities enables us to contemplate more fully the threats now facing urban life, whether the catastrophic damage that will likely be wrought by climate change, wars and terrorism that deliberately target cities, or violence resulting from increasing social division. Just as acceptance of one's own mortality can lead to a freer and more compassionate life, so the

## Destruction

same in cities might transform the built environment into something far more humane, richer and meaningful than it currently tends to be. In a city ruled by a form of global capitalism that seems hell-bent on continuing and accelerating its 'creative' destruction, there is an urgent need to foster a radically different approach to destruction – one that regards it an inevitable product not just of capitalism, but rather of any society that fails to acknowledge and accept limits, vulnerabilities and endings.

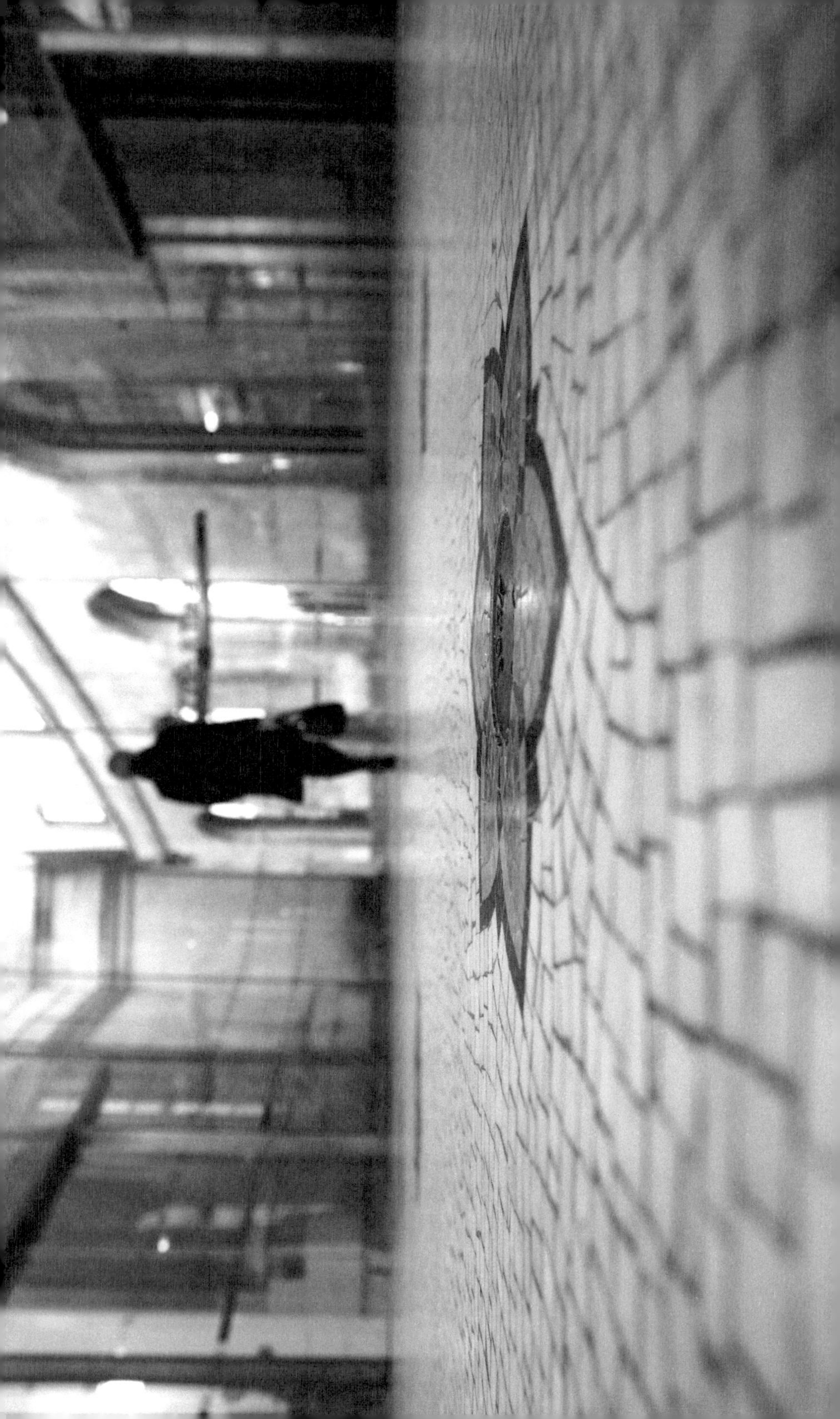

### Destruction

## *Flower* – Sarah Sayeed

Flowers are symbols of life itself. From time immemorial flowers have offered us a life filled with happiness and hope. Maybe we buy flowers that have been picked in a field by someone else, or pluck them from the soil, lovingly arrange them to adorn our living spaces. Their symmetry and unrivalled, pristine beauty open the door for the hope we desperately need as humans. Their fragrance is the root of our spiritual health and well-being, and the scents of flowers adorn every aspect of our lives. And across Manchester, the gardens of Platt Fields and Fletcher Moss offer us the experience of the natural splendour of flowers; on the edges of the school playing fields flanking the banks of the River Mersey, wild flowers blow in the cool soft breeze.

But sometimes flowers represent something much more ominous. In the covered space that now connects Manchester Town Hall and the Central Library, the large mosaic floor gives away the secrets of a tragic event, told in some of its red and orange five-petalled flowers. The flowers are the Lancashire rose, the symbol of the historic county in which Manchester used to sit, until the creation of Greater Manchester in 1974. Eighteen of these mosaic roses are inscribed with names at their centres: each one of those killed in the Peterloo massacre on 16 August 1819.

Perhaps no event in Manchester's modern history has had more impact on radical change and reform in the city. On the morning of 16 August 1819, at least 60,000 people flooded down Windmill Street and Oxford Road and assembled in the fields fronting Peter Street to ask peacefully for the right to decide who would represent them in Parliament. They had come from all areas of the

**72** (Opposite) Mosaics on the floor of the building connecting City Library and the Town Hall Extension, representing those injured and killed in the Peterloo massacre on 16 August 1819

## Manchester: Something rich and strange

Manchester region – from Salford, Saddleworth, Bury, Stockport, Middleton, Oldham, Withington and beyond. The crowds consisted of men, women and children, and the majority of them were workers from the Lancashire cotton mills that surrounded Manchester. The Peterloo casualty list – eighteen dead and many hundreds injured – outlines the names of many individuals in the crowd, and they included spinners, weavers, watchmakers and blacksmiths. These workers were coming to ask for the right to vote and were championed by Henry Hunt, a proponent of universal suffrage.

This gathering had already been declared illegal by the Manchester Magistrates, who were behind the dispatching of the cavalries who caused the many fatalities and injuries. The Magistrates were also strong supporters of Lord Liverpool's Tory government, who were fiercely resistant to expanding the franchise. As people began to come into the centre of Manchester for this peaceful protest, Yeomanry cavalry and the 15th Regiment of Light Dragoons were dispatched to march into and upon the crowds. And so they did, charging into people with ruthless abandon, cutting them down as they went along. Protestors were crushed, their shoulders dislocated, ankles and loins seriously hurt; parts of skulls were slashed off, bodies were stabbed, heads were bruised by truncheons and many endured severe beatings. These were flowers that had been trampled on.

The mosaic flowers now inscribed with the names of those killed at Peterloo are easily missed, and even when noticed their significance and meaning is not immediately apparent. As the fragments of mosaic stone assemble together to form flowers in space, the names of those killed at Peterloo glisten through the circles of ruby-red glass at their centres. There was Mary Heys of Oxford Road, who was pregnant and trampled to death by the horses. Mary died the day after Peterloo. Then there was Sarah Jones from Silk Street, who had seven children and was beaten to death with a truncheon.

## Destruction

In her poem 'Unnatural', Bengali poet Maya Choudhury pictures flowers as vulnerable prey 'attacked' by ravenous bees:

> A dandelion bites down hard, basal leaves tearing concrete,
> Floret blooming as a hungry bee hovers, licks yellow spring smiles
>
> In summer the fluffy moons stalk the night-air dream
> Of spitting seed spearheads, floating past
>
> Brick brownfields
> To the woods, barging into bluebells, knocking their
> vainglorious purple flowerheads off.

As one walks through the entrance to Manchester Central Library, it seems no coincidence that those lost at Peterloo are remembered through the fragments of a mosaic. Their lives were clearly shattered that day, but one thing remains with each flower. And that is a hope for humanity, for the future lives of us all. May we never again have to experience such cruel death in the face of fair and truthful protest.

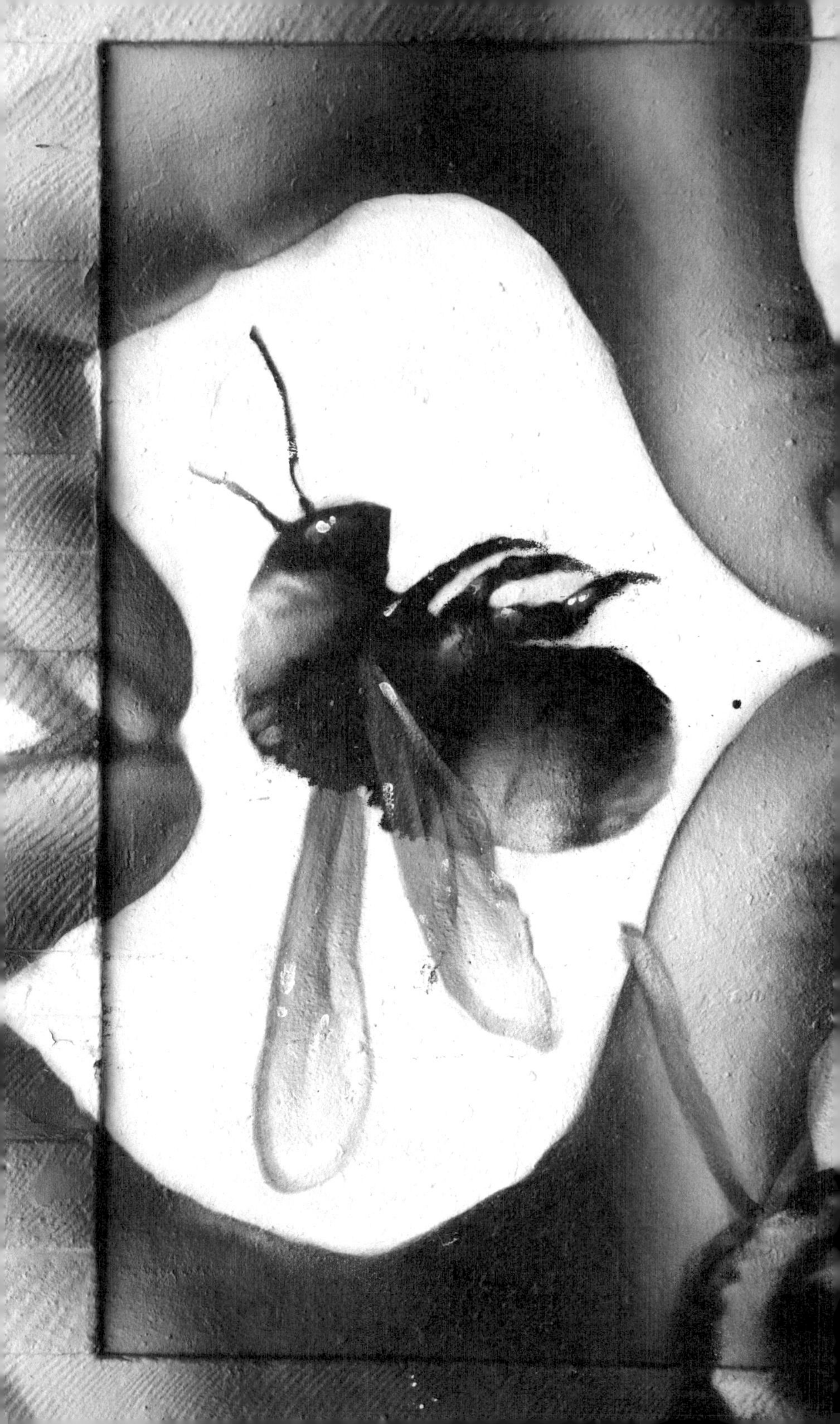

## Destruction

## *Bee* – Paul Dobraszczyk

For over 150 years, the bee has been a symbol of Manchester. The city's coat of arms was given royal approval in 1842 – even though Manchester didn't officially become a city until 1853 – and it included a globe covered with bees. This was not only an obvious symbol of industriousness, but also a reflection of the fact that, by the 1840s, Manchester had become the world's pre-eminent industrial city, defined by its global domination of the cotton industry. From then on, bees became part of the image of the city and were incorporated into the floor mosaics of Manchester's most important civic statement – the Town Hall, completed in 1877 – as well as some of the buildings of the co-operative movement, where bees are equated with an equitable form of labour, one that isn't based on the exploitation of workers. Even as the city's principal industry went into catastrophic decline after the Second World War, bees still featured in Manchester's civic iconography, but reduced to a more prosaic role as labels for the city's lamp posts and rubbish bins.

The significance of the bee in the city was changed forever in the wake of the terrorist atrocity carried out just after an Ariana Grande concert ended at the Manchester Arena on 22 May 2017 – a suicide bomb attack that left twenty-two people dead and sixty-four injured. Many of the victims were children, the youngest being 8 year-old Saffie Rose Roussos. Hours after the attack, illustrator Dick Vincent posted a hastily drawn image of a bee on Instagram, together with the caption 'Stay strong our kid', and, in the following days, bees appeared everywhere in the city. This equating of the bee with resilience chimed strongly with the

**73** (Opposite) Bee mural by Qubek in Stevenson Square in the Northern Quarter, painted shortly after the Manchester Arena terrorist attack on 22 May 2017

defiant mood of the city. When a vigil was held for the victims on 23 May in Albert Square, the same design was seen surrounded by flowers at a memorial near the cenotaph.

Bees also began appearing on the bodies of Manchester's residents. After Stalybridge tattoo artist Sam Barber launched the Manchester Tattoo Appeal on 25 May, hundreds of people were seen queuing for bee tattoos – the proceeds donated to a fund for the victims of, and families affected by, the attack. As reported by the *Manchester Evening News*, people of all ages waited patiently for bee tattoos. They wanted to identify with those affected by the atrocity, not least the parents of one of the victims – 15 year-old Olivia Campbell – who both had the bee emblem tattooed on their hearts, together with Olivia's name and birthdate.

Three years on from the attack and the bee has re-emerged as one of the principal emblems of the city, often accompanied by messages of defiance – whether 'We stand together', 'Stronger together', 'Unity is strength' or 'Bee strong Manchester'. The Bee in the City festival in the summer of 2018 saw dozens of bee sculptures appear all over the city, accompanied by slick corporate marketing that initiated a city-wide trail for visitors and residents alike (see 'Sculpture', p. 76). At the same time, window stickers have appeared in many premises, with bee badges and stickers now sitting alongside football shirts and postcards in the city's souvenir shops. Some have stickers on their car bumpers or windows; others have bee trinkets, bee-emblazoned boxes or even bee wallpaper. Dozens of bee murals have also been painted onto buildings in the city, particularly in the Northern Quarter, where street art defines the look and feel of the area. Foremost of these artists is Qubek – tag name of Russ Meehan – who painted a bee mural on the old public toilets in Stephenson Square two days after the attack. In early June 2017, Qubek was commissioned by the *Manchester Evening News* to paint a large bee mural on the side of the Koffee Pot cafe on Oldham Street. Taking up an entire wall, this mural unequivocally equated the bee with the victims of the attack, each of its twenty-two bees representing one of those killed, bar the terrorist himself. Here, Manchester's principal newspaper endorsed the bee as a symbol of 'Manchester's indomitable spirit'. Since then, Qubek has been overwhelmed with commissions to paint bees, whether civic projects that seek to draw diverse communities together, such as one he undertook in October 2017 with children attending Stanley Grove primary school in Longsight, or as emblems for businesses seeking to identify with this new collective spirit. Qubek has even been commissioned to paint large-scale bee murals on private homes in Chorlton and Offerton.

This renewed sense of civic identity and unity is clearly a powerful response to a tragedy that was shocking in its brutality and senselessness; yet it risks turning the bee into something sacrosanct – a powerful response to a tragedy that was shocking in its senselessness (see also 'Spirit', p. 28). Qubek may have become the leading image-maker of bees in the wake of the terrorist attack, but he was actually using bees in very different ways previous to it. For instance, in October 2016, Qubek painted a bee on a hoarding advertising 'luxury student apartments' in Hulme, questioning whether such accommodation could ever be afforded by most Mancunians. In May 2016, he painted an aggressive-looking bee on another hoarding in Back Piccadilly, together with the slogan 'Save our banks; kill our poor!' He also painted a cubist-style bee mural in 2016 near the Co-operative building in Angel Square, with the slogan 'So much to answer for', a reference to The Smiths 1984 song 'Suffer Little Children', which is about the Moors Murders. And even in the months after the attack, Qubek has used bees to symbolise something quite different from defiance in the face of tragedy. In a recent mural painted near the Southern Cemetery in Barlow Moor, bees revert back to their association with industry – here the references are to the Manchester Ship Canal, built in the 1890s.

The malleability of symbols like the bee is important because it allows them to remain open to multiple interpretations. One of Manchester's bees demonstrates this beautifully. On Canal Street

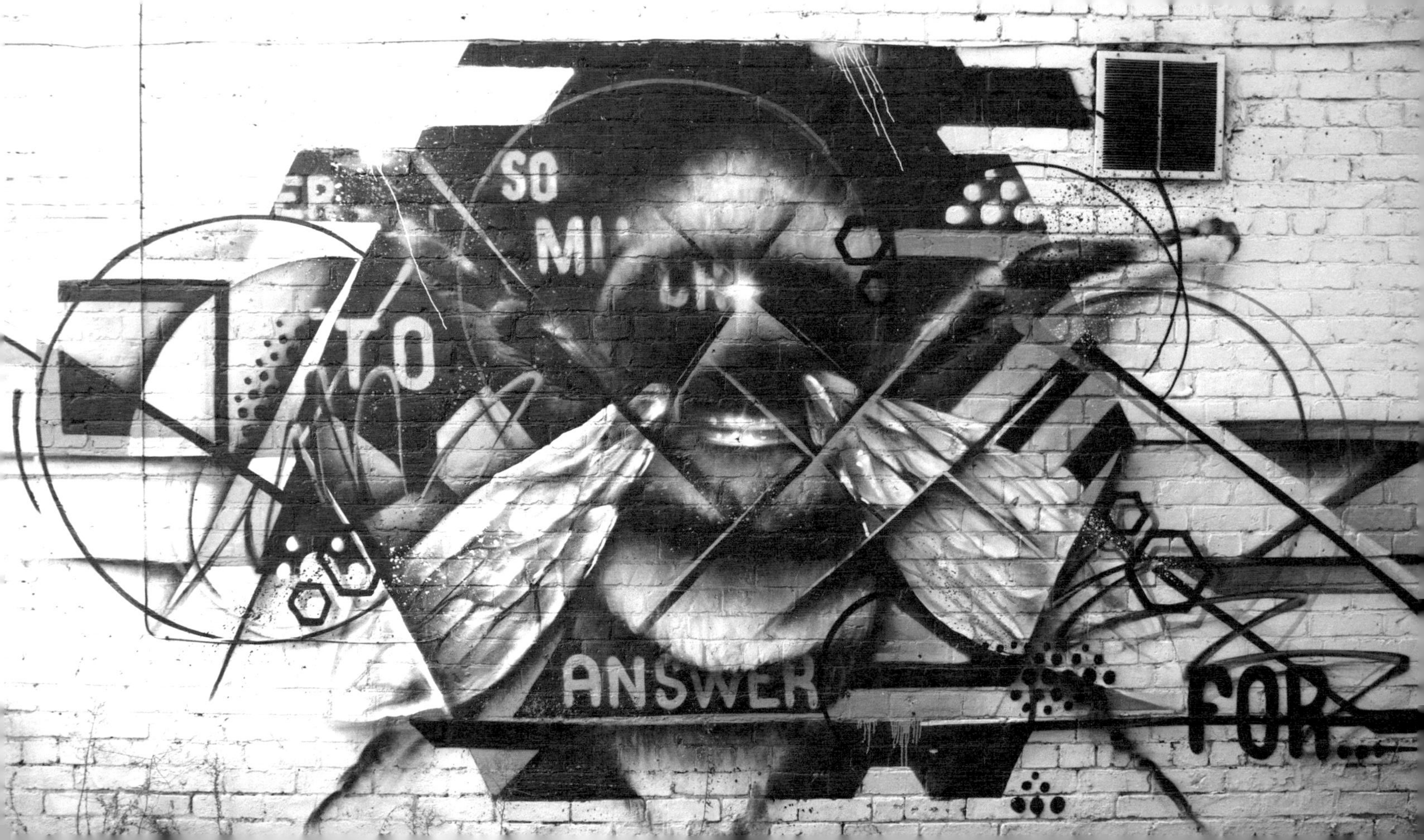
SO
TO
ANSWER
FOR

## Destruction

in the city's Gay Village is a lamp post sporting bees placed there by the city council – the bee as symbol of civic authority. An unknown person has added the colours of the rainbow to the bee's abdomen, together with a rainbow umbrella above its head, to protect the delicate bee from the inevitable Manchester rain. Subverting a symbol of civic order into one that celebrates both diversity and vulnerability turns the meaning of the bee on its head. We may need to be strong in the face of terror; we may need to be unified and defiant; but we also need to acknowledge our vulnerability and to accept the need for protection against any unity that is enforced or exclusive.

**74** (Opposite) Bee mural by Qubek near Angel Square, painted in 2016

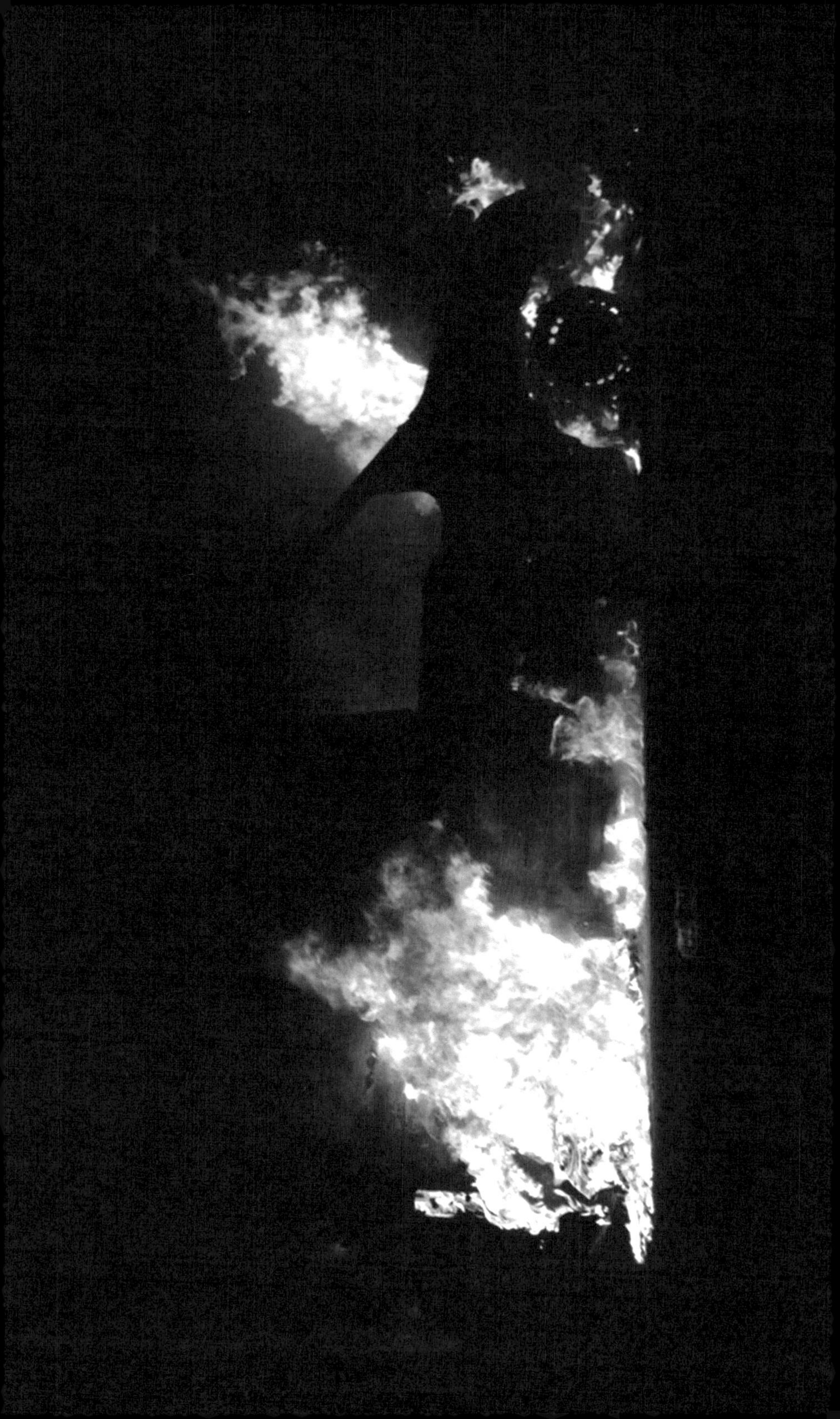

# Destruction

## *Riot* – Sarah Butler

*Piccadilly Gardens. There are no buses, no cars, no trams. The traffic noise replaced by shouts, whistles, running feet, breaking glass, burglar alarms. The smell of traffic and coffee and Greggs pasties replaced with cigarette smoke and weed, and the sharp, choking stink of burning plastic.*

*Two boys try to lever the shutter away from a shop window. The metal rattles and groans, but isn't quite ready to break. Further towards Market Street, a crowd surges around Primark's doors – people running inside and coming out with their arms full, coat hangers clattering to the ground.*[1]

9 August 2011. The riots arrived in Salford and Manchester city centre. They were always going to. Just a matter of time. England's geography folded in on itself – one city igniting another. Was it any different here than in Bristol, Birmingham, Liverpool? Did it mean anything different? Did it mean anything at all?

Hundreds of thousands of words were thrown at the problem – newspaper stories, tweets, government reports. Why did the riots happen, they asked, what did they mean? Was it the impact of austerity; inequality; a disconnect from the democratic process? Or the demonstration of 'Broken Britain'; feral youth; moral bankruptcy?

Perhaps neither. Perhaps both. Perhaps those things and a hundred thousand others.

The days during and after the riots were filled with overarching narratives and sweeping generalisations. Despite some journalists' attempts to interview rioters, we heard very few of the myriad of individual stories which made the riots.

As a novelist, I am drawn to individual stories, to specific details. I resist the overarching narratives and sweeping generalisations that abounded in those days during and after the riots. If I had to pick, I'm in the austerity and inequality camp. I could make an

75 (Opposite) Burning car after Manchester riots in early August 2011

argument about Manchester's glitzy regenerated city centre that excludes poorer communities and physicalises the inequalities of the city. But I can't help thinking that there were as many reasons for those riots as there were people who took part in them.

*On Mosley Street, two men aim kicks at a newsagent's window. A third hits a fire extinguisher against the glass until it punctures, cracks fanning out like a spider's web. They keep on until the window gives way, the glass crumbling to leave a hole big enough to walk through, head high. The three men duck into the shop and more follow them, coming out with wine, crisps, beer. One man has a tin of shaving foam; he shakes it up and starts spraying, yelling at the top of his voice, white foam spurting over the pavement, the broken glass, the tram lines.*

I wrote *Before The Fire* in response to the media's vilification of young people during and after the riots. I wanted to explore the story of one young man who ends up involved in the Manchester riots for his own complicated and specific set of reasons. Again, I try to resist grand statements, but if I was trying to say anything with that novel, it was that everyone had their own story, which intersected with the riots in their own particular way.

*Jessops is smashed up, the shutters peeled back and the shelves stripped bare. The ground outside HMV is littered with CDs and broken plastic cases. Down by Topman, a handful of police officers in riot gear stand, the visors raised on their helmets like they are taking a break from welding.*

*Miss Selfridge is on fire. Flames surging out of the shop window, gushing black smoke up over the bricks into the cool early-evening sky. Groups of people stand and watch, the blaze repeated over and over again on tiny phone screens held up to catch the action.*

The geographer Steve Pile suggested to me that perhaps there might be such a thing as 'riot space' – a space which superseded the specific places where the 2011 riots happened. A kind of non-space, where Manchester was folded into Bristol was folded into Leicester was folded in Wolverhampton was folded into London. And all these spaces were repeated over and again on television, social media, in newspapers; so this riot space is not only concrete, but also narrative, verbal, fictional and institutional. A space that

## Destruction

is remade each time we reperform and reproduce the riots through language, court sentences, documentaries and stories.

The riots began with a specific set of circumstances in Tottenham – the shooting of Mark Duggan, the poor police-handling of a peaceful protest – but by the time they had spread as far as Manchester, geography seemed to be less important. Yes, specific circumstances affected the exact nature of the riots in each place (the Salford riots were seen as organised and criminal, the Manchester riots as opportunistic), but for that night it was as though Manchester had stopped being Manchester – turned instead into a film set; a nightmare (or dream, depending on your viewpoint) – a dystopic, imagined place.

*The Arndale Centre. A crowd of people by the locked doors, trying to kick their way in. The glass holds as long as it can, but they don't give up until they're in – lifting the broken glass like a curtain to slip inside.*

I sit writing this and realise it is the anniversary of the riots. Seven years on and it is as though they never happened. Deleted from our collective memory and narrative. They don't fit. They are uncomfortable to think about. We have Brexit to worry about now – never mind that the riots showed the country's deep divisions and anger long before the referendum was on the table, and I would argue that ignoring the individual stories that underpinned the riots paved the way for the referendum's result. Have they changed the city? I'd argue not – though perhaps it would be better for all of us if they had.

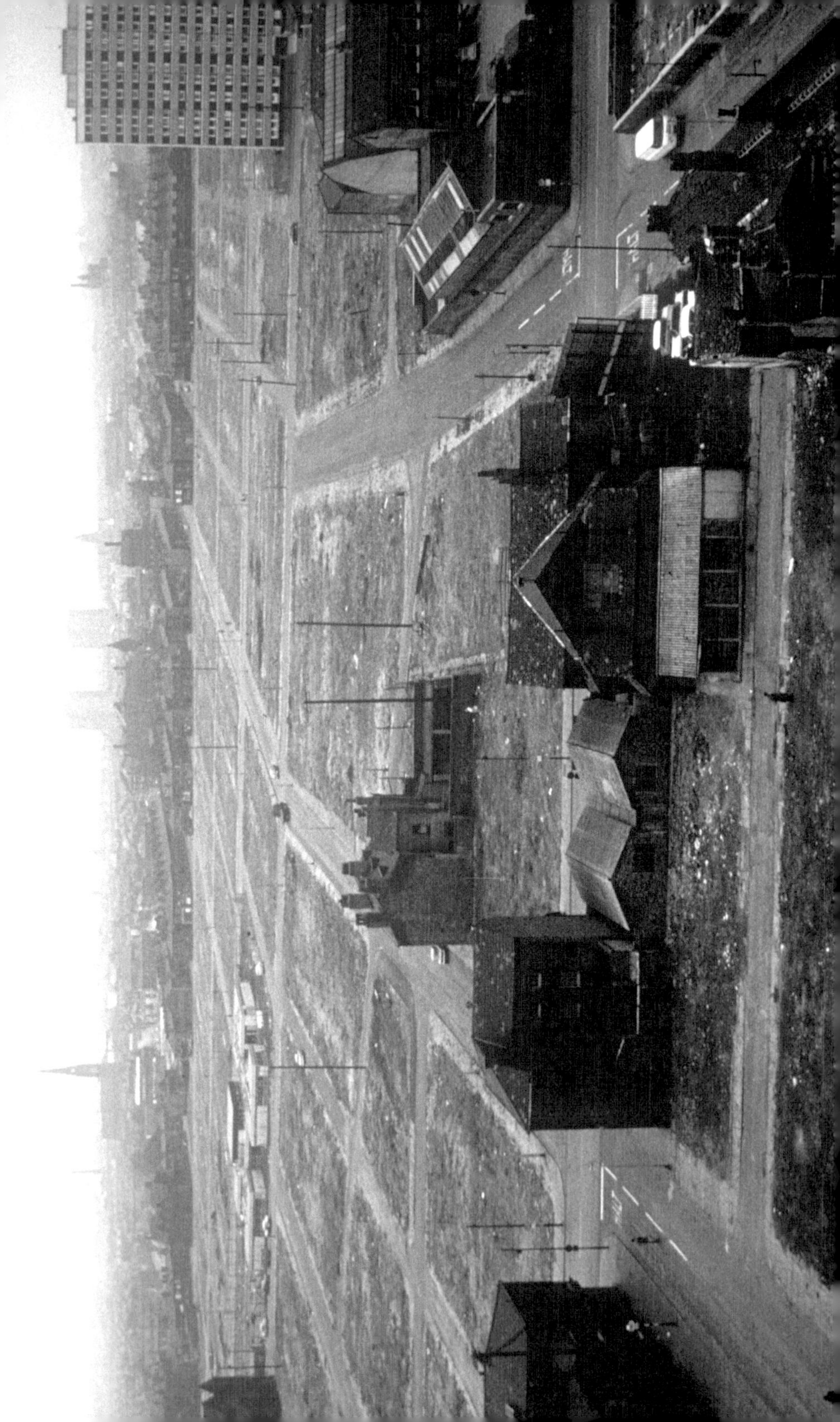

## Destruction

## *Atom* – Steve Hanson

This late 1960s image of Hulme is so powerful. The Victorian houses in the image are long gone, but so are the Hulme Crescents which replaced them in the early 1970s. The overstated story that Manchester is a co-operative city full of socialist radicals has a flipside: that Manchester's real revolution was industrial, not political.

Friedrich Engels, in the 1840s, in his father's factories, saw men referring to other men as 'hands', and doing so to their faces. When he saw this he noted the conditions that forced socialism, co-operativism and trade unionism to the surface of social life in Manchester. The emerging proletariat had to be atomised in the urban environments first, in order to be forced into new patterns of political togetherness. Industrialism came before, not the politics that opposed its uprooting effects.

The story of the atom in Manchester, then, is first the story of social atomisation. They might have been packed together in factories but they could not hear each other and were effectively atomised by the division of labour. They no longer owned a 'craft', although this has been overstated, as the machine loom took skill to operate and maintain. It is poetic, then, that Manchester's other story as 'a city of science' often reproduces the trope of the city as the place where the atom was first split. It is also poetic that John Cockroft's contribution to the process, creating particle colliders, drew on his skills wiring his parents' factory waterwheel up to dynamos. Cockroft took his entrance examination for Cambridge in 1914, the day before Archduke Ferdinand was shot in Sarajevo. Later, he studied under Ernest Rutherford, taking part in research which irrevocably changed the face of the world.

**76** (Opposite) View across Hulme showing areas cleared for redevelopment – taken from the extension to the Manchester College of Art and Design (the current Chatham Building) around 1966

## Manchester: Something rich and strange

The move into the nuclear age can be tracked through a couple of generations and one family, on this site. Clearly this is an exceptional situation, but it gives an indication of the extent to which all that is solid did melt here during late modernity. On the wall of the Rutherford Building at the University of Manchester is the Latin motto *Arduus ad solem* ('Striving towards the sun'). This Enlightenment credo refers to several myths – for instance, that of Icarus, who flew towards the sun and fell as the wax in his wings melted. Also lurking on this spot is Mary Shelley's Frankenstein: 'Rutherford's room', in Manchester University, has been investigated, as, in the past, some of those who inhabited offices above, below, and to the sides, died of cancer. In this we can read another old and strong myth related to Victor Frankenstein – that of Prometheus. In the 1980s, Manchester had many signs boasting that it was a 'nuclear-free city'. All but one of these signs have now disappeared, and the Peace Gardens, where the first Occupy camp in Britain was sited in 2011, have vanished. The 'nuclear-free city' signs can be viewed as a series of repeated alibis at the surface of the city – ones that have since receded.

If we could psychoanalyse a city, it would be tempting to suggest that these signs were symptoms of collective guilt, yet hubris is almost always given as the dominant characteristic of Manchester. The 'nuclear-free city' sign was an alibi. These alibis begin with John Cockroft's naive belief that nuclear energy would end all wars and bring world peace. Here was a man who lived only in the theoretical realm. Here was a man who popped into the University of Manchester to pick up some papers, then forgot all about his car and his wife waiting in it, before getting the train home. This is how the world really was changed here in Manchester – by anonymous-looking, distracted men. Scientists, industrialists, economists and capitalists, and they brought the whole world to the brink we are now facing.

Many other texts relating to Manchester, from research on male isolation, to records by The Smiths and Joy Division, still testify

## Destruction

to the city as a place of social atomisation. The shift to atomic physics has its parallel in the shift to an atomised social world. From Manchester capitalism and industrialism, to graphene – a substance that is stable only in itself; that these processes began in Manchester before spreading virally, globally, is no coincidence. John Cockroft's biography contains a vignette of his brother, who was lame in one leg. During a childhood game he missed his footing, grabbed hold of the waterwheel in the family mill, and went spinning around it, the electron around the nucleus, the individual, now on a new trajectory.

There's a strong connotation of post-war Europe to this Hulme photograph, but also of post-bomb Hiroshima. Epping Walk Bridge, the site of the famous image of Joy Division captured by Kevin Cummins in January 1979, speaks to the idea that Manchester is now a post-industrial, Cold War city. This idea has become a lightweight trope in many ways, through the simplistic idea of Joy Division as a 'post-industrial band'. This image of Hulme speaks to the violence of capitalist accumulation, the way in which it leaves so much destruction in its wake. The violent clearances seen in the image break through into new forms of capital accumulation – the cogs and gears of what we now call 'gentrification'. The Birley building of Manchester Metropolitan University sits where the Hulme Crescents once did. Birley is an atom: a self-sufficient island of high-tech energy production, with its own heat pumps and power. Only a little gas is piped in. This is more than a metaphor: Birley mirrors the ways in which the public and private have moved in this era more widely, and not just in this area. The rise of gated enclaves all around the region are a parallel phenomenon to this. In retrospect, the image that accompanies this article seems to premonitor our current urban landscapes. It is an augur. Our hyperreal spectacles of consumer individualism can be traced back to the point when the Industrial Revolution had to invent, through sheer seat-of-the-trousers necessity, 'Manchester Capitalism'. The Kevin Cummins image seemed to want to tell us that the money and will of industrialism had irrevocably thawed. But its attack was double-edged. On the one hand it is a deeply, morbidly mournful image; on the other it seems highly critical of socialist mass planning. None of this is just incidental detail. This worn photograph of Hulme, of an 'atomised' and atomising landscape, in a city that contributed a great deal to the development of the atom bomb, is for me also a cipher for atomised individualism. We may all think we are individuals now, but that is, in itself, a mass collective illusion. In this photograph of a Hulme once again caught between phases we find a rare, beautiful and terrible trace of the continuation of that idea in physical form.

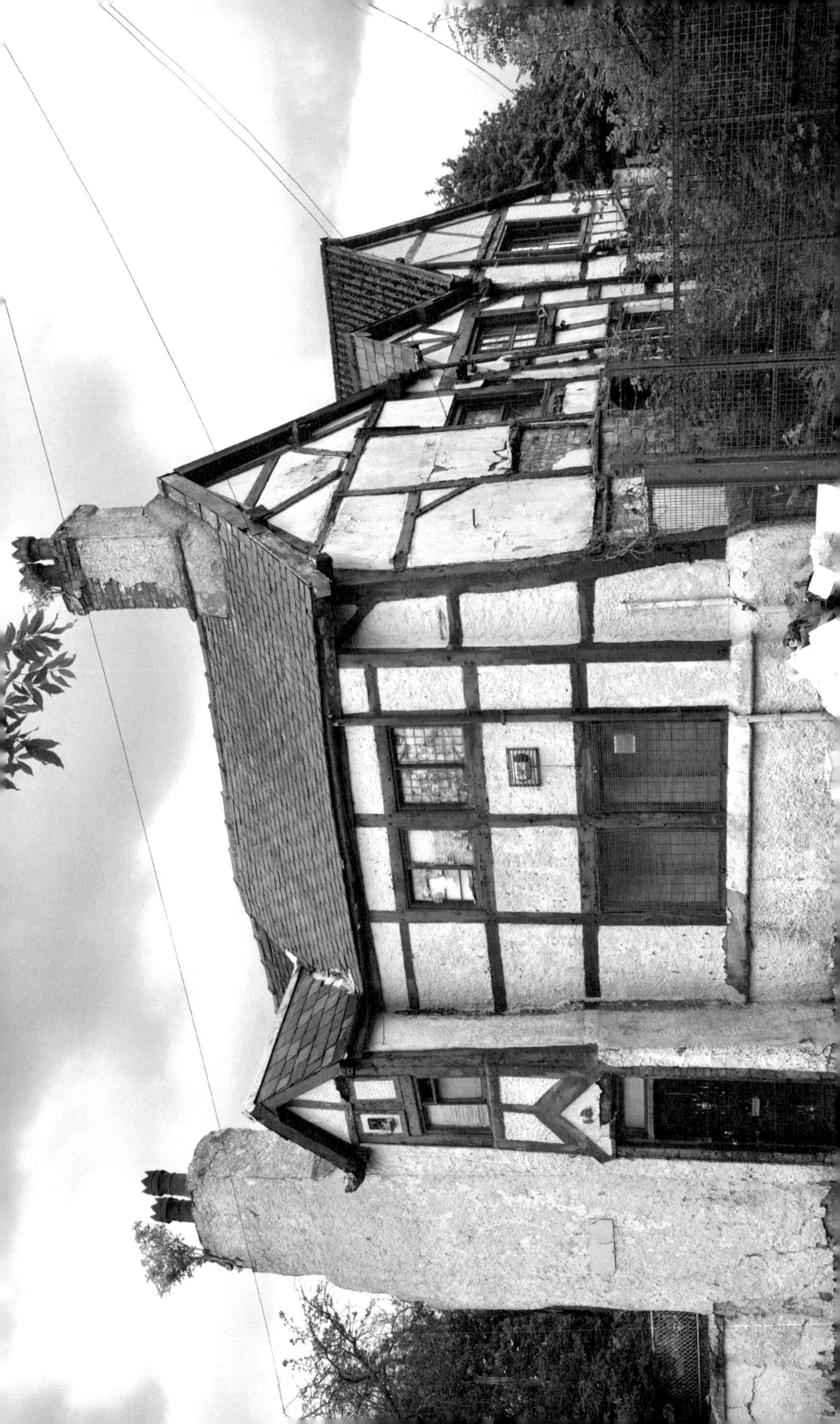

Manchester: Something rich and strange

## *Tudor* – Paul Dobraszczyk

A ubiquitous building type over the last hundred years or so in Britain is the Tudor-style house: the dream of any self-respecting middle-class aspirant; the waking nightmare of most professional architects and critics. Unlike its other revivalist cousins – neo-Georgian, Gothic Revival, neoclassical – it has never been respected enough to be called anything other than 'Mock' Tudor, as if it were an entirely imaginary style. Yet, just like any other copycat style, the Tudor refers back to a real form of architecture, or rather a type of building that characterised the period in Britain from 1485 to 1603, when the monarchy finally shed its Norman roots – and its basis in France – and, at least in the popular imagination, became fully British – namely during the reigns of Henry VII, Henry VIII and Elizabeth I.

In the Manchester region, genuine Tudor buildings cling to life precariously, long since swallowed up by either industrial buildings or, later, vast housing estates. The wrecks are all too present, often the subject of plaintive appeals from local residents or the city's newspapers. Wythenshawe Hall – a sixteenth-century timber-framed former manor house standing in splendid isolation in the middle of Wythenshawe Park – was badly damaged after a fire was deliberately started there on 15 March 2016; its fate is now uncertain, despite assurances from Manchester City Council and the charity group the Friends of Wythenshawe Hall that the building will be restored and put to public use.

Nearby is an even older building, Baguley Hall, probably built in the fourteenth century, making it one of the oldest (and pre-Tudor) medieval timber-framed halls in North West England. It stands anachronistically among Wythenshawe's endless residential streets, mostly built en masse in the 1920s and 1930s to create a

**77** (Previous page) Remains of Hough Hall in Moston in 2017

## Destruction

new garden-city suburb of Manchester (see 'Gardens', p. 272). After being used for many years by the council for storage, it was acquired by the Ministry of Public Buildings and Works in 1968 and is now in the care of English Heritage. Surrounded by a high fence and obscured by overgrown vegetation, Baguley Hall is both an obdurate survivor and poignant reminder of just how difficult it is to find new uses for old buildings, especially when their very oldness is the quality that is valued.

Sadder still is Hough Hall in Manchester's northern suburb of Moston. Probably built at the end of the sixteenth century, and long enveloped by Victorian terraces, it has been mostly empty for decades – only partially used by its last owner as a commercial business up until 2005. Today, its dilapidation is extraordinary: plaster is crumbling, accelerated by the plants that have found sustenance from it, while the distorted timber beams have none of the picturesque qualities we so admire in other surviving Tudor buildings.

Of course, there are a few celebrated Tudor buildings in Greater Manchester that have gone on to find other uses that cherish rather than resist their ancientness. Ordsall Hall in Salford, built in the fifteenth century, was sold by its long-standing owners, the Radclyffes, in 1662. It was eventually acquired by Salford Council in 1959 after centuries of use as variously a school for clergy, a working men's club and a radio station. Refurbished between 2009 and 2011, the hall is now a free museum hosting exhibitions, interactive displays and a cafe. The City of Manchester still has its most famous medieval building, Chetham's School and Library, founded in 1421 as a priests' college for the nearby Collegiate Church (now the cathedral). Dissolved by Henry VIII in 1547, Chetham's was subsequently acquired by the Stanley Family and remained in their hands until the Civil War. It has been a school since 1653 until the present day – now one of the most esteemed private music schools in Britain. But perhaps the most stubborn survivor is the Old Wellington Inn, built in 1552 and located next to the cathedral in Shambles Square. Having miraculously survived the bombs of the Luftwaffe, the pub and its seventeenth-century neighbour, Sinclair's Oyster Bar, only escaped demolition in the 1970s when they were raised up 15ft and literally lifted out of the ground. Spared once more after the IRA bomb of 1996, they were moved again to their current location as part of the more recent redevelopment of the city centre (see also 'Medieval', p. 143).

All the Tudor buildings that still stand in Greater Manchester – other examples include Clayton Hall, Bramall Hall in Stockport, Wardley Hall and Worsley Old Hall in Worsley, and Hall i' th' Wood in Bolton – survive not as the result of careful preservation, but because new uses have been found for them in the face of destruction or redundancy. Because they are of relatively simple construction – brick, timber and plaster – and organic in their evolution, Tudor buildings are eminently adaptable, even as this inevitably leads to the loss of their authentic architectural identity. Indeed, it could be argued that nearly all Tudor buildings that survive are 'Mock' Tudor, bastardised by centuries of adaptation. And even those buildings that are seemingly irrevocably lost – like Hulme Hall, which was demolished in 1840 to make way for the Bridgewater Canal – live on in other ways: the building's fifteenth-century carved oak panels were saved and rehoused in Worsley Old Hall, later to be transferred to the new home of the local landowners, the Egerton family.

Back in 1972, when Hough Hall was scheduled for demolition under a compulsory purchase order, local residents organised a one-off festival to demonstrate their resistance to the council's plans – children made Tudor costumes and walked around the market on Moston Lane enlisting support from shoppers.[2] Today, children are encouraged to dress up in Tudor costumes in both Ordsall and Bramall Hall, and, on a visit to Ordsall, my daughter willingly obliged by donning chain mail. The recent popularity of Tudor histories – perhaps most notably the BBC series *Wolf Hall* (2015) and *The Tudors* (2007–10) – with all their sensational sexual

### Destruction

and political intrigues and lavish costume design, demonstrate that the appeal of the Tudors is most definitely not limited to children. In the popular imagination, Tudor buildings and their inhabitants signal a golden age in British history – a time when the elusive but much-coveted notion of Britishness revealed itself most strongly. Of course, this is mostly a myth, and a dangerously seductive one at that in these post-Brexit times; but perhaps we can at least celebrate Tudor architecture for its exemplary adaptability – its seeming ability to be moulded into any shape, its very lack of authenticity its greatest strength.

### Notes

1  The italicised parts of this chapter are edited extracts from Sarah Butler, *Before The Fire* (London: Picador, 2015).
2  See www.manchestereveningnews.co.uk/news/local-news/save-hough-hall-1147451.

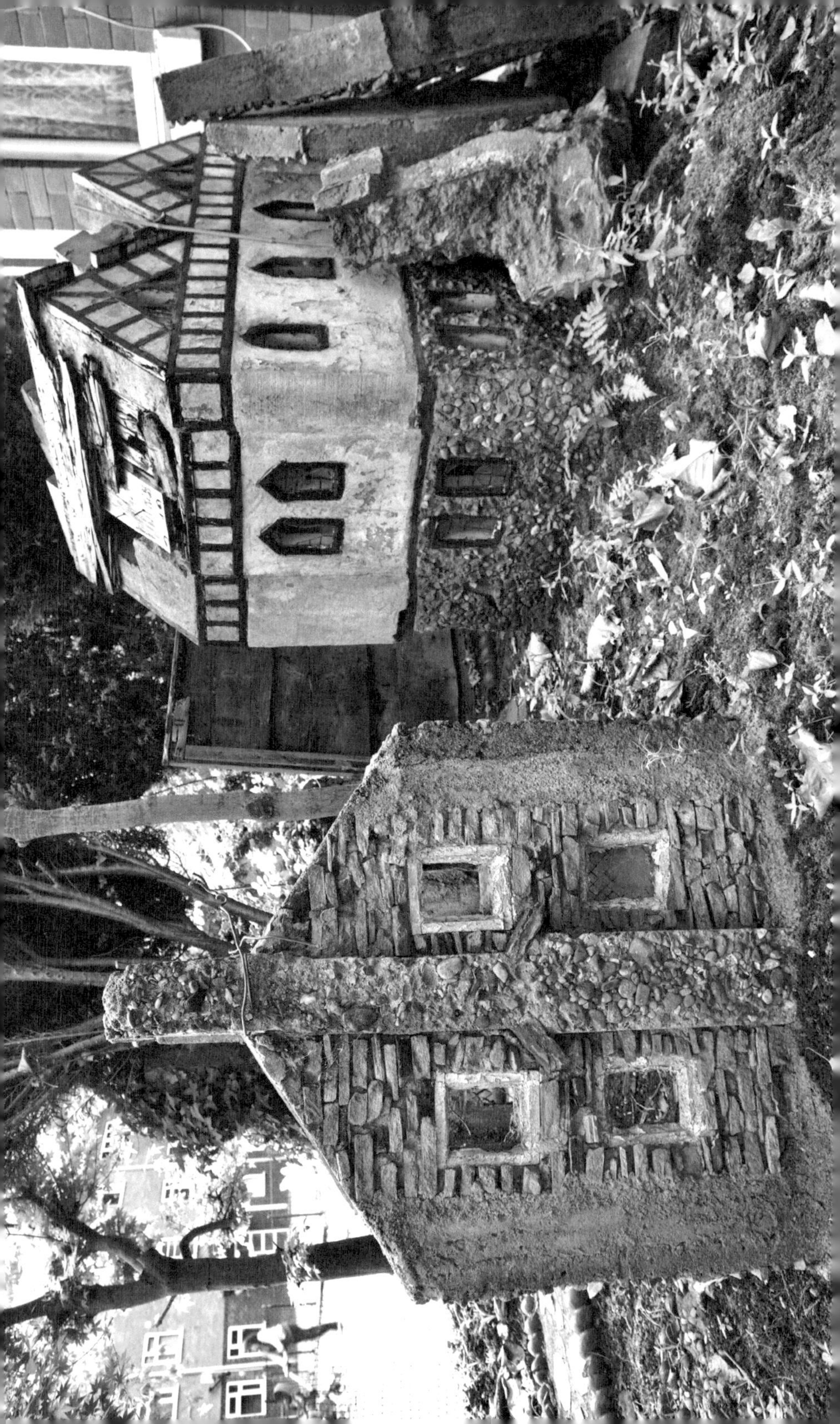

# Home

It's nice to be out in the morning
When you've got somewhere to go
But seeing the same old faces
That can make you feel so low
Ardwick Green where the grass is grey
Beswick, Hulme, and Harpurhey
Whalley Range where the tomcats roam
They're not the sights of Rome
But it's home
    Herman's Hermits, 'It's Nice to be Out in the Morning', 1968

How do we find and make a home in the city? It is not simply a matter of housing (though that is as hot a topic in Manchester as elsewhere) but also of identity, belonging, connection, community – something you might find in a laundrette, a mosque or a city park as much as within the four walls of a flat or house.

Home is anything but a straightforward concept. We tend to associate it with safety, comfort and stability, but it can also be a place of violence, abuse and uncertainty. And its counterpoint, of course, is homelessness, a problem that has become more and

**78** (Opposite) Ruins of a miniature village made by Alan Teague in his garden at 380 Slade Lane, Levenshulme, from the 1970s onwards (the remains were removed in 2017)

more visible, particularly in Manchester's city centre, over recent years, as Steve Hanson documents. As well as those sleeping on the streets, Manchester has a vast and often hidden homeless population occupying low-quality unsupported temporary accommodation, as Sarah Butler explores in 'B&B'.

On becoming the first elected Mayor of Greater Manchester in 2017, Andy Burnham pledged to end homelessness in Manchester and declared he would donate 15 per cent of his mayoral salary to a new homelessness charity. It is a knotty and complex problem however, and sometimes the rise of luxury towers and lack of affordable housing in Manchester's centre seems to mock Burnham's aspirations.

Manchester is a city of migrants who have made it their home, who have been shaped by the city and have in turn shaped it – from Rusholme's 'curry mile' to the shops and businesses of Cheetham Hill and Longsight. As Jonathan Silver points out in 'Synagogue', and Qaisra Shahraz discusses in 'Immigrant', we should be wary of ignoring the moments of violence and racism which have stained the city's past and present. However, Manchester is a city which prides itself on its diversity and togetherness, something brought to the fore after the Arena terror attack of 2017.

How and where we feel at home in Manchester's spaces will vary from person to person, but it is without a doubt a city that generates a fierce sense of pride and belonging in its inhabitants, old and new. To claim the moniker Mancunian is to align oneself with the city's history of innovation, rebellion and perseverance. A complex, contested home, it might be, but it is a home all the same.

**79** A rough sleeper outside a bank in Piccadilly Gardens

## *Homeless* – Steve Hanson

The Town Hall homeless protest camp was set up on 15 April 2015, when around thirty protesters camped outside Manchester's most important civic building. There were articles expressing solidarity in the Salford *Star* and support from various groups, as well as the comments of the controversial figure Sir Richard Leese, long-term leader of Manchester City Council, who expressed his view that chalk graffiti drawn on the Albert Memorial by the protestors 'just demonstrates these people have no respect for the city, or the people who live in it'. His hawkish comments are still noted in Manchester left-wing circles.

Anna Baum has provided an overview of the context for the Manchester homeless camps. She explains that 'the town hall cut homelessness funding, including to the city's flagship Booth Centre project, by £2m in 2015'.

The city's case for clearing the camps was that 'the continued occupation of these sites' might 'present a health and safety risk', in the context of 'the proximity of the camp to the public highway and the lack of facilities available', that 'prevents or deters members of the public from the use of the land'.[1]

The use of 'health and safety risk' as a tool to socially cleanse the homeless camp is notable, as Leese is a Labour politician, and health and safety legislation has long been part of the repertoire of Labour resistance, emerging from trade-union activism.

The point to be made here is that the strategy itself makes no guarantee for its ethical application. On 27 April 2015, an injunction was served for the protestors to move from the Town Hall. Baum comments that the 'protest camps reveal how systems of social cleansing work'. The details of this system seem to be right on the surface here, all the bare wires showing:

A Mr Walthall, representing the council, said 'there is no running water, no washing facilities and no toilets. This presents a health and safety hazard.' He also said the 'camp's position prevented the public's right to walk in the square'. Yet, as Baum points out, 'Mr Walthall, and the austerity agenda, are condemning these people to live without these facilities on a daily basis.'[2] The encampment in St Ann's Square was tucked into the centre and had no real pedestrian access issues. At these points, nineteenth-century stigma and the 'unwashed masses' rise from the cultural unconscious, for which Judith Walkowitz's work is a crucial touchstone.[3]

Between 5–6 May, Manchester Council banned homeless people from using the library. The library claimed that the protestors were 'attempting to occupy' the building, as the camp 'claimed equal rights to use the facilities'. G4S security were employed to deal with the situation. The homeless were refused access to toilet facilities in the library. On 7 May, the camp won the right to stay another week at the Town Hall site.

On 19 May, the St Peter's Square eviction was executed. Bailiffs came at 8 am, some occupants were already packed, others attempted non-violent resistance. The BBC showed photos of protesters in masks. On the same day, the group set up camp in St Ann's Square. On 25 May, the Spring Festival of Markets was moved due to the occupation.

An injunction was then posted in St Ann's Square, specifically against the establishment of a 'protest camp'. In response, the camp removed all of its protest banners and waited for whatever would come next. Being homeless is tolerated, but organising as the homeless is now criminalised. This camp was then controversially cleared, and the council put all the sleeping bags from this occupation into a skip. Rumours suggest they were burned.

This point is not just interesting incidental detail; it is a main political juncture. When the focal centres of city neoliberal governance are disrupted by those who are not part of its programme – consumption, tourism, spectacle – they are cleared from those spectacular surfaces, as key events have to be relocated due to the occupations.

## Manchester: Something rich and strange

In St Ann's Square, glasses of prosecco were being drunk in full view of the homeless camp, as Manchester City Council worked elsewhere on an injunction to remove them from the surface of this consumerist space. Challenges by local group Manchester Left Writers to Cllr Nigel Murphy's involvement in the clearing of the space remain unanswered. The sick, bleak irony of a ban on tents in a city centre now full of them, and serving expensive food and drink, is on one level a polemical point, but on another it represents the wider income gap in Britain. It also shows Manchester to be what the late Rosemary Mellor described in 2002 as a 'hypocritical city'. Mellor's comments have only become more acute over the years and are backed up by the damning Centre for Research on Socio-Cultural Change/London School of Economics report on Manchester in 2016.

The homeless protesters were denied legal aid in their court battle with the city council, and the council eventually won an injunction to ban the protesters from camping anywhere in the centre of Manchester. The court's decision means 'anyone who erects a tent in the city centre without permission from the council could face up to two years in prison'.[4]

The St Ann's Square homeless camp became particularly loaded against the backdrop of the Dig the City and Manchester Jazz Festival. These breezy summertime celebrations in the city centre suddenly had a very visible sign of their opposite, and in the 'independent food and artisan crafts' market that was relocated, we see 'The Hipster' reflected. That largely vilified, contested figure seems to personify these contradictions and tensions at an iconic level. The hideous logic of strivers and skivers on national television, in the form of *Dragon's Den* and *Benefits Street*, are two further sides of this cultural issue in Britain, with skivers on one side and strivers on the other.

It is also important to point out that ethnocentrism has not been suddenly solved in these 'cosmopolitan' spaces, and that we simply need to 'deal with' class equality and economic privilege – because the other event mirroring this one in St Ann's Square in July 2015 was the so-called 'Calais Crisis'. BBC reports bellowed about how Britain's economy was 'booming' and 'these people' wanted to break into that, from Europe and elsewhere. In St Ann's Square, we could see the 'economically necessary' figures, the excluded of consumer capital, emerging from their tents from time to time.

Later, an almost favela-sized encampment by Piccadilly station was eventually cleared. Some of the tents could later be seen down towards Ardwick Green; these were tolerated, but the spectacle could not be interrupted. Visitors disembarking from trains and heading to taxi ranks would not see the reality of Manchester's homeless population. The same was true of the encampment by Manchester Metropolitan University under the Mancunian Way on Oxford Road, known as The Ark – it was cleared before freshers' week. Later, this space became a cool centre of consumption known as Hatch. Its Brick Lane aesthetics and hip container units are geared to making money from the student population.

This is just the recent pre-history of the Manchester homeless situation. The number of homeless rose by 40 per cent in one twelve-month period, and Manchester currently has the highest number of deaths of homeless people in the country.

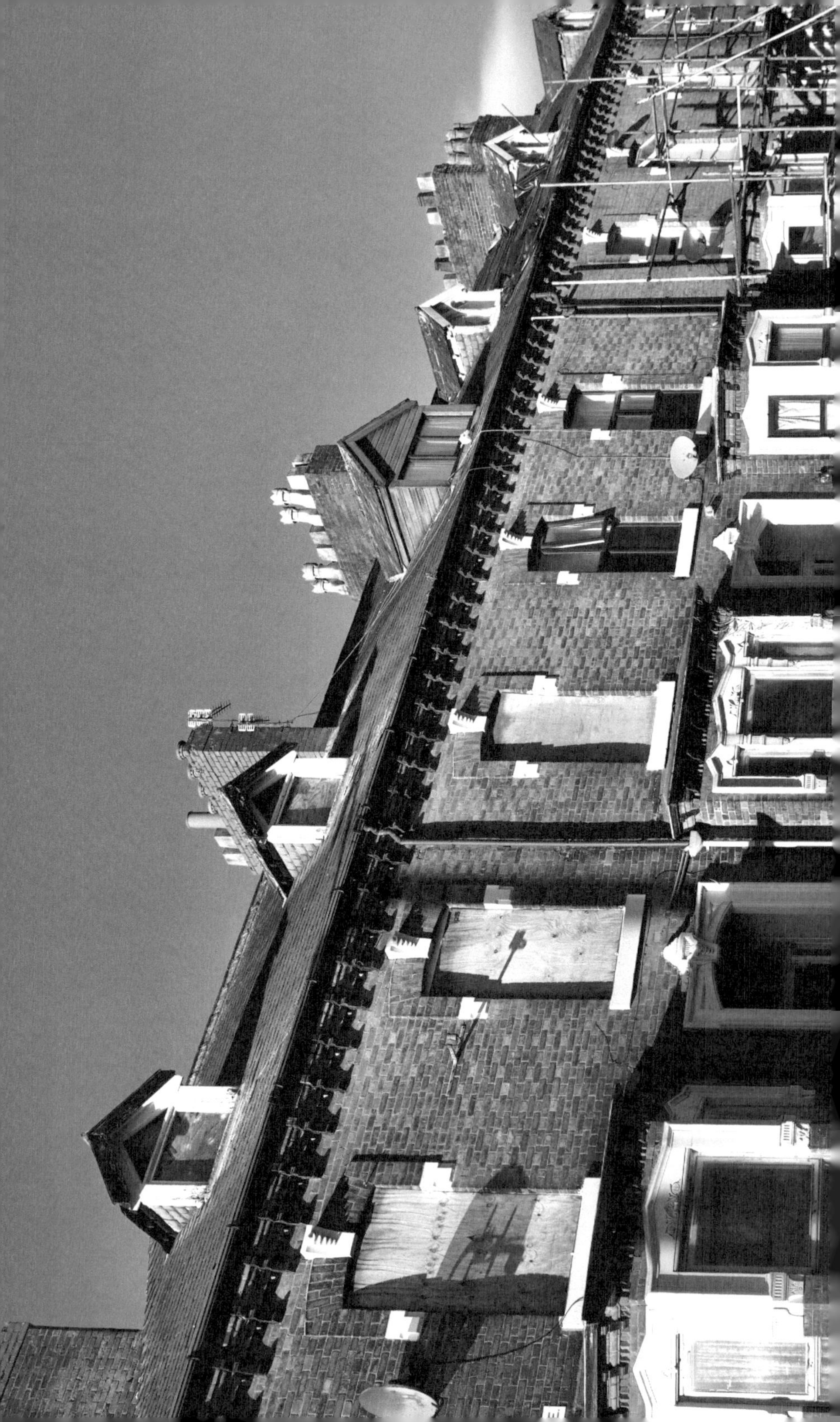

# Home

## *B&B* – Sarah Butler

East Manchester. A once-grand Victorian terrace. Bay windows. Elegant chimney stacks. Brick detailing. Four houses are boarded-up, smoke-damage blackening the walls of one; the front gardens left to grow wild. Most of these houses are B&Bs. Not the kind you might be familiar with. They aren't listed on tourist websites. There are no signs outside; no flyers with local attractions on the bedside tables; no daily cleaning or fresh towels. These are places of last resort.

### *Bedroom*

*I could stand in the room and touch both sides. It was filthy. You could literally push the door in. The three walls of my room were plasterboard, painted. So you can hear them breathing next door. You can hear everything, smell everything, it's horrible, man.* – Stuart[5]

It's as though the walls are made of paper. Every time someone walks past they shake. Every time someone in the next room breathes, or farts, or coughs, he can hear it. The carpet's brown, dirt and hair locked into its pile. By the bed there's a burn mark the size of a dinner plate, the synthetic fibres melted into black lumps. There's nothing in here save a single bed; a sink with a mirror tile screwed off-kilter to the wall above it; a chest of drawers meant for a kid's bedroom. It smells of damp and old fags and feet and something else he'd rather not think about – something rotten.

It's estimated that over 70,000 individuals and families[6] live in unsupported temporary accommodation across England, 50,000 of those in B&Bs – temporary, insecure, substandard housing which has a drastic impact on residents' mental and physical health.

**80** (Opposite) Unsupported temporary accommodation in Openshaw

Residents experience increased anxiety, higher drug and alcohol use, increased social isolation and risk of premature death. They share filthy bathroom facilities, regularly out of order; often have no access to cooking facilities and often feel harassed and intimidated by other residents and in some cases by the management.[7] There are approximately 500 individuals and families living in B&Bs in Manchester, and an estimated 1,200 in Greater Manchester.

### Dining room

*I can't have the breakfasts there because my cholesterol's up here. He just slaps it in the pan. Two eggs. Two bacon. It's all grease though. I put some weight on eating all that for two months. I said to him, can I use the kitchen? No, he locks it up.* – Frank

He has to pay a top-up – thirty-five quid every two weeks – and what for, he'd like to ask. An hour's heating a day and the grottiest breakfast you can imagine. His cholesterol's through the roof as it is, without a sea of grease every morning. Cheap bacon, cheap sausages, fried in cheap oil. Cheap beans, cheap bread – the kind that bungs you up if you eat too much of it. He shouldn't complain – there's people with no food to talk of, but it gets him down all the same. He walks past those Northern Quarter cafes sometimes – sees people with their French toast and smoked salmon, their poached eggs and sourdough bread – and he can't decide if it makes him angry or sad.

In 1972, Shelter widened their traditional definition of homelessness, stating that a person was homeless if they lived in 'conditions so bad that a civilised family life is impossible'.[8] Charities have been campaigning for the hidden population living in unsupported temporary accommodation to be recognised as homeless, and for the role of unsupported temporary accommodation in the homelessness 'system' to be recognised in legislation, policy and initiatives aimed at reducing or ending homelessness.

# Home

## *Outside*

*I'm never there. I'm always out. I just go out for a walk. I hate it there. It does my head in.* – Suni

He goes out, not because he has somewhere to go but because he can't stand to be in that place. He walks. Mooches. Goes down the canal, or follows the bus route to Ashton, Beswick, Piccadilly. Even walking in Manchester rain is better than being in there. He got given a coat at one of the churches and it keeps the worst of it off. He does the rounds of the places – Tuesday pies in Openshaw, Thursday soup in Hulme, Sunday lunch in Ancoats.

There are places to go. There are people trying to help. Justlife was formed in 2008 to actively reach out to the residents of Manchester's homeless B&Bs: building trust, gathering help, working and campaigning for transformation. Its name came from a desire to change the despair and acceptance repeated over and over again by residents to the charity's founders: 'It's just life.' Over the past three years, Justlife has helped over 2,000 hidden homeless individuals living in unsupported temporary accommodation.

## *Bathroom*

*I couldn't have a shower in that place. I have a stick and there were no bars to hold onto, so I couldn't stand up, and it was dirty. I had a sink in my room. That's all I had to clean myself.* – Charles

The place has got three bathrooms, but there's only one shower working and he has to wait an hour and half before he can get in. It's small – cold and dank with a crap shower over a narrow bath; sink grimed with dirt; shit-smeared toilet. There's a window, but someone's covered it with a bedsheet. It feels like showering in a tomb.

It's January, but the heating's only on for an hour in the afternoons, so he's wearing as many clothes as he can: two jumpers, jeans, a jacket, scarf, three pairs of socks. He's brought a plastic bag to shove his clothes in so they won't touch anything. He undresses, keeping his socks on until the last minute, trying not to look at the floor, or the grime in the bath, or the stains on the tiles, or the mould on the walls. He tries not to think about how cold the water will be. He tries not to think.

20

Cossell Fletcher

# Manchester: Something rich and strange

## *Synagogue* – Jonathan Silver

Walking down a street in Broughton in the winter sunshine of early 2019, a construction site is visible next to a school. Much of the structure remains hidden by the scaffold. However, at the sides, part of the new building protrudes and hints at an architectural style that is quite different to the surrounding suburban homes. And a render of the completed building, on a panel fronting the site, lets passers-by see its final form. The new synagogue, completed in late 2019, holds a remarkable story that unfolds from its striking similarity to a building hundreds of miles away in western Ukraine. It will become an important site of remembrance, celebration and everyday life for the Chortkov Hassidic dynasty.

Chortkov, or Czortków as it is known in Polish, was located in the Galician province of the Austro-Hungarian Empire before becoming a part of Poland in the interwar years, and is now located in western Ukraine. It was an important centre for Hassidism, through the Chortkov Hasidic dynasty established in 1865 by the first Rebbe of Chortkov, Rabbi Duvid Moshe Friedman, a major figure in Central Eastern European Jewry. By the time the Second World War broke out, many of the 6,000 Jews in the town faced an uncertain future. The leader, Rabbi Nochum, managed to flee before the German army arrived, but many of the dynasty's followers did not. From 1941, the Nazis had turned a part of the town into a ghetto and Jews were murdered in mass shootings or sent to labour camps. This genocide continued into August 1942, when the ghetto was surrounded and 300 Jews were shot on the streets in an orgy of murder. Another 3,000 were put on trains and sent to the horrors of the Belzec extermination camp. By the time of

**81** (Previous page) Construction of a new synagogue in Broughton, Salford, in January 2019

liberation by Soviet forces, only 100 Jews in the town were thought to have survived.⁹

Remarkably, the dynasty continued, now co-led by Rabbi Yisroel Friedman, the Rav of the Chortkover Kloiz, who has made his home in Salford. The story connected to this new building in Salford offers a stark reminder of the violence visited upon Jews and their religious buildings, of the power of architecture to convey histories of places far beyond their location and, of course, the remarkable story of the survival of the Chortkov dynasty, and the sanctuary provided to new arrivals in areas such as Broughton. The violence visited upon the Jews of Chortkov, and their survival, has found a resonance in the built environment and prompts us to consider further the ways in which synagogues bear witness to violence against the Jewish population in the conurbation.

The history of Manchester's Jewry began in the 1770s with various visiting merchants, but the population remained small primarily because the city 'could not compete for security with Liverpool, where tolerance to Jews was longstanding'.¹⁰ Those who met in the Manchester Hebrew Congregation in a Garden Street warehouse from 1796 never exceeded 100 persons. The hostile environment for Jews in Manchester, prompted by general anti-Semitism and the suspicions of manufacturers having their secrets stolen, accelerated during the Napoleonic Wars and the Aliens Act of 1793. After the war, Manchester became less xenophobic and the community began to develop. By August 1824, construction began on a synagogue in the Old Town in the courtyard of the Lamb Inn on Toad Lane.

The Manchester Reform Synagogue, founded on Park Place in 1858 by German-Jewish migrants, was described as the 'cathedral' of Manchester's Jewish population in Cheetham Hill. It was bombed during the Manchester Blitz of 1 June 1941 as waves of German aircraft attacked the city. The building, alongside many treasured records and possessions, was destroyed. The synagogue subsequently moved to central Manchester on Lloyd Street, opening in 1953.

After the horrors of the Luftwaffe's bombs, and despite growing public awareness of the Holocaust and extermination camps such as Belzec, Manchester's synagogues continued to experience violence. The 1947 pogrom against Jews is a forgotten episode in the history of a city that considers itself a friendly and welcoming metropolis. On Friday 1 August 1947, disturbances were experienced across Britain. The origins of these attacks were rooted in the geopolitics of the Palestine Mandate and growing attacks by Zionist militants against the British. The hanging of two British soldiers by the Irgun terrorist group provided a spark that led to anti-Jewish attacks in Liverpool, Leicester, Hull and London. By Sunday the violence had spread to Manchester's Cheetham Hill district. An angry mob attacked the Great Synagogue, tearing down the canopy before surrounding a dancehall in which a wedding celebration was taking place, chanting 'Death to the Jews'.[11] Walter Lever, a local Jewish resident, wrote that on Cheetham Hill Road:

> Someone here and someone there thought it would be a good idea to show the Jews what real Englishmen thought of them. They found stones and brickbats, and flung them at shop windows and private houses, at synagogues and club rooms … All premises belonging to Jews for the length of a mile down the street had gaping windows and the pavements were littered with glass.[12]

The violence visited upon Manchester's synagogues remains visible in recent years and seems to be a sad constant in the city. In 2016, a man was arrested in Prestwich threatening worshippers as he took an axe out of his car; in 2017, a man leaving a synagogue was threatened with murder and a stone was thrown through the window of another. Other incidents include arson attacks on Jewish restaurants in 2017 and a spate of attacks on Jewish cemeteries. Meanwhile, everyday racism amounted to 200 separate incidents in 2016 alone.[13] Synagogues across Greater Manchester,

# Home

a conurbation that houses the largest Jewish population outside London, are places of spirituality, community, love and celebration stretching back to the first such (temporary) space in 1786 on Ainsworth Court, Long Millgate. But they are also sites which carry and convey, navigate and experience, the violence of anti-Semitism both near and far – a reminder to Mancunians never to forget that this ancient hatred remains alive in the city.

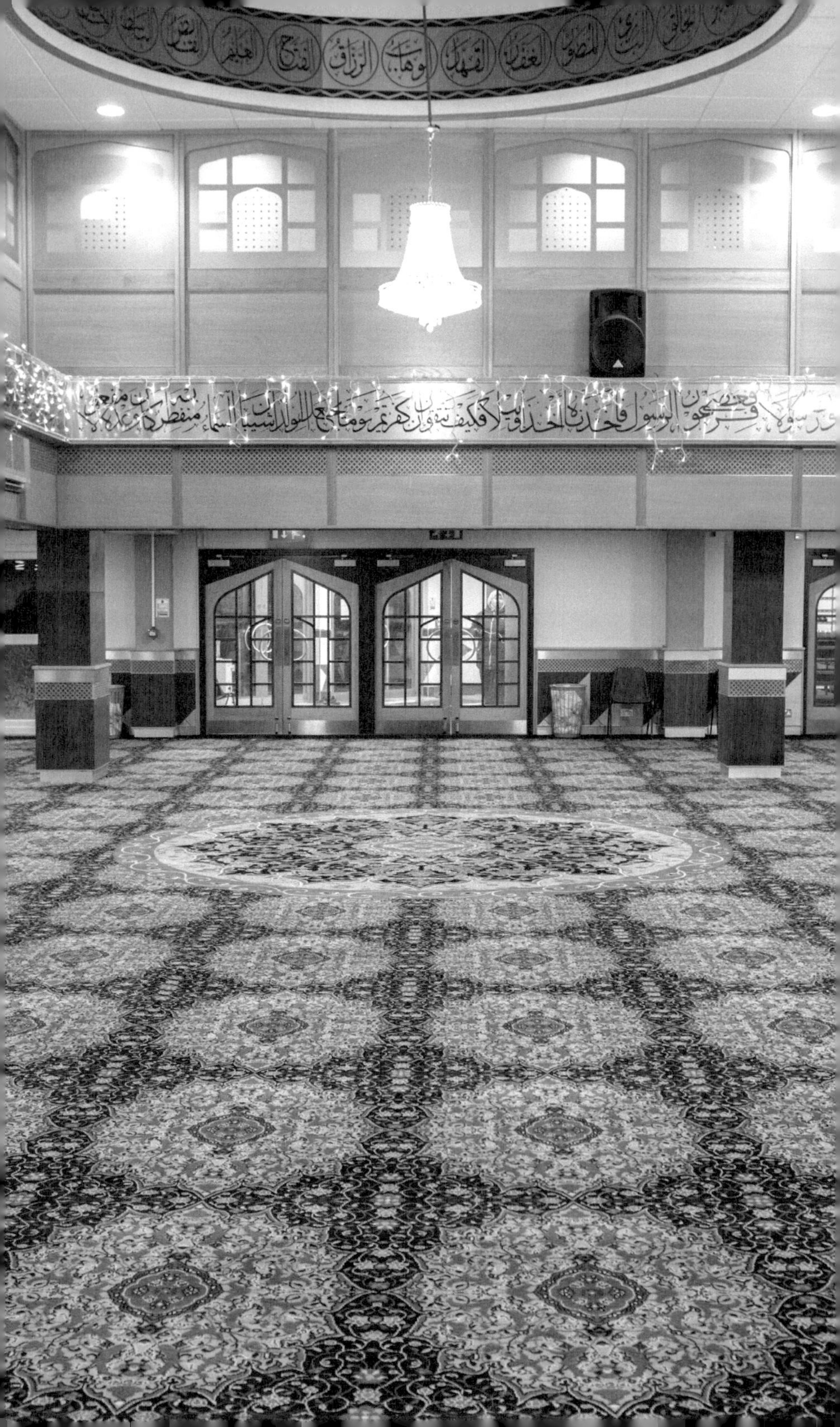

## Mosque – Qaisra Shahraz

Like a synagogue, a mosque is also a place of worship. No matter where it is, a mosque is the heart and hub of a Muslim community. It might be a small place consisting of just two simple rooms, a prayer room or a meeting place, and a bathroom for ablutions. Or it could be a large purpose-built building, able to accommodate hundreds of people. As prayer (*salah* in Arabic) is one of the five pillars of Islam, a place to pray together is a basic necessity.

Manchester Central Mosque, or the Jamia Mosque as it's popularly known, was the first mosque to be built in Manchester. Starting its life as a semi-detached house purchased by Manchester's Muslim community in 1948, it was reconstructed as a purpose-built mosque in 1970. It has become a famous landmark in the leafy inner suburb of Victoria Park, and is two streets away from the lively Curry Mile in Rusholme. For three decades it was the largest central mosque for the city's Muslim community, which is predominantly of Pakistani origin. For much of my own life it was my local place of worship. It is the place where my deceased mother was given a special ceremonial bath known as *ghusl* before her burial, and also where her funeral *Janaza* prayers took place in the presence of hundreds of people, including family members, friends, relatives and well-wishers from across the UK.

Mosques are not only places of worship; they also provide spaces for meetings, social activities, lectures, seminars, community and youth events, Eid festival prayers and celebrations, wedding ceremonies (*Nikah*), and religious education for children and adults. Their doors are always open, especially during the month of Ramadan, for everyone including students and travellers visiting the city. Yet, since the terrorist attack on the Christchurch

**82** (Opposite) Interior of the Manchester Central Mosque in Rusholme

mosque in New Zealand, these buildings are having to become more secure in order to protect worshippers.

For me, the best time of the year to visit a mosque is during Ramadan, when late-evening prayers called *tarawih* are offered while men and women listen to recitations from the Holy Quran. All mosques try to read the entire Quran; the imams (known as *hafiz* if they have memorised all of the text) recite it, and they can be either men or women. Each evening, two *huffaz* take it in turn to recite a whole chapter of the Quran as part of the prayers. It's clearly hard work to memorise such long passages, but it's also exciting to be one of the worshippers.

There is a special atmosphere in a mosque during Ramadan. Then, mosques are open to the public offering evening meals, which are free, so that guests, including students away from their families, can break their fast or just join in gatherings and eat together. As hospitality is at the heart of Islamic etiquette, so feeding people during Ramadan is reckoned to be an especially good deed. In Manchester, many Muslim charities become very active during this month offering the fast-breaking meal in Piccadilly Gardens and on the campus of the University of Manchester, not only to Muslims, but also to feed the homeless.

I also enjoy visiting the mosque on the special spiritual night of the twenty-seventh fast. On this night, I join other women in prayers and listen to the *khotbah*, which is the imam's special spiritual lecture, and the next morning we have our breakfast (*sehri* in Arabic) to begin the day's fast.

It is not mandatory for women to pray in the mosque in the way it is for men. However, there are special rooms set aside in which women can pray. Many non-Muslims view this as a form of segregation, yet it is similar to the practise in Orthodox Jewish synagogues and is not a form of discrimination against women. Rather, it is simply to give women privacy and space to themselves. With the prayer sequence involving much physical activity – rising and prostrating on the ground – I prefer to pray standing beside other women. I would not feel comfortable standing next to a man while praying. Prayers require attention, without being distracted by who is standing near us.

Many women are and have been at the forefront of building, managing and financing mosques. My own mother, for example, had a mosque rebuilt in her home town of Gujrat in Pakistan. She contributed to both the funding for the entire building and also the design of the rooms, tiles and carpets. And centuries ago, Fatima al-Fihri founded and funded a place of learning for children and adults in ninth-century Fes, Morocco, a madrasa that would later became the first university in the world – the University of Al-Karaouine in 859 CE.

In Muslim countries, mosques are traditional centres for art-making, whether painting geometric patterns on tiles, using calligraphy for the writing of the Holy Quran, architecture, carpet-weaving or lantern-making. Mosques are manifestations and reflections of a country's artistic heritage. Hence, the architecture of the mosques I have visited in other places, whether in China, Pakistan, India, Turkey, Germany, Spain or the UAE, is dictated by local taste, materials, skills of the artisans and designs. For example, I noted the preference for the rich blue colour of tiles in the mosques of Samarkand in Uzbekistan and Marrakesh in Morocco. My favourite mosque outside Manchester is the white Sheikh Zayed Grand Mosque in Abu Dhabi, where I savour every moment of sitting in its splendid white interior, among its marble pillars and gorgeously rich carpets.

Manchester's Jamia Mosque has hosted many community and interfaith events that I have helped to organise, for We Stand Together, Faith Network 4 Manchester, as well as a Muslim Arts and Culture Festival in 2018, where we offered public tours of the mosque and celebrated its interior artwork and architectural features. Its doors are always open for Muslims and non-Muslims alike.

Fax: 0161 256 4518
A to Z PHONES
CONVENIENCE STORE
UNLOCKING - REPAIRING - INTERNATIONAL CALLING CARDS
0161 257 2574
Chatkhara's
0161 225 2552
hungryhouse
Chatkhara's
Takeaway & Restaurant
Free Delivery
0161 225 2552
BELIEVE.
SONS
Lycamobile
OPEN

## *Immigrant* – Qaisra Shahraz

I read and hear about immigrants. I meet them in my everyday life. I have taught them for nearly fifteen years. I am dismayed that there is constant negative news in the media about immigration and refugees. I am disappointed that some politicians appear to have no qualms about using immigration as a topic to whip up racism to win them votes. I hate it when migrants are scapegoated for economic problems and when they become easy targets for vilification and hate. Remember the targeting of the Eastern European and Polish communities after the Brexit referendum, resulting in the tragic death of a Polish man in Harlow, Essex in August 2016?

Then I remember that I, too, am an immigrant. Or rather, I was one many years ago, travelling from Lahore in Pakistan to Manchester at the age of nine. Having lived in Manchester for over 80 per cent of my life, it's difficult to believe and accept at times that I could still be called an immigrant, or that I am indeed a migrant by background.

Pakistani I might be by origin, but Britain is my home, and Manchester is my beloved home city, the place where I live, work, study and have raised my family. As an author I have written about the lives of immigrants: my novel *Revolt* (2013), for example, captures the feeling of displacement immigrants often feel – of being lost between two worlds.

In my latest book, *The Concubine & The Slave-Catcher* (2017), I focused on my father's generation in a story called 'Escape', exploring what it was like for these men who arrived in England in the 1960s. Men who, like my father, were invited to come to the UK through the voucher system, as Britain was in need of workers after the Second World War. Where is their sense of belonging?

**83** (Opposite) Shops and restaurants on Stockport Road, Longsight

## Manchester: Something rich and strange

'Escape' traces the life of an immigrant called Samir, who arrived in the UK over fifty years ago – typically it was the men (like Samir) who arrived first, often staying with friends when they got here. I still marvel at how it must have been for my father's generation of immigrants. They would have arrived in a new place, knowing very few people or the language, and often ended up living in wretched conditions in shared rooms, and called racist names by skinheads. I remember, as a child, Enoch Powell's infamous 'Rivers of Blood' speech. It frightened the immigrant adults and children like myself. We were made to feel so unwelcome, which is a horrible experience to go through.

Since then, Manchester has become a hub of well-settled communities from around the world: Europe, Asia, Africa. People have migrated to the city for various reasons: fleeing war, poverty or oppression. As communities have settled over a period of time, areas of Manchester have become associated with distinct immigrant groups. For example, Longsight and Cheetham Hill have been popular with the Pakistani communities; Moss Side and Rusholme with the Somali community. Shops of all kinds meet the needs of various immigrant communities. Walking through Rusholme, down the famous Curry Mile, one can see the changes. Now, Middle Eastern restaurants are replacing the Asian ones.

Since the 9/11 terrorist attacks, Muslim immigrant communities all over the world have felt marginalised, under threat, unsafe and isolated. Yet it makes me, as a community and international peace activist, work harder to build bridges and to raise awareness. I remind people that there are terrorists in all faiths and communities, including Jo Cox's killer and the New Zealand far-right terrorist who massacred over fifty Muslims in Christchurch. Yet no one equated his atrocities with his faith – Christianity. Why is it that the tag 'Muslim' is applied only to terrorists who come from a Muslim background?

Yet, despite ongoing prejudice, and especially after the Arena attack in 2017, Manchester remains an amazing example of

## Home

diversity and multiculturalism. I often tell my students in Germany, who are studying my short story 'A Pair of Jeans' as part of their Abitur (the equivalent of A level English Literature in Germany), that Manchester is the best example of a city that truly welcomes immigrants as well as flourishing itself as a result. I describe myself to those students as a British Muslim woman of Pakistani origin. I then go on to remind them that, for me, all three of my identities are of equal importance. They make me who I am. My Muslim identity affects the realities of everyday life – for example, I eat halal meat and address other Muslim men and women as brothers and sisters. I greet all Muslim people with the greeting words 'Asalam-o-Alaikum' meaning 'May peace be upon you.' Islam itself means 'peace'.

Similarly, I regard my Pakistani heritage as enriching – something to be celebrated. I am so glad that I can speak two languages of Pakistan. I have a wardrobe full of elegant Pakistani party garments. I love my curries and chapatis. When I see an elderly person from Pakistan, of my father's age group, I automatically switch to either Punjabi or Urdu out of respect for them. In all other contexts English is my first language, including when conversing with my children. When I was writing my first novel, *The Holy Woman* (2001), someone asked me, 'Which language do you think in?' I automatically replied, 'In English of course.' I could not think or write in any other language. In short, I am happy with my immigrant status, finding it a very enriching experience, and would not have it any other way.

Wash & Dry
CLEAN MACHINE LAUNDERETTES
Wash & Dry
Wash & Dry
CLEAN MACHINE LAUNDERETTES
Wash & Dry
DAMIEN ST.
36
36

# Home

## *Laundrette* – Peter Kalu

I go in and it hugs me like an old friend. It still has the 1970s signage. I always associate laundrettes with flare-pant-sporting, fur-coated footballers, because back when few families had washing machines, laundrettes were the smart investment for star soccer players thinking ahead to their non-playing days. Heading to a washer, I slip back to this boom time when the set of twelve industrial washers, twin rows of six Candy big box dryers (plus the mini Apollo 11 spin-wringer tucked into a corner) were the essential fixtures of this fluorescent-lit, makeshift youth club where I whiled away time in the evenings, dreaming that George Best might drop by in his white Rolls Royce and fluffed mink coat to throw us smiles and empty the coin boxes.

Suddenly I'm 12 and being ordered to tug the family washing in a granny shopping trolley down Burton Road to the laundrette. The sight of me makes me laugh, my youthful doppelganger skinny as a pole, scrunched face hauling my weight in siblings' dirty clothes. I snuck in with sellotape in my pocket to stick the coins onto. This was so, after slipping the coins into the money slot, when the metal coin box snub flicked back to release those coins and enrich George Best, instead of falling, my money just hung there on the sellotape and I got to pull it out and spend it on Chewits instead. As sweet as stolen pears.

Occasionally, as a lonely student in Edinburgh I visited a municipal laundrette with a bundle of clothes, simply for the company I'd find. They are places where civility – across languages, age groups, cultures, dress styles and different degrees of sobriety – takes place. Where the art of being a citizen can be practised – all the mores and means of greeting another stranger and making polite, gracious conversation that simply acknowledges each other's right to

**84** (Opposite) Laundrette on Damien Street, Levenshulme

breathe the same civic air. I used to take my guitar – to practice chords, and in case I met someone there, because strumming a guitar, however badly, is a great ice-breaker.

I get on with my business, loading a washer. A man in brogues rocks up alongside me and cracks open the neighbouring washing machine. He plucks clothes out of a bin liner, stuffs them into the drum, loads powder, then expertly works the dials. He turns and exits, leaving my clumsy efforts in his wake. I see his silhouette later, outside, smoking Russian cigarettes, leaning on a car.

I stay inside, people-watching. Particularly fetching is the furtive folding of underwear. There is a civic decency in averting your eyes as such items get folded. Women have a nonchalance about this that men generally do not achieve; most men throw all their dried clothes into a bag and haul it off to some more private place for separation. The women watch with indifferent eyes as others smooth socks with small holes, joke underwear, holey T-shirts. An entire family genealogy, lifestyle and bunch of personalities gets stacked before your eyes.

Three women stand about by the rocket-wringer and chat in Polish and English as a fourth looks on, distracted. Meanwhile, the attendant is sitting strategically on a low bench in a corner by the dryers, reading a tabloid. She is not to be disturbed. She knows the rule about how long dried laundry is allowed to merely sit in a machine while others tap feet to signal annoyance as their washed, wet clothes wait in those indestructible cheese-hole plastic buckets. The most fought over items are the dryers. A laundrette is a space full of cycles. And always the dryer cycles are out of sync with the washers – the dryers unable to toast clothes as fast as the washers disgorge them. Added to that, the minuscule amount of time your drop of coin buys you of a dryer and, if aggravation is to be found in a laundrette, it is always centred around the dryers.

The queue isn't too bad this evening and my wet wash is nowhere near done. It's hot in here, I muse. It always is. The flat above the laundrette is the one home that never needs heating, I guess. I

## Home

wonder if it rents out at a premium because of that. Laundrettes have numerous kinks and folds in their time–space fabric. The language of the signage is curt youth court and baroque Victorian. No loitering. No sitting on machines by order of the proprietor. Clientele availing themselves of washers have priority in use of dryers. Your custom is esteemed. It is mid January and tinsel signs sit along the list of prohibitions and flattery: 'Merry Christmas. Happy Festive Season'. I ponder the absence of any soap vending in the laundrette and the presence within fifty yards of any laundrette of a shop selling soap. In contrast, in France they have washing machines at drive-ins that dispense their own soap. *Chacun son goût.* My eyes have accidentally parked on a washing-machine drum and I start trying to make out tops from trousers, bras from towels. The destruction rate of bras is probably higher than 10 per cent; the underwires always work their way loose in the end. Apart from bras, among other metal and miscellaneous objects hated by proprietors must be coins, pens, chewing gum, batteries, teeth. If you poke around in the machines' lint-catchers over the course of a year you'd find all those, plus the standard orphaned socks and squat, brown, drowned fleas and bed bugs.

I look up and out at the View-Master through the shop window. I watch cars limping along, humans shuffling, congregating with grunts and headshakes, dogs wandering back and forth the way that stray dogs do. Inside, the kaleidoscopes of the spinning dryers: the hypnotic turns of clothes become Jackson Pollock explosions of wet colour, or the blowing white sheet sails of ships, or the party you once went to all those years ago. Spinning dryers have that wagon-wheel effect on my mind, always plunging me into memory. The washing machines, on the other hand, instil a bizarre vigilance with their seemingly chaotic stop–start and slosh anti-clockwise-now-clockwise rotations, the sudden lurches into hyperspeed, then the lulls when nothing appears to be happening until you notice that waterline slowly creeping up, and it starts again.

There is a sudden extract from a Jane Austen costume drama as

## Manchester: Something rich and strange

a crying woman runs in with a bridesmaid's dress that she hastily shoves into a large front loader, soap added from the box in her fluttering hand, coins dropped into the slot. She whizzes out again. I look up into the ceiling fluorescents and imagine.

There is always a telephone number, stuck up somewhere, for when things don't work. Ring it, and if you say the right combination of words or oaths, either the owner, or the owner's hireling, will appear. They are indistinguishable in disposition: pissed off, sceptical, suspicious. You've rubbed the bottle and summoned the sore-headed genie. He comes toting a grubby magic toolkit, and it usually takes him five minutes to either bang metal into place and pronounce the machine fixed, or attach a sign saying 'Do Not Use'. Today though, everything is moving smoothly. I'm done with drying. I fold my clothes, smalls and all. Then I'm out.

### Notes

1. Anna Baum, 'Manchester Homeless Protest Camp 2015', available at http://bit.ly/1MKrdkb (accessed 17 June 2020).
2. Ibid.
3. See Judith Walkowitz, *City of Dreadful Delight: Narratives of Sexual Danger in Late-Victorian London* (Chicago: University of Chicago Press, 1992).
4. Natalie Bloomer, 'Manchester homelessness camp likely to shut after protestors denied legal aid', *Politics* website, 3 August 2015, available at www.politics.co.uk/news/2015/08/03/manchester-homelessness-camp-likely-to-shut-after-protestors (accessed 17 June 2020).
5. All names have been changed to protect identities.
6. Alex Rose and Bill Davies, *Not Home: The Lives of Hidden Homeless Households in Unsupported Temporary Accommodation in England* (Manchester: IPPR North, 2014), p. 13.
7. Ibid., p.18.
8. Shelter, *The Grief Report* in 1972, cited in Christa Maciver, *Lifting The Lid on Hidden Homelessness* (Manchester: Justlife, 2018), p. 8.
9. J. Thompson, 'Repairing the past. Confronting the legacies of slavery, genocide, and cast', *7th Annual International Conference Yale University*, 2005, pp. 1–20.
10. Bill Williams, *The Making of Manchester Jewry* (Manchester: Manchester University Press, 1976), p. 37.

11 See www.jta.org/1947/08/05/archive/britons-arrested-for-attacks-on-jews-in-liverpool-manchester-saiford.
12 W. Lever, *Jerusalem, Your Name is Liberty* (Tel Aviv: Massadah, 1951).
13 See CST, *Antisemitic Incidents Report 2016* (London: Community Security Trust, 2017), available at https://cst.org.uk/data/file/b/e/Incidents%20Report%202016.1486376547.pdf (accessed 17 June 2020).

# Notes on contributors

**Becky Alexis-Martin** is a lecturer in Cultural and Political Geography at Manchester Metropolitan University. Her research considers the cultural significance of existential threats, including climate change and nuclear warfare. She is the author of *Disarming Doomsday: The Human Impact of Nuclear Weapons since Hiroshima*, published in 2019.

**Clare Archibald** is a Scottish poet and writer interested in articulation, movement, nuance and the interplay of words, sounds and images. She is widely published and has performed her hybrid work in diverse settings – from book festivals to car parks and woods. She is currently making an experimental art film, *Can You Hear the Interim*, as practice-based research for her postgraduate MSc, is developing a site responsive album, *Birl of Unmap*, with composers Kinbrae, and has a hybrid pamphlet forthcoming with experimental art and literature publishers Gorse. She also runs Lone Women in Flashes of Wilderness – www.lonewomeninflashesofwilderness. For more information see www.clarearchibald.com.

**Jenna C. Ashton** is a lecturer and Programme Director of Heritage Studies in the Institute for Cultural Practices, University of Manchester. Her research, practice and teaching concerns the development of collaborative and creative feminist methods

## Notes on contributors

and analysis for applied heritage and theory, and working at the intersection of heritage, arts, activism and social justice. She holds a number of advisory and trustee roles in the UK and internationally. In 2019, in collaboration with diverse women artists, she co-founded CIWA (the Centre for International Women Artists) – a collective artist studio and gallery in Manchester.

**Natalie Bradbury** is a writer based in Greater Manchester interested in art, education, architecture and cities. Her PhD, from the University of Central Lancashire, was entitled *Pictures for Schools: Art, Education and Reconstruction in Post-war Britain*. She has a chapter in *Women's Periodicals and Print Culture in Britain, 1918–1939: The Interwar Period* (2017), focusing on the twentieth century co-operative women's magazine *Woman's Outlook*. Her art and cultural journalism has appeared in publications including *a-n*, *Art Monthly*, *The Modernist*, *Corridor8*, *Creative Tourist*, *The Co-operative News*, *Big Issue in the North*, *Manchester Confidential* and many more.

**Cassie Britland** is a true crime and travel writer based in Sydney, Australia. She is the former executive editor of *Midnight Echo*, Australia's premier horror fiction magazine, and the current managing editor of the *Wotif Insider* and *Live Lastminute* travel blogs. Cassie is currently working on her first book – the true story of her ancestor, Mary Ann Britland, the first woman executed at Manchester's Strangeways Prison. Find out more at www.cassiebritland.com.

**Sarah Butler**'s work explores ideas of home, belonging, identity, family, and urban landscapes. She has three novels published in the UK and with fourteen international publishers: *Ten Things I've Learnt About Love* (2013), *Before The Fire* (2015) and *Jack and Bet* (2020). In November 2018, she published a novella, *Not Home*, written in conversation with people living in unsupported temporary accommodation in Manchester. She lectures part-time

## Notes on contributors

in Creative Writing at Manchester Metropolitan University. Sarah also explores the relationship between writing and place through participatory projects. Recent writing residencies include writer-in-residence on the Central line; at Great Ormond Street Hospital; and *Stories From The Road* – a project exploring personal stories of Oxford Road, Manchester. www.urbanwords.org.uk | www.sarahbutler.org.uk.

**Paul Dobraszczyk** teaches at the Bartlett School of Architecture, University College London. He is the author of *Anarchist Architecture* (forthcoming in 2021); *Future Cities, Architecture and the Imagination* (2019); *The Dead City: Urban Ruins and the Spectacle of Decay* (2017); and *Iron, Ornament and Architecture in Victorian Britain* (2014). He is co-editor of *Global Undergrounds: Exploring Cities Within* (2016) and *Function and Fantasy: Iron Architecture in the Long Nineteenth Century* (2016). Paul also created the photographic website www.stonesofmanchester.com.

**Martin Dodge** is Senior Lecturer in the Geography Department at the University of Manchester. His research focuses on digital technologies, urban historical geography, and the politics of maps and visualisation. He has also co-edited a series of books on the development of cartographic ideas: *Geographic Visualization* (2008), *Rethinking Maps* (2009), *Classics in Cartography* (2010), *The Map Reader* (2011), *Mapping – Critical Concepts in Geography* (2015) and *Mapping Across Academia* (2017). Much of his current research is on the history of Manchester and he has co-curated several high-profile public exhibitions on aspects of the city, including *Mapping Manchester* (2009), *Infra_MANC* (2012) and *Making Post-war Manchester* (2016). His latest co-authored book, *Manchester: Mapping the City* was published in 2018.

**Nick Dunn** is Executive Director of Imagination, an open and exploratory design research lab at Lancaster University, where he is Professor of Urban Design. Born in Salford, Nick lives in

Manchester. His work responds to the contemporary city, which he explores through experimentation and writing on the nature of urban space. He has written numerous books on architecture and urbanism. A keen nightwalker, his book *Dark Matters* (2016) is a love letter to nocturnal Manchester and Salford.

**Tim Edensor** is Professor of Social and Cultural Geography at Manchester Metropolitan University and a research fellow at Melbourne University. He is the author of *Tourists at the Taj* (1998), *National Identity, Popular Culture and Everyday Life* (2002), *Industrial Ruins: Space, Aesthetics and Materiality* (2005), and *From Light to Dark: Daylight, Illumination and Gloom* (2017) – as well as the editor of *Geographies of Rhythm* (2010). Tim has written extensively on national identity, tourism, ruins, mobilities and landscapes of illumination and darkness. He is currently co-editing *The Routledge Handbook of Place*, and completing a project about lithic materiality in Melbourne.

**Steve Hanson** works as a lecturer, writer and researcher. He has taught at Goldsmiths, and in the sociology departments at Manchester Metropolitan University, the University of Salford and the University of Lincoln. He has worked as a research assistant for the University of Oxford and central government, and as an ethnographer on research for City University and London Metropolitan University. His first book, *Small Towns, Austere Times*, was published in 2014. He has written chapters on urbanism, including a chapter with Mark Rainey in *The Routledge Handbook of Henri Lefebvre, The City and Urban Society* (2019). An experimental volume, *A Shaken Bible*, was published in 2020. Steve has published journal articles for *Street Signs*, *Cultural Studies*, *Visual Studies*, *Social Alternatives* and the *Journal for Critical Education Policy Studies*. He has also written a column on Manchester-related matters for *Open Democracy*, and many essays for artists, including work for the Bradford Ways of Looking festival catalogue, and Charlie Meecham's Oldham

Road Revisited project for the People's History Museum. He lives in Manchester.

**Clare Hartwell** is an architectural historian. She is the author of the *Manchester Pevsner City Guide* (2001) and *The History and Architecture of Chetham's School and Library* (2004), and co-author of revisions in Pevsner's *Lancashire: Manchester and the South East* and *Lancashire: North, Cheshire and Derbyshire* in the Buildings of England series.

**Joanne Hudson** is an architect, educator and maker. After studying architecture at the Manchester School of Architecture and working in professional practice, she completed a PhD in human and cultural geography in 2013 at Manchester Metropolitan University. In 2014, she moved to Liverpool where she now teaches architecture at Liverpool John Moores University. Her research focuses principally on the relationship between spatial planning practices and the production, (re)production and use of wastelands and derelict spaces – what she terms 'informal spaces' – and developing new design strategies in relation to affordable housing.

**Peter Kalu** writes short stories in styles ranging from the realist to the surreal to the carnivalesque. They can be found in various anthologies, including *Closure* (2015), *A Country To Call Home* (2017) and *Seaside Special* (2018). He also writes novels and poems. Until recently, he ran a carnival band. More at www.peterkalu.com.

**Andrew McMillan** is a poet and Senior Lecturer in the Manchester Writing School at Manchester Metropolitan University. His two award-winning collections of poetry are *physical* (Guardian First Book Award, Somerset Maugham Award) and *playtime* (Polari Prize).

## Notes on contributors

**Sean R. Mills** is a neuroscientist at the University of Southampton, where he researches how people perceive the world through touch. He lives in Manchester.

**Brian Rosa** is an independent scholar based in Barcelona, Spain. He holds a PhD in Human Geography from the University of Manchester and was formerly Assistant Professor of Urban Studies and Geography at the City University of New York. He is the co-editor, with Christoph Lindner, of *Deconstructing the High Line: Postindustrial Urbanism and the Rise of the Elevated Park* (2017).

**Morag Rose** is an artist, activist, academic and anarchoflaneuse. She worked in the voluntary sector across Greater Manchester for fifteen years before completing her PhD 'Women walking Manchester: desire lines through the original modern city' (University of Sheffield, 2018). In 2006, Morag founded Manchester psychogeographical collective the Loiterers Resistance Movement (LRM), and has performed, presented and exhibited widely. She is a lecturer in Human Geography at the University of Liverpool, a member of the Walking Artists Network, and is currently working on a number of publications. Her interests include protecting and promoting public space, accessible architecture, creative mischief-making, Americana music and *Dr Who*.

**Sarah Sayeed** is a writer who has received numerous poetry and music commissions over the last fifteen years, with a focus on plays and scriptwriting since 2016. Writing credits have included the radio drama *My Heroes are Behind Me* commissioned by BBC Radio 5, and the *Knives and Forks* stage-play extract for the Royal Exchange's Memories of Partition project. Her first full-length immersive play *Descent*, co-written with David Calcutt, has been commissioned by Midland Actors Centre. In 2018, Sarah was selected as writer-in-residence at the Jaipur Literature Festival and commissioned by Durham Book Festival to write *Sophia for*

## Notes on contributors

*Sophia*, based on the life of Sophia Duleep Singh. Sarah is based in Brighton and is currently working on her first book of short stories.

**Qaisra Shahraz** is Executive Director of MACFEST (Muslim Arts and Culture Festival) and author of *The Concubine & The Slave-Catcher* (2018), *Typhoon* (2014), *The Holy Woman* (2013), and *Revolt* (2013). She is also a scriptwriter, former Ofsted inspector and a peace and gender activist. She is a Fellow of the Royal Society of Arts, a literary judge, and adviser to Asia Pacific Writers & Translators. Qaisra has won several prizes, including the prestigious National Diversity, Lifetime Achiever Award in 2016 from the University of Salford. She has been widely recognised for her work, and was the No. 1 Most Influential Woman in Manchester in 2017 and in the 2018 Muslim Power 100 list.

**Jonathan Silver** is based at the Urban Institute, University of Sheffield, and is an urban geographer focused on researching inequality across cities, technology and environment. His work explores comparative methodologies and theories to think about infrastructure systems through research in Ghana, Uganda, South Africa, Senegal, the USA, and in recent years in his home city of Manchester.

**Matthew Steele** is a researcher and writer on architecture and urbanism. He is currently completing his PhD on the architectural profession's engagement with historic places of worship in England in the post-1945 period. He is a regular contributor to *The Modernist* and co-investigator of the Sacred Suburbs project (2014 to present). Recent publications with A. Connelly include: 'Surveying Greater Manchester's Sacred Suburbs', in *Modern Futures*, ed. Hannah Neate and Ruth Cragg (2016); and *Sacred Suburbs: A Guide to Greater Manchester's Post-war Places of Worship* (2015).

## Notes on contributors

**James Thorp** grew up in Manchester and graduated from the Manchester School of Architecture in 2011. Since then he has worked in architectural practice before returning to academia to undertake a PhD in Design at Lancaster University in 2018. He co-authored *Decades*, a pamphlet exploring the post-war architecture of Manchester, published by The Modernist Society in 2017 and supported by the Heritage Lottery Fund.

# Photo acknowledgements

The editors, contributing authors and publisher wish to express their thanks to the below sources of illustrative material and/or permission to reproduce it.

Photo Clare Archibald: p. 229; photo Jenna C. Ashton: pp. 155, 233; photo Natalie Bradbury: p. 95; photo Cassie Britland: pp. 46, 178; photo Paul Dobraszczyk: pp. 3–24, 35, 51–4, 61, 69–83, 100, 109, 117–28, 136–42, 150, 165, 186–94, 207, 222, 241–50, 267, 276, 284–8, 299–304, 312, 326–7; photo Nick Dunn: pp. 42, 91, 202, 259; photo Tim Edensor: pp. 86, 212; photo Steve Hanson: pp. 307; photo Richard Hopkins: p. 290; photo Joanna Hudson: pp. 210, 254; photo Peter Kalu: p. 133; photo Matthew Kowalczuk: p. 280; courtesy Manchester Metropolitan University: p. 64; courtesy Manchester Metropolitan University Special Collections: p. 294; artwork Sean R. Mills: pp. 31, 198, 237; photo Brian Rosa: pp. 146, 173; artwork Morag Rose: pp. 27, 105; photo Darmon Richter, p. 168; photo Jonathan Silver: pp. 38, 58, 317; photo Matthew Steele: pp. 160–3, 217, 271; courtesy University of Manchester: p. 112; photo Tim Woodward: p. 322.

# Index

Note: page numbers in *italic* refer to illustrations

accidents 196
alcohol 200–1, 221n.9, 314
alleyways 153, *241*, 242–4, 249
Ancoats 6, 28, *38*, 39–40, 123, *128*, 131–2, 161, 199–200, 218–19, 220, 224, *237*, 238, 315
animals 119, *250*, 256, 261–2
archaeology 59–63, *61*, 147
arches 44, *146*, 167, *173*, 174–7, *210*, 210–11, 232
architecture
   Arndale Centre 29, 53, *64*, 65–8, 89, 145, 293
   Beetham Tower *3*, *80*, 126, 147
   Chetham's School and Library 87, 140, 144, 301
   Co-op buildings 111, *122*, 123–7, *125*, 285, 287
   Daily Express Building *128*, 131–2
   Etihad Stadium *150*, 151–3
   Free Trade Hall 226
   Gothic 19, 44, 52, 59, 70, 143, 144, 180, 187, 300
   Haçienda nightclub 175, 227
   Hulme Crescents 66, 78, 111, 226, 243, 295, 297
   Maine Road stadium 151–4, 218
   Manchester Cathedral 44, 53, *64*, *69*, 70–2, 87, 140, 144–5, 301–2
   Manchester Town Hall 52, 55–6, 65, 88, 144, 205, 281, 285, 308–9
   medieval 140–1, *142*, 143–5, 300–2
   mills 6, 29, *38*, 40–1, 110, 115, *139*, 140, 218, 234
   St Ann's Church *75*, 78, 87, 88
   Trafford Centre 67, 93, 171

Beswick 76, *150*, 151, 218–19, 305, 315
blitz 71, 145, 277, 302, 319–20
Bolton 39, 78, *139*, 157, 234, 302
Bradford 41, 193, 195, *217*, 218–21
breweries 40, 176, 201, 219, 221n.9, 239–40
bricks 29, 39, 41, 44, 78, 110, *117*, 118–21, 124, 126, 137, 140, 153, 154, *174*, 174, *186*, 188–9, *194*, 196, 206, *210*, 210, 215, *217*, 219–20, 227, 230–2, 256, 274, 283, 292, 302, 313
bridges 25, 36, 37, 67, 78, *91*, 92–4, 124, 149, 164n.3, *222*, 260, 297
Burnage 193, *212*, 213–15, 272
bus stop 30, 36, *100*, 101–4
Brexit 9, 226, 293, 303, 327
Brown, Ford Madox 144

345

# Index

Britland, Mary Ann 47–9, *178*, 179–82, 187–8, 199
Burnham, Andy 111, 306

Calvino, Italo, *Invisible Cities* 11–12
canals
    Ashton 98, 218, *250*, 268
    Bridgewater 41, 97, 268, 302
    Manchester Ship 93–4, 129, 171, *207*, 208–9, 268, 269, 275n.4, 287
    Peak Forest 88–9
    Rochdale 119–20, *191*, 197, *267*, 268–9
cancer 57, *237*, 238–40, 249n.2, 296
capitalism 22, 28, 40, 53, 60, 84–5, 123, 200, 208, 269–70, 279, 296–7, 311
car parks 77, 193
car wash 111, *133*, 134–9, *136*
Castlefield *42*, 44, *80*, 141, 147–9, 174, *191*, 269
cathedral 44, 53, *64*, *69*, 70–2, 87, 140, 144–5, 301–2
cemeteries 167, *178*, 179–81, 287
Cheetham Hill 251, 306, 319, 320, 328
chimneys 25–6, *38*, 39–41, 50n.7, 134, 137, 140, 181, 188, 270, 313
Chorlton 96, 162, *259*, 260, 287
churches 70–2, 78, 87–8, 114, 144, 169, 180–1, 196, 219–20, 277, 301
City Council, Manchester 9, 66, 98, 218, 228, 232, 243, 274, 289, 300, 301, 302, 308–10
climate change 26, 41, 252, 266, 278
clothing 113, 115, 199, 256, 315–16, 331–4
    *see also* cotton
coal 41, 87, 98, 110, 195, 201, 203–5, 218, 219, 242
    *see also* smoke
cobbles 2, 28, 87, 89, 123, 152, *241*, 242–3, *245*, 246–9, 278
Cold War 264–5, 297

Collyhurst *86*, 87–9, 224, *229*, 230–2
colonialism 22n.8, *61*, 60–2
concrete 13, 33, 44–5, *64*, 65–6, 89–90, *91*, 92–3, 134, 170, 172, 243, 251, 265, 283
convent 224, *229*, 230–2
Co-operative movement 111, *122*, 123–7, *125*, 130–1, 285, 295
    *see also* architecture, Co-op buildings
*Coronation Street* 92, 174, 249
cotton 1, 7–8, 20, 40–1, 55, 59–60, 65, 79n.3, 81, 84, 110–11, 113–16, 138n.1, 140, 218, 236, 238, 243, 282, 285
crime
    Moors Murders 48, 287
    mugging 97, 184
    murder 47–50, 119–20, 179, 199–200, 252, 287, 318, 320
    terrorism *284*, 285–9, 306, 320, 323, 328
    violence 13, 20, 49, 56, 60, 184–5, 278, 306, 319–21
Cummins, Kevin 297–8
cycleways *see* transport, cycling

darkness *42*, 26, 43–5, *100*, 110, 167, *183*, 203–6, *290*
Davyhulme 93, 171
decolonisation *see* colonialism
De Tocqueville, Alexis 192
Dibnah, Fred 39
Dickens, Charles 26, 203
Didsbury 135, 246, 248
demolition 13, 39–40, 79, 145, 153, 220, *225*, 243, *276*, 277, *294*, 302
devolution 5, 8, 22n.3
Dukinfield 164, *178*, 178–81, 190n.2
dye *see* industry

elections 11
Engels, Friedrich 9, 22n.5, 40, 84, 204, 277, 295
engineering 113, 118, 148–9, 170, 268
essence 8, 28–30, 252

# Index

factories 25, 111, 113, *117*, 118, 126, 130, 140, 195–7, *212*, 213–15, 230, 236, 295
Factory Records 85, 227
festivals 11, 43, 286, 302, 309, 310
films 17, 19, 55–6
First World War 34, 126, 170, 213, 238
flowers 29, 130, 180, 235, 269, 275n.10, 278, *280*, 281–3, 286
folklore 252, 270
football 8, 18, 28, 141, 286, 331
   Manchester City *150*, 151–4, 195, 218
   Manchester United 29, 152

gangs 13, 29
gardens 57, 78, 97, 126, 131, 231, 251–3, 260, 266, 269, *272*, 272–5, 281, 296, *304*, 313
garden villages 272–5, 301
Gaskell, Elizabeth 56, 203
Gay Village 57, 184, 269, 289
Geddes, Patrick 7, 22n.4
Gorton 96, *254*, 255–7, *277*
Gothic 19, 44, 52, 59, 70, 143, 144, 180, 187, 300
graffiti *see* public art
Greater Manchester
   creation of 5–8
   geography of 5–11, 18–21, 40, 96, 260
   governance of 22n.3, 260, 306

hair 17, 141, *155*, 156–9
heritage 9, 28, 76, 89, 98, 116, 126, 131, 144, 147–9, 175, 236, 301, 325
hills *10*, 48, 93, 180, 251
Hollaway, Tony 71–2, *73*, 78
homelessness 2–3, *4*, 75, 78, 135, 174, *210*, 214, 305–6, *307*, 308–11, 314–15, 324, 334n.1, 334n.8
hospitals 238–40, 247, 249n.2, 266
hotels *35*, 36–7, 45, *83*, 85, 116, 130, 226

housing
   terraces 29, 40, 78, 153, 154, 224, 226, *241*, 242–4, 249, 301, *312*, 313
   tower blocks *3*, 5, 9, 53, 141, 306
Hulme 66, 78, *109*, 111, 161, 220, 243–4, 266, 287, *294*, 295, 297–8, 302, 305, 315
   *see also* architecture, Hulme Crescents

illness *see* cancer
imagination 5–6, 11–12, 18–19, 43, 76, 174, 214, 252, 275n.6, 303
immigration 17, 135, 230, 236, 306, 327–9
Industrial Revolution 9, 26, 29, 39–41, 87, 140, 147–8, 218, 270, 295, 297
industry
   brickmaking 110, 118–21, *217*, 219
   car washing 111, 134–7
   chain-making *212*, 213–15
   coal mining 41, 87, 98, 110, 218–19
   cotton production *see* cotton
   dyeing 110, 118, 193, *194*, 195–7, 199
   foundries 120, 215, 255
   newspapers 66, 111, *128*, 129–32
   retail 53, *64*, 65–8, 87, 93, 115, 124, 216

John Rylands Library 19, 88, 130

Kazmi, Basir 17

Labour Party 9, 56, 228, 308
language 22, 137, 171, 236, 328–9, 331, 333
laundrette 305, *330*, 331–3
Levenshulme *14*, 96, 132, *304*, *330*
libraries
   Chetham's School and Library 87, 140, 144, 301
   John Rylands Library 19, 88, 130
   Manchester City Library *280*, 281, 283, 309

*347*

# Index

lighting 43, 151, 180, 204
literature 15, 18, 22n.11, 26, 203, 223
London 17–19, 52, 70, 126, 129, 131, 167, 170, 175, 226, 252, 292, 321
Longsight 126, *136*, 287, 306, *326*, 328
Lowry, L. S. 13, 219, 221n.10

Mancunian Way 15, 33, 44, 169, 311
maps 107, *112*, 114–16, 120, 179, 181, 223, 224, 262, *263*
marketing 7, 19, 28, 123, 159, 192, 286
markets 66, 98, 145, 302, 309, 310
Marx, Karl 84
medicine 130, 200–1, 224, 238–40
medieval 65, 70, 140, 141, *142*, 143–5, 246, 262, *299*, 300–2
memorials *54*, 119, 126, 154, 170, 278, *280*, 281–3, *284*, 286, 308
Miles Platting 161, 164, 193, *194*, 195–7, 252
mills *6*, 29, *38*, 40–1, 110, 115, *139*, 140, 218, 234
money 20, 82, 84–5, 88, 114, 135, 189, 230, 298, 331
monsters 252, 270
moors *10*, 26, 47–8
Moors Murders *see* crime
mosques 305, *322*, 323–5
Moss Side 13, 22n.9, 56, 78, 152–3, 218, *241*, 244, 277, 328
Moston 120, *299*, 301–2
murals 97, *109*, 126, 130, 144, 164n.2, *284*, 286–7, *288*
museums
    Manchester Museum *57*, 58–63, *59*
    Rochdale Pioneers Museum 124
    Science and Industry Museum 44, 118, 147, 148
music 2, 8, 18, 32, 111, 131, 151, 157, 226, 301

nature 20, 26, 119, 180, 247, *250*, 251–3, *254*, 255–8, *259*, 260–1, 269
    *see also* parks

neurology 32–4
Newton Heath *117*, 118–21
nightclubs 111, 175, 176, 227
night-time *see* darkness
NOMA 123, 126, 130–1
Northenden 262, 273
Northern Powerhouse 2
Northern Quarter 29, 68, 77, 123, *202*, 264, *284*, 286, 314
nostalgia 8, 193, 235
nuclear technology 170, 238–40, 252, *263*, 264–6, 278, 296

Oldham 40, *46*, 47–9, 130, 164, 215, 244, 247, 282
Old Trafford 114, 130, 143, 152
Ordsall 79, 208–9, 301, 302
Oxford Road Corridor 25–6, *35*, 36–7

parks 25, 47–8, 78, 96–7, 119, 169, 251–2, 260, 300
Peak District National Park 88, 252
Peterloo massacre 21, 53, 129, 226, 278, *280*, 281–3
photography 19, 47, 145, 158, 187, 189, 297–8
Piccadilly Gardens 55, 184, 261, 291, *307*, 324
Pitfield, Alice *155*, 156–7, *233*, 234
plants 113, 244, 257–8, 301
poetry 15–16, *16*, 17, 283
poisoning 49, 57, 179, 197, 199–201, 222n.7
pollution *24*, 41, 50n.7, 94, 120, *202*, 204, 238, 251, 252
    *see also* smoke
post-industrial 2, 20, 40, 111, 116, 119, 121, 175–6, *191*, *194*, *202*, 255, 269, 297
poverty 9, 124, 203, 287, 292, 313–15
prison *see* Strangeways Prison
protest 159, 188, 282–3, 293, 308–10, 334n.1
public art 20, *69*, 72–3, *73*, *75*, 76–9, 97, 126, *285*, 286, *288*
pubs 49, 152, 153, 219, 220

348

# Index

quarries *86*, 87–90, 98

racism 15, 106, 227, 306, 320–1, 327–8
radioactivity *see* nuclear technology
radium 224, *237*, 238–40, 249n.2
railways *see* transport
railway stations 45, *95*, 96, 130, 147–8, 175–7, 218, 255
rain 12–17, *14*, *16*, 20, 28, 49, 108n.2, 205, 249, 251, 289, 315
redevelopment *see* regeneration
regeneration
   high-rise buildings *1*, 2, 77, 129, 147, 243
   housing 22n.2, 40, 120, 124, 126, 153, 176, 177, 216, 243, 272, 274, *294*, 305–6, 313
religion
   Catholicism 230–2
   Islam *322*, 323–5, 328–9
   Judaism 17, *317*, 318–21, 324, 334n.10
retail *see* shops
riots 49, 167, *183*, 188–9, 278, *290*, 291–3
rivers 25, 81, 147, 170, 246, 251
   Mersey 98, 171–2, *259*, 260–2, 281
   Irk 87, *165*, *168*, *222*
   Irwell 44, 77, 148, 149, 208, 209
Rochdale 123–4, 247
Roman period 143, 147, 161, 246
ruins 20, 47–8, 143, *212*, 213–16, *225*, 269, *276*, 278, *304*
Rusholme 152–3, 306, *322*, 323, 328
Russia 157, 234–5

Salford 2, 5, 17, 44, 53, 79, 82, 92, 97–8, *122*, 126, 143, *147*, 148–9, 161, 213, 282, 291, 293, 301, 308, *317*, 319
Salford Quays 77, 129, 208–9, 215
schools 55, 76, 79, 87, 97, 144, 152, 162, 163, 197, 231, 232, 266, 277, 281, 287, 301, 318
sculpture *54*, 55–7, *75*, 76–8, 286

Second World War 2, 8, 18, 57, 111, 154, 240, 256, 285, 318, 327
senses 26, *31*, 32–4
sewers *see* underground, sewers
shops 20, 36–7, 53, 65–8, 96, 111, 130, 152, 153, 286, 306, *326*, 328
Shudehill 29, 32–3, 67, 123, 131
Sissay, Lem 15, *16*
skyscrapers *3*, 5, 9, *10*, 53, *80*, 126–7, 141, 147, *173*, 306
   *see also* architecture, Beetham Tower
slavery 55, 60, 114, 140, 332n.9
smoke *24*, 25, 26, 40, 50n.7, 187, *202*, 204, 292
   *see also* pollution
sport 162, 218
   football 2, 8, 18, 28, 141, 151–4, 218
   swimming 37, 56, 141, *160*, 161–4, *163*
stained glass 53, 70–4, *73*, *69*, 79n.4–5, *229*, 231
Stalybridge 179, 286
statues *see* sculpture
steel 33, 44, 76, 77, 78, 93, *146*, 149, 154, 215
Stockport *24*, 96, 98, 200, 215, 302
stone 48, *52*, 81, *86*, 87–90, 94, 98, 181, 196, *202*, *245*, 246–9, 282
Strangeways Prison 167, 179, *186*, 187–90, 199
subterranean *see* underground
suffragettes 53, *54*, 56, 188
swimming pools 141, *160*, 161–4, *163*
symbolism 17, 26, 28, 49, 62, 67, 71, 76, 84, 115, 141, 167, 235, 278, 281, 285–9
synagogues *317*, 318–20, 323, 324
   *see also* religion, Judaism

television 19, 292, 310
terrorism
   1996 IRA bomb 22n.1, 67, 71, 85, 145, 302
   2017 Arena attack *284*, 285–9, 306

## Index

textiles *see* cotton
trade *see* industry
trade unions 295, 308
Traherne, Margaret *69*, 71–2
transport
  buses 13, 29, 30, 32, 36, 66, 67, 82, 98, *100*, 101–3, 248, 291, 315
  canals 41, 45, 76, 81, 87–8, 93–4, 97, 98, 113, 119–20, 129, 147, 152, 171, 174, *192*, 197, 208–9, 218, 251, 252, *267*, 268–70, 287, 302
    *see also* canals
  cycling 13, 32, 82, 89, *95*, 96–8
  motorways 44, 67, 82, *91*, 92–4, 130, 260
  railways *42*, 45, 81, 87–8, *95*, 96, 98, 131, *146*, 147–9, 167, *173*, 174–7, *210*, 218, *222*, 232, 255
  taxis 36, 101–3, 135, 311
  trams *31*, 32–3, 129, 166, 220, 248, 274, 292
  tramways 88–9
trees 26, 78, 181, 252, 264–6
Tudor period *142*, 278, *299*, 300–3

underground
  canals *267*
  culverts *165*, 170, *222*
  Guardian Telephone Exchange 265, 275n.2

railways 66, 166–7
sewers *168*, 169–72
tunnels 66, 126, 170, 220, 265
universities 15, 77, 129, 201, *225*, 226, 239, 264, 296, 297, 311, 324, 325

Venice 52
viaducts *12*, 44, 98, 141, *146*, 148, *173*, 174–7, *210*
Victorian period 5, 19, 48, 52, 70, 97, 111, 114, 116, 126, 145, 147, 148, 164n.2, 167, 169–70, 174, 199, 238, 242–3, 246, 295
violence *see* crime

walking 15, 29, 36, 43–5, 47, 52, 82, 93–4, *105*, 106–8, 119, 152–3, 171, 181, 184–5, 188, 230, 251, 260–1, 268–9, 315
warehouses 52, 110, *112*, 114–16, 126, 175, *202*, 205, 238
waste *see* pollution
waste ground 29, 87, 107, 193, 197, *207*, *250*, 251, *254*, 255–8
weaving *see* cotton
Whalley Range 29, 96, 244, 305
Wigan 98, 162
work *see* industry
Wythenshawe 162, 253, *271*, 272–5, 300